THE HEBREW LITERARY GENIUS
AN INTERPRETATION
BEING AN INTRODUCTION TO THE READING OF THE OLD TESTAMENT

LONDON: HUMPHREY MILFORD
OXFORD UNIVERSITY PRESS

THE
HEBREW LITERARY GENIUS

AN INTERPRETATION
BEING AN INTRODUCTION TO THE
READING OF THE OLD TESTAMENT

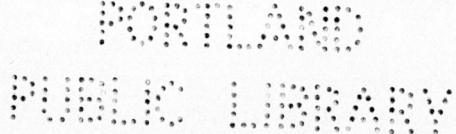

By DUNCAN BLACK MACDONALD, M.A., D.D.

SOMETIME SCHOLAR AND FELLOW IN
THE UNIVERSITY OF GLASGOW
HONORARY MEMBER OF THE ARAB ACADEMY OF DAMASCUS
PROFESSOR EMERITUS OF HARTFORD THEOLOGICAL SEMINARY
AND HONORARY CONSULTING PROFESSOR
IN THE KENNEDY SCHOOL OF MISSIONS

PRINCETON · PRINCETON UNIVERSITY PRESS · 1933

COPYRIGHT, 1933, PRINCETON UNIVERSITY PRESS

PRINTED AT THE PRINCETON UNIVERSITY PRESS
PRINCETON, NEW JERSEY, U.S.A.

To
The Joint and Honored Memories
of John Nichol
and James Robertson
Sometime Professors in the University
of Glasgow

CONTENTS

Prologue xvii
The attitude of the book and of its author—The Hebrews and Jehovah—Methods of interpreting the Old Testament—The Romantic Awakening—Lowth—Herder—The literary approach—The folklore approach—Sir Walter Scott and romantic literature—Results of too much "criticism"—The Old Testament fallen on evil days—Method of this book—The dedication, its tribute and reason.

Chapter I 1
Recent folklore development—The ancient Hebrews in the modern Near East—Hebrew literature and Arabic literature—Hebrew ideas and Islam—How to read the Old Testament for literary effect.

Chapter II
A study of literature—And of life—How the Hebrews expressed themselves—Their relation to Jehovah—His reality—The People of Jehovah—Secular and sacred were one—The Hebrew miracle—The Hebrew secret—The essential characteristic of their mind and literature—Ruled by ideas—Subjectivity expressed objectively—Platonists, not Aristotelians—The Hebrew poetic mind—Emotion—No word for "poet"—The Arabic word and its meaning—The playing child—Only lyric poetry—The dramatic lyric—The epic lyric—The Song of Deborah—The didactic lyric in the Psalms—Song and impulse of the moment—Contrast the sonnet.

Chapter III 20
Three classes of poets: lyric; semi-dramatic; absolute dramatic—Illustrations—Hebrew poetry and Hebrew prose—Arabic parallel—Job and the poet of the Colloquies—Dramatic lyric in Job—The structure of the book—Attitude in Speeches of the Lord—Prologue and Epilogue—Job's daughters.

Chapter IV 33
No epic in Semitic—How far a drama—Origin of Greek drama—Joyous side of Hebrew religion—The laughing Reason—Mani-

festations in song and dance—Muslim parallel in ritual step; "limping beside the altar"—David's orgiastic dance—No epic ballads to sing—Scraps of Hebrew lyric—Sword song of Lamech—Arabic parallel—Song of the Well—Arabic parallels. David as law-giver in song.

Chapter V 40

David as sacrosanct figure—Psalter—House of David—This a creation—The real David—His life and songs—David for Amos —David in Ezekiel—Materials for his life—Books of Samuel— Stories in them—History as reconstructed by prophetic guilds— The original David—A racketeer—But a great soldier and statesman—Nabal and Abigail—Bathsheba—Absalom—Shimei—Wise Woman of Tekoah—Gulf between this David and David of Ezekiel—A poet, singer, musician—His *Diwan*—Vanished, except fragments—Suppressed?—Parallel of Imr al-Qais in Arabic—A model for later psalm-writers—Surviving fragments—Psalm xviii—Character of David in it—His relation to Jehovah—Self-humiliation of Jehovah—Beginning of "self-emptying" of Christ —Parallels and contrasts in the old poems of the Arabs—The personality of Jehovah—The Unseen for Arabs and Hebrews— Psalm xxiii—David as prophet—The last words of David—His laments—Arab parallels—David in the Psalter—Imitation in Arabic—Our failure before the contradictory figure of David.

Chapter VI 58

The anonymity of Hebrew literature—The songs of the people— The Book of the Upright—Arabic parallel—The Book of the Wars of Jehovah—The Hebrews a singing people—Relation of music to song—Modern illustrations—Song renders the emotion of the singer—Weakness, therefore, in Hebrew form—Parallel and contrast in Arabic—Hebrew literature romantic—The romantic in art as opposed to the classical—Western illustrations— Three stages of the romantic: primitive; revived and reviving; sophisticated—The Hebrews, great artists, playing children; primitive and modern—Their literature universal.

Chapter VII 64

The phenomenon of the Hebrew prophets—Their relation to song —Their origin, machinery and apparatus—Their place in the life of the Hebrews—Dynamic literature of the Hebrews: poetry;

philosophy; prophecy—The source of each—The prophets as channels for influences from the Unseen World—The reality of the Unseen—Contact with it, legitimate and illegitimate—That world as source of prophecy, soothsaying, poetry—Poetry under spirit influence—Invoking the muse—Subconscious production of verses—Prophecy connected with poetry, soothsaying, ecstatic religious emotion—Balaam—The last words of David—The prophet and soothsaying—Samuel as clairvoyant and prophet of Jehovah—"Man of God"—Meaning of Elohim—Seer—*Nabhi*—Arabic derivation—Gazer, i.e. scryer—Witch of Endor—Possessor of an *'ōbh*—Appearance of Samuel—"False Prophets"—Different tests—Relation of prophet to God—Moses, a unique case—Automatic speech—Amos—Interpreter of the actions of God—In the counsel of God—Parallel in Islam—On the outside, a fool, insane—"Man of the spirit"—"Spirits" in the Old Testament—Micaiah and Jehoshaphat—External sign when speaking in the spirit—Parallel in Islam—Jehovah in his court—Different pictures—Saul and the evil spirit from Jehovah—Muslim parallel—Saul "prophesies"—Story of Eldad and Medad—Hebrew knew no devils—Satan, the Adversary, prosecuting attorney in the divine court—The prophet as madman—Type of language of diviners in Arabic and in Hebrew—"Prophecy" as ecstatic religious emotion—Saul among the prophets—Darwish Zikr—Prayer meeting or perfunctory ceremony—David's dancing—Ritual dancing step—"Prophesying" by the Temple Choir—Muslim parallel—Tongues and prophets in the New Testament—Parallels in Islam—Parallel of Greek oracles.

Chapter VIII 84

Unique development among the Hebrews of this relation to the Unseen—The seer of the mind of Jehovah—Yet seer of the Unseen—Foretelling—The prophets as "defeatists"—"Good" and "bad" Kings—Moral defeatism—Contrast with Christian Church—Possibility and reality of foretelling—Theories of time in modern physics—Evidence for actual foreseeing—Charles Richet—Andrew Lang—Precognition in flashes—Micaiah's vision—The gathering of prophetic utterances and construction of prophetic books—Example, Amos—Writing in Syria from thirteenth century—Gathering of Words of Amos—Parallel of discourses of Christ—Construction of book—Parallel of Koran—Book of Amos contrasted with Book of Isaiah—Contrast of Book of Jeremiah—The prophet-theologian—The prophet as artistic writer—Conscious foretelling—The prophetic tract—Apocalyptic—The revenge of the mendacious seer.

Chapter IX 93

The Semites a story-telling people—Subjectivity in their stories—Ideas worked out in acts of persons—The reservoir of folklore tales—Stories that came to the Hebrews—How they passed them on in legend and used them in literature—Use of legends in Book of Judges—Broken to a scheme of history—Arabic parallel—Legends of David—Of Elijah and Elisha—The Book of Genesis the work of a great artist and philosopher—Unified by him—Contrast with Exodus—This creator personally unknown—The fundamentals of life for him—His ideal for Israel—His use of the pre-patriarchal stories—The two stories of Creation—The place of man in the world—Creation of light—A divine spirit brooding on the abyss—Prologue to Fourth Gospel—Wordsworth's ode—"In Our image, according to Our likeness"—World very good—Philosophical position—Mystical implication—Creation a begetting—This First Narrative new?—Second story—Garden Story—Folk-tale—The fairy garden—Its two trees—Man—The Beasts—"A help corresponding to him"—The attraction of sex—Parallel of Plato's myth—The serpent—Man acquires a conscience—Divides him from beasts—The different curses—On the serpent—On woman—On man—All reproduce basal facts of life—Toil—From the dust and to the dust—Man driven out—But the human family begins—Doctrine of the Fall—Paul—Apocalypse of Ezra—Varying status of Fall in Christian Church—The First Narrative a preface by the philosopher to his book?—Cain and Abel—The two Hebrew ideals of life—The Rechabites—The philosopher rejects this attitude—Sin has nothing to do with the mode of life—Abel and Ecclesiastes—The House of Cain—It produces arts and crafts—The case of the East against the West—The Sons of God and the Daughters of Men—Contending of the divine spirit in mankind—Use by Ecclesiastes—Legend of the Flood—Used as basis for the assured cycle of nature—Guaranteed by Jehovah's covenant—Table of descendants of Noah—Turned into picture of the philosopher's world, racial, linguistic, geographical, national—Tower of Babel—Arabian parallel—Abram—The greatest fact of the world, the people of Israel—Psychological study of individuals in a family—Contrast with Virgil's use of Aeneid—Men and women of Genesis—They are real—Were they historical?—Story of Joseph—The Hebrew race against the world—Its triumph—The will of Jehovah.

Chapter X 121

Other types of stories—Ruth—"Short story"—Dialect story—One of the Five Rolls—Their different qualities—David's Moabite ancestress—La Princesse Lointaine—Folklore elements—Boaz—Note of family unity—Stories by religious artists—Popular legend used didactically—Book of Jonah—Its relation to Book of Tobit—Folk-story of great fish—Character of Jonah—Parable of Jonah—Moral apologue—Why among the Prophets?—Book of Daniel—Very compound—Three Daniels—I. Ancient sage of Ezekiel—II. Younger contemporary of Ezekiel in Babylonian exile—Folklore stories (chapters i-vi)—III. Writer of Apocalypse (chapters vii-end)—Calls himself Daniel and writes 167-165 B.C.—How were these three brought together?—Story of Job—Job of legend patient throughout—Parallel Chaucer's Patient Griselda—What the poet of the Colloquies did to the Legend—Story of Balaam—Most strangely thrust into the Law itself (Numbers xxii, 2-xxiv, end)—Complete contrast to other references to Balaam in Old and New Testaments—Popular legend of a great diviner—Hostile use of legend by official Israel—Sympathetic moralizing use by this story-teller—Legend of Habakkuk in Greek additions to Daniel—Historical romance in Hebrew—Exodus—Had philosopher of Genesis any part in it?—Doctrine of "becoming" in Hebrew thought—Even of Jehovah—"I become what I become"—Exodus a débris of romance-fragments—Experience of present writer in Cairo—Historical tales by his donkey-boy—Parallels of Arabic romances—How far historical—The fable—Not native to Hebrews—Two tree-fables only—Book of the Stories of the Trees of Lebanon?—No fable in old Semitic—Came into Arabic late from Africa and India—Fable of Jotham—Fable of Jehoash—Was there a fable-center in North Syria?—Greek evidence—Egyptian Aramaic evidence—Other foreign stories of the Hebrews—Esther—Tobit—Story of Ahiqar and framework story of *Arabian Nights* kin to these—All go back to fifth century B.C. at least—Their very different fates—Did the Hebrews reach true history?—What is history?—The *Investigations* of Herodotus—The Hebrews very early reached a philosophy of history—Examples: That of Amos, the

CONTENTS

Prophets and the Nazirites—That of the prophetic guilds—That of the Law—The racialism of the philosopher of Genesis.

Chapter XI 145

The Hebrews and the Unseen World—The shudder before the Weird—A primary emotion—Most strong for the romantic mind —Kinship of religious attitude to imagination in poetry—Susceptibility to in-breaking from an unknown world—Western examples —Something beyond the world of sense—Contrast the classical attitude—Clearness and system—Map of Greeks reached abodes of gods and of the dead—The voyage of Odysseus—Journey of Aeneas with the Golden Bough—No shudders—Change with Lucian and Apuleius—Invasion from East—Classical system broken in pieces—A romantic world-system has come—A barrier between Seen and Unseen—Peace for early Christianity in rule of the Risen Christ—Similar result from destruction of Scandinavian mythology—Their parallel to situation for ancient Hebrews—Semitic mythology broken—Only débris surviving in Old Testament as poetic imagery—Effect of unique personality of Jehovah—Two worlds of Seen and Unseen and Jehovah dominant—No Heaven or Hell in Old Testament—The State of the Dead—In the desert the solitary-grave conception—The Babylonian Hades—For the Hebrews the two were confused—The pious dead and their relation to Jehovah—Necessarily an abiding one—But no place for them—God not the God of the dead—Enoch—Elijah—Muslim parallel—A belief later, in some undefined future spiritual existence—Ecclesiastes and Genesis reject it—Job's surmise of a physical resurrection and existence in this world—Ezekiel's vision of Valley of Dry Bones—These not spiritual immortality—Led to apocalyptic visions only—In three Psalms a deep assurance of continuance of intercourse with God —These are the beginning of a true doctrine of immortality—Otherwise the spirit world was dreadful in its vagueness—Its inhabitants impersonal and nameless—Messenger of Jehovah to Manoah—The Wrestler with Jacob—Parallel of nameless Jinn of the Arabs—Only personality the official Adversary—"The accuser of the brethren"—Cross of Archangel Michael—Angels with names only in Apocalypse of Daniel—Ghost stories—The Witch of Endor and Samuel—Immediate contact with spirit world—Vision of Eliphaz—Vision in Abraham's covenant—All have horror of human flesh before the Unseen—Assyrian army smitten before Jerusalem—Contrast to Greek army before Troy

CONTENTS xiii

—Belshazzar's Feast—"The fingers of a man's hand"—The romantic touch on the shuddering nerve.

Chapter XII 159

The world of visible nature—Hebrews had no "Nature" as an abstract personality—Jehovah filled whole background—An order in the world by the will of Jehovah—Man's place in the world—Two views—The world created as habitat for man—Man only part of the world and the world God's toy—Psalm civ—Man minimized in this picture—But man is Nature's priest—Jehovah looking at the earth—But the light is His garment—Speeches of the Lord in Job—Man insignificant—Moral blindness of the Lord—Love of animal creation—Parallel in Arab desert poetry—Also contrast—Man a discordant element—Man has disturbed peace of nature—A glorifying of beast-life—Parallel in Swift's Gulliver—Broad Hebrew feeling for wild life in nature—Beasts copartners with man—Another Jehovah, separate and lofty—Product of exile—Strange poem in Isaiah, chapter ii—Development of this picture in Islam—Man looking at nature—Is carried beyond to Jehovah—On the way to pantheism of Wordsworth—The world the Face of God—Muslim parallel—Simplicity of Hebrew diction—No adjectives in Hebrew—Touches of description make pictures—The lonely word—Saw the far horizon—Contrast of Amos and Robert Burns.

Chapter XIII 171

The Hebrews had philosophy—Summary of previous examples of this in book—Genesis philosophical throughout—Jehovah a "becoming" God—Platonists, not Aristotelians—Wise Woman of Tekoah—Book of Jonah—What is philosophy?—Thinking rationally about life—Three accepted bases—Personality of Jehovah—Man, the thinking percipient—The physical world—Jehovah the metaphysic of the Hebrews—The character of Jehovah—Man mentally and morally free—Man had a moral sense—Might doubt if Jehovah had—The physical world abiding, objective, real —In perpetual change—But no phantasmagoria—The obscuring myth of "Wisdom"—Two meanings of Hebrew word *hochma*—Reason and wisdom—The difference—Fundamental idea in that word—Controlling, ruling, guiding—Examples of application to arts and crafts—Women have full share—Book of Proverbs—Its contents—Success in life—Be good and you will be successful—A

CONTENTS

reasoned, *a priori*, position—Wide extremes—Doctrine of worldly success—Doctrine of Reason speaking in life—The world rational—In harmony with nature—Can man think God's thoughts?—Two views—Job xxviii denies—Man cannot reach absolute reason—For man only the fear of God—Yet reason is objectified to God—The relation of man's reason to the fear of Jehovah—Rival guides in life—Authority in the Law and the Prophets—Reason in the soul of man—In Genesis—In Psalm i—In Psalm ciii—The tears of human things and trust in Jehovah—"The beginning of reason is the fear of Jehovah"—"The beginning of reason is 'get reason' "—A sceptic as to knowing Jehovah—Personifying in Hebrew rhetoric—Reason becomes she—How she speaks in and through the world to men, her sons—Provoked to scornful laughter—Delighting in her sons—Her house for training—Personified Folly, a contrasting figure—Thus a revelation in the world—Intelligible to men because they are children of Reason—A rational bridge between God and man—No systematic treatise on philosophy—Must piece together—Proverbs viii culminates in the Fourth Gospel—Development in Islam—Butler's Analogy—Inner light—Prologue to Fourth Gospel—Logos is "reason," not "word"—"In the beginning"—"Light" of Genesis—"The true light"—Reason the only begotten son—Become flesh—Centuries of unknown development between—Not the Logos of Philo—Not the *Memrá*—Difference of Fourth Gospel from other three—Utterances of this divine Reason—A constructive theory—But not arbitrarily imposed—Similar utterances in Matthew and Luke—Different possible biographies of one man—A possible interpretation of Christ—A contemporary record—Other theories of the world—Not "very good"—Or not rational—Appeal to the facts of life—Modern humanism—But Hebrew scheme has Jehovah behind it—Therefore criticism of Jehovah—Reasoned scepticism as to Jehovah's goodness—Or as to possibility of knowing Him—Evil as folly—Treatment of the fool—Folly is almost hopeless—Distinction among fools—"The blunderer"—Prophets came to use this word for "sinner"—Philosophers kept "blunderer"—A hard-headed, rationalistic attitude to sin—But not optimistic—Hebrews pessimists as to improvement in man—Due to his created nature—Yet there is a divine influence upon him—Either authoritative and external—Law and Prophets—Or from within—A spirit implanted in man—Or the voice of nature—Image and likeness of God—In Proverbs neither Law nor

Prophets—Only divine Reason speaking through life—In Book of Job many views on human suffering—For poet problem of unmerited suffering—Other treatments of Job in present book—Could God answer challenge of Job?—Or of poet?—The poet knew the Prologue and God had no answer to it—But Job did not—Job's ignorance like ours—Has God an answer to us on unmerited suffering?—Job's moral sense *must* be in God who made him—No Hebrew sceptic sees this—And few modern philosophers—We have to explain ourselves and we are parts of the world—The poet created Job and Job expressed the poet—But Job still was Job—The dramatic, pathetic, and esthetic elements obscure the philosophical issue.

Chapter XIV 197

Book of Ecclesiastes greatest product of Hebrew thinking—Pushes utilitarianism of Proverbs to an ironic end—Also a great creation in literature—I. Evokes Solomon from his tomb—He gives his experience in life and as to usefulness of wisdom—Connection with Solomon's dream—Qohéleth, "collector," a name for Solomon—Had "collected" everything—II. Then author speaks as himself—We know nothing about him outside of his book—Meaning of "Ecclesiastes"—"The Preacher"—"Ecclesiastes" was a gentleman farmer of old family—Also business man—Aristocrat of best type—Sympathetic with sorrowful and oppressed—"They have no comforter"—The government of his time—Wide experience in life—Always saw two sides of everything—The part of a wife in life—Wrote as an old man—A book of self-revelation—Qualities in this type of literature—Western parallels—A great personality; a great book—Friendly, lovable—Manifold influences on later world literature—Steadfast courage in facing life—Admonition always to go on—What makes life worth while?—III. His philosophical scheme—Compound of school of Genesis and his own experiences and speculation—Opposition of God and man—The toiling, unresting universe—An order in the universe—Confirmed by God—Man must accept—Doctrine of conformity—Toil in the mind of man—To make ultimate reality unattainable—The fear of God—What is this fear?—What is his God?—Man of the dust—Returns to dust—What is "spirit" in man?—Comparison of passages in Genesis and Ecclesiastes—All is transitory—Development of doctrine of "becoming"—Evading God's curse—Nature of "God" for Ecclesiastes—His own moral norm—God's norm, amoral—"Good before God"—Blunderers—His own constructive philosophy—"The All possesses Time"—An occasion for every event—The event and its opposite—All come round and fit in—Arranged to keep man in his place—But happiness in work while working—A gospel of work and an evasion of the curse—"Judgment" the coming of the opposite—Thus the world is not "vain" or "empty" but transitory—Fill the flying moments with flying work and flying joy—But there is no progress—This round of events only a screen between God and man—If God is irritated He may strike through it—The blunderer—Parallel in Muslim theology—The primitive Semitic attitude—Ecclesiastes and woman—Parallel in Genesis—Later Jewish attitude to Eve—This, too, in Ecclesiastes but not his personal feeling—A literary convention—"A wife whom thou lovest"—"Remember thy well of water"—Parallel figure in Proverbs and the Song—IV. The book as a guide to life—Practical conclusions carefully balanced—Life is many-sided—Not a fatalist—But a thorough conformist—A pessimist?—A scheme of life—He faced life gallantly—Life is good and sweet—Live full, joyous lives—St. Paul and "Rejoice in the Lord"—Not a hedonist—His joy in work—Face death steadily—No terror in it—An escape from transitoriness—To do one's part by life—A cynic as to God—Because a conformist—But not as to life—Life a reality to be lived—This cynicism inevitable for the Conformist—V. His place in philosophy—Doctrine of "becoming" leads to transitoriness—The thing and its opposite—Joy in doing—The worth of life—The body as House of Life—Its breakdown an escape—The appendix—The book in circulation—How in the Canon?—Its appeal to many types of mind.

Epilogue 216

Note on Hebrew Old Testament 221

Index (of Scripture References) 223

PROLOGUE

I AM well aware that this book will be strange and even repellent to two very different classes of readers. To the specialist in Old Testament criticism it will seem unscientific and even visionary and to the worthy people for whom their Bible is still Sacred Scripture and the Word of God it may well seem destructive of their basis for eternal truth and even frivolous. To these last let me say that I am far nearer their position than they may at first think, and that the specialist may quite possibly classify me and my book as reactionary. The truth, I think, is that while all precise doctrines of inspiration and inerrancy—in any degree at all—have for me gone by the board I have come more and more to recognize an eternal purpose in the history of the Hebrew people and a unique guidance behind them and in them. He who has once accepted the theistic position and realizes what it means will have little difficulty in taking this further step. I have therefore tried to show the Hebrew people expressing their innermost self—and selves—in their literature and to bring out very clearly that in the end this forces us back to the fact of Jehovah and His choice of them as His own peculiar people. What lies behind that fact I do not know, but it, as the Hebrews knew it, is an unshakable fact of history. It is, so far, unexplained and it seems unexplainable. The guesses at explanation, through a tribal god of the Kenites and the like, are simply ludicrous; and the story the Hebrews themselves told of the revelation in the Mount may be strange but is not ludicrous.

There the critical specialists will join issue with me at once. That I cannot help, for I begin from an essentially different philosophical and literary position. I am a theist and I can recognize what are the consequences of that position; I am a student of literature and I believe in taking peoples as they show themselves clearly in their literatures. I do not believe, either, that literature can be profitably studied in a concordance any more than botany can be profitably studied *in horto sicco*. It must be studied as a thing alive, bearing its own life in it and having its own laws of life. That holds of the literature of every people and it holds of the literature of the Hebrew people. This is no new discovery as to the Hebrews. It was made already in the eighteenth century as a part of what we commonly call the Romantic Awakening. At that time the attempt was made to present the mass of literature which we call the Old Testament from a fresh point of view. Of course no view is fresh in the absolute sense. For of every way of looking at every thing there have been ancient adumbrations and even full statements. These would, then, being perhaps premature, fall into oblivion of a kind and the normal and usual attitudes would reassert themselves. For a position or method to live it must come as a stage in a process of continuous development. Otherwise, it is born into an alien environment; it looks too far forward and has to wait another age to be really appreciated and fully understood.

So with the interpretation of the Old Testament. The history of that interpretation is full of premature attempts at fresh viewpoints. Each of these attempts had its origin in some drift of thinking about human life and literature, apart from the steady course of what would call itself, by preference, Old Testament science and apart from the studies of the schools. Each was a cross-fertilization from outside of the schools and while, in a sense, the products lived, they could not be said to flourish. Their time was not yet come. Illustrations of this, and also of the fundamental attitude in the fresh attempt of the present book, are to be found in the work of Bishop Lowth (1710-1787) and, a generation later, of the German Herder (1744-1803). Both were products of the Romantic Awakening. Romanticism, of course, had never really disappeared; it had at the most been asleep; and when Alexander Pope died in 1744 there were signs everywhere of a return in literature to nature as opposed to art. Especially did this show itself in a recognition that each national literature was the spontaneous, even automatic, expression of the genius of each people. The more primitive peoples and their literatures, as opposed to the more sophisticated literatures of modern Europe, here came to their own; and with that grew the feeling that each people as a whole was responsible for its own literature and not a select group of litterateurs. The dictum, "Das Volk dichtet," applied here in a much wider and truer sense than to the ballad problem. And each poetry, it was recognized, could only be fully understood in the environment which produced it. So came Goethe's saying, "He who will understand a poet must go to the poet's land." An early expression of this reaching out into the life of the people for the sources and explanation of its elemental literature is to be found in Collins's great *Ode on Popular Superstitions* (1749). Thomas Gray was interested in Scandinavian, Celtic, and Old English literature from 1760 on. Macpherson's *Ossian*, with all its sins upon its head, appeared in 1762-1763. Percy's *Reliques of Ancient English Poetry*, loaded with other and different sins, appeared in 1765. Chatterton, the great imitator of genius, died in 1770. The workings of the spirit of the age dragged Samuel Johnson from Bolt Court and Fleet Street to the recesses of the West Highlands of Scotland in 1773. A year later Thomas Warton's monumental *History of English Poetry*, monumental for the early forms and sources of that poetry, began to appear. Earlier than almost all of them, but part of the movement of the same swelling wave, were the lectures on the Old Testament of Robert Lowth in 1753. His *De Sacra Poesi Hebraeorum* struck, for the Bible, a new note. Academic lectures, delivered in Latin, they yet recognized that the poetry of the Old Testament was the poetry of the Hebrew people as a people. It might be advisable to call it "sacred" but that made little difference for Lowth; he knew that there were all kinds of poetry there and he made that clear. His study was a study in pure literature and he kept as free as he could from all archeology, theology, history, and "higher criticism"; the texts he read and emended freely. Later, when his book was taken up and edited by Michaelis it was loaded with a burden of school-learning, but Lowth himself had cared nothing for these things and had kept away from them. His was the case of a brilliant classical scholar who had taken the trouble to learn to read Hebrew easily and who was concerned only to apply his literary experience in the Greek and Latin classics to the understanding of the ideas and literary forms of the Semitic texts before him. Just because he was of the first swellings of that wave he could use for his comparisons only the two literatures which he knew thoroughly, those of Greece and Rome. He, therefore, was constrained to find epics and dramas and odes and the other forms of classical literary art in the far simpler and quite differently constructed literature of the Hebrews; he applied a set of classical norms to an essentially romantic material. But, however that may be, it is his glory to have recognized that the Old Testament is the literature of the Hebrew people—the expression in words, used with art, of all that had come to them. With Herder the matter went further. He came, a generation later, when many primitive literatures were accessible in translation. From his title, *Vom Geist der hebräischen Poesie* (1782-1783), the word "sacred" has vanished and it is the "spirit" of the poetry of the Hebrews for which he searches. He has little need of classical parallels, for he is what we would call now a "folklorist." The conception of the people, as a whole, spontaneously expressing itself in its literature has arrived.

Why did not more come of this rich and significant beginning? Why was it possible that, practically in our own day, a man of university and classical training like Mr. Gladstone could write such a book as *The Impregnable Rock of Sacred Scripture* and another, of academic status, could write on *The Divine Library of the Old Testament*? The answer can only be that the time was not ripe. On one hand the learned commentary of Michaelis on Lowth was significant as showing how much was yet to be done in lexicography, grammar, history, antiquities, textual and higher criticism before the way was really cleared for psychological and esthetic considerations. Lowth and Herder, carried on the wave of the Romantic Awakening, had looked over and beyond these details, but the details remained and had first to be cleared away. On another side, their attack had brought home to many minds that the Old Testament, whatever sacred and theological associations it might have, could be regarded also as part of the literary expression of the human race. We know how Sir Walter Scott read the Bible, and especially the Old Testament, with his children and explained it to them. If he had only left to us some record of these expositions among his *Tales of a Grandfather* we would have had a unique exposition of a great romantic literature by one of the greatest of modern romantic artists. But we can see that ancient art flashing into new light when his Rebecca sang,

> By day along the astonished lands
> The cloudy pillar glided slow;
> By night Arabia's crimsoned sands
> Returned the fiery column's glow.

The picture in the mind of the ancient Hebrew romantic artist is lifted for a moment clear away from the obscurations of our modern higher critics and rational expositors by passing through the mind of another and kindred poet. When the Abbot of Iona in *The Lord of the Isles* turns to De Bruce and, struck by the spirit, changes his curse to a blessing—"I bless thee and thou shalt be blessed!"—it is the enigmatic figure of Balaam that is suddenly reconstructed for us and put, alive, before us, free of all questions of exegesis. And his Brian in *The Lady of the Lake* shows how far he had entered into the obscure psychological problems of what we, covering our ignorance with a word, call "prophetism." Brian was not Elijah, but he was of his kin. The mind of a poet, thoroughly at home in the figures and ideas of his own medieval world, saw and recognized in their reality those strange Hebrew appearances. And we, looking at the Old Testament in these flashes, through his eyes, are lifted above all problems of history, criticism, analysis, documents, all things local and of the garment of time, to see those figures and happenings *sub specie eternitatis*—bare pictures, ideas, emotions, that can be of any time or place. That freedom the Romantic Awakening wrought for Scott.

And now in our day, the methods of criticism, of the analysis and dating of documents and of the apparatus of learning generally, have run themselves to a stop. Critics of critics of critics have become more interested in each other than in the literary reality before them. The addition of another Isaiah to that anonymous crowd seems more important than the heart-cry, "Comfort ye, comfort ye, my people!" A suspected crack in the unity of Ezekiel's Book is more than the problems of Ezekiel's strange and cracked personality, than the majesty of the Valley of Dead Bones or the glory of the Burden of Tyre. Critics are now fairly devouring each other. And through it all, and because of it all, the Old Testament has fallen on evil days. A battle-ground of professional critics cannot interest the multitude, even those that read and think. If that is all that is in the Old Testament—a jumble of historical and critical problems—we need not take any account of it, is their attitude. And yet the men and women of the Old Testament—their sensations, emotions, ideas—are exactly the same as ours at the present day. On the side of giving a mirror to life and all varieties of living, the Old Testament, it is safe to say, is more modern than all of the New except the words of Christ Himself. The rest of the New Testament is theology, and some of it very ancient and moth-eaten theology, but the Old Testament is the very life and thinking of the whole of the Hebrew people and their life and their thinking, *sub specie eternitatis,* are exactly our own.

All this assuredly being so, I can only entreat the specialist to believe that I do not approach these problems in ignorance of their details and difficulties. A lifetime of study of the Hebrew and the Arabic literatures now lies behind me, and I can refer those who might be inclined to question my so-called scholarship to my earlier, specialist, writings on these literatures. On the basis of these long-continued specialistic studies I now dare to write a non-specialistic book. I write it because I venture to think that something of the kind is needed.

This book, further, makes no attempt at being a systematic treatise; system is abhorrent to literature and treatise is a word of ill omen in connection with the Old Testament. Its object, rather, is to suggest, and no more, a different way of regarding the mass of Hebrew writings from that most in use among us. To open, if it may be, certain vistas and prospects which may be found fresh and full of meaning for the life and thinking of the People of Jehovah. To see anything from a new angle is to see often a quite new thing, and it is the hope of this book that the Old Testament as seen from its window may have a novelty not unattractive.

All learned apparatus has been suppressed; the text stands for itself and tries to be intelligible by itself. But it presupposes that the reader will make constant use of his English Old Testament. When these pages were in the free-hand stage of classroom lectures the Old Testament was the only text-book prescribed. The lecturer used it in the Hebrew and translated from the Hebrew as he went; the class used one or other of the English versions. No other method was possible as the vast majority of the class had no knowledge of Hebrew, while the course of lectures was in Hebrew literature and not in the English Bible. Thus arose the free translations from the Hebrew which are scattered through the following pages. When they differ from the current English versions (King James, the Revised and all the private versions), it is for good and sufficient reasons. There does not exist in English a translation of the Old Testament which is trustworthy throughout, and many show a lamentable ignorance of ordinary Hebrew grammar and usage. It is still the glory of the King James Version that, for all its manifold inaccuracies, it has rendered the spirit of the Hebrew Scriptures into perfect English. There is that at least to the credit of James VI of Scotland and I of England. The appended note on the structure of the Hebrew Bible as the Hebrews themselves put it together seemed necessary.

In the following pages I recognize that there will be found much repetition. That was in part inherent in the plan of the book, for certain elements in Hebrew thinking kept recurring and each time had to be given their place and weight with due explanation for each situation. That is how life is constructed, and, as the Greek said, you cannot split it in two with a hatchet. Neat little watertight classifications may be possible in a text-book; they are not possible in any statement of the life of a people. But, again, some of the repetition was of intention. There is much ignorant writing at the present time which presents Jehovah as a bogey-god and the Hebrew people as Calvinists of the most objectionable type. These ideas seem to be a hang-over from theological speculations of the past to which no theologian now pays any attention, and the original responsibility for which rests with certain western schools of theology, especially from the Reformation on, and not with the theological thinking and religious aspiration of the Hebrew people. To those, also, who summon us to follow the guidance of the Greek mind I would suggest that they consider the depth and originality of Hebrew speculation on the origin and meaning of the world, on the rationality of the world, on the relation of the divine Reason to human thinking and on that strange development of Hebrew joy and gladness in life, the laughing Reason of the eighth chapter of the Book of Proverbs. If the light-hearted, philosophical Greeks reached anything like this last I do not know of it.

The dedication is the belated tribute of an old man to the two teachers whose living words most helped him as a student in his youth. And if, perchance, beyond this silence, in some Elysian Fields—for sure I am that no dreary Hades or Sheol can hold those spirits—it may come to their knowledge that their names have been thus gratefully if strangely joined, there under the true eyes of that Eternal Wisdom, whom they both sought and followed and have found, they will understand. The attitude and the methods of this book are essentially their own. From John Nichol I learned to see beyond literature the philosophy of the minds and the races that produced it, and from James Robertson I learned to recognize in the modern Semitic East the same workings of thought and emotion that produced our Old Testament. How far they would accept my results I have no means of knowing. I never heard John Nichol deal with the Old Testament and he may easily have lumped it, with Carlyle, as Jewish old clothes. James Robertson felt I was right as to the Prophets, but thought me rash as to the pre-patriarchal stories. On both I was following his own clues.

This preface has reached a length altogether contrary to usage. It might be called an Introduction and I shall call it a Prologue, to balance the Epilogue, but its essential characteristic is that in it I speak directly and personally to my possible future readers. Hereafter I shall not presume beyond the occasional "we" of the lecturer.

Finally, I wish to express my gratitude to my some-time student, Mrs. W. M. Mackensen, for much loyal labor and patient care in the preparing of the manuscript of this book for the press. I am deeply in her debt.

CHAPTER I

ON READING THE OLD TESTAMENT

OUR time has seen a great development of interest in folklore and these modern studies of the ideas and usages of the masses of the people have reached the Near East. Collections have been made of songs, proverbs, stories—popular literature in the widest sense. The modern dialects of Arabic and Aramaic have been booked in texts, lexicons and grammars. The manners and customs, the superstitions (as we call them), religious usages and beliefs, have been recorded and studied. And when all this is done, the astonishing fact comes out that these peoples today, living there in Syria, reaching back into the desert and north into the mountains and south into Egypt, are in all essentials of fundamental thinking and living, one with the masses of people in the pages of the Old Testament. The Canaanites are there; the Hebrews are there; the Arabs are there; the Arameans are there; the Phoenicians are there—still surviving, although they may call themselves by other names. Even the tremendous fact of Islam and the apparently overwhelming invasion of the Arabs have changed little but the names. In consequence, these modern folklore researches have come to be of the first importance for the interpretation of the Old Testament.

And, again, another and even more precise possibility of interpretation has showed itself. The Hebrews, it has become plain, were simply an Arab clan which, under strange and unique guidance, entered Palestine and settled there. But they remained Arab, although they denounced the name. And their literature, throughout all their history and to this day, in its methods of production and in its recorded forms, is of Arab scheme and type. Every kind of literature in the Old Testament, with the partial exception of the Psalms, finds a pigeonhole for itself in the great scheme of Arabic letters. Many even of the Psalms find their parallels, in the poems of the desert. And, further, while the Hebrew literature has often a spirit, a variety of picture, and an essential life lacking in that of the Arabs, it is, in comparison, small in amount. There may survive in the Old Testament a single specimen of a type of which a dozen are to be found in Arabic. When, then, the literature of the Hebrews is considered as to the literary types which it contains the key is to be found in the far wider Arabic literature. And, still more, it is not only for the literature of the Arabs in the desert, the cousins in blood and form of life of the Hebrews, that this comparison holds. In all the later development of the literature produced and written in Arabic the types persist and the curious rhythmic form, for example, in the Psalms of Ascent can be paralleled today in Arabic songs sung in the African Tripoli. In this preservation of old, fundamental, Arab types the influence of Islam has been strong. It has so preserved words, ideas, forms of literature, social forms, religious institutions and usages that these in modern Islam are often the counterpart of those of the old Hebrew days in the Old Testament. The commonest Hebrew word for "prophet" is a borrowed word, from an Arabic root, which came with the institution itself from the desert; the organizations and usages of the prophets in the Old Testament with their so-called "schools" are closely the same as those of the Muslim darwishes and their fraternities at the present day; the mixing in and influence on the politics of their time, exercised by the Hebrew prophets, is strangely paralleled by that of the Saints of Islam and was feared and resented by the Kings of Islam in much the same way as by the Kings of Judah and Israel. Even such a problem as that of the domestic affairs of Hosea can be paralleled in Islam. As a consequence of all this, our widening knowledge of Muslim institutions and their intimate workings is bringing out into fresh light the living reality of the life and thinking of the Hebrews in the Old Testament. This is infinitely more important and more illuminating than any knowledge which has been derived from Assyrian or Babylonian sources. It is a light of comparison and a light also of contrast. For while it shows a basal original unity—of race, language, and fundamental institutions—it shows also one strange and overwhelming difference. The Hebrews were dominated by the personality of Jehovah, and there is no such personality behind the world of Islam. Allah is not Jehovah any more than he is the God and Father of our Lord Jesus Christ.

In what spirit, then, and along what paths, must this approach to the Old Testament be carried out? First, it is necessary to turn away from that exclusive preoccupation with the theological ideas of the Prophets, on the one hand, and with the legislation of the Pentateuch, on the other, which has so long dominated Old Testament Introduction. There are other aspects of the Hebrew literary genius—expressing the workings of Hebrew experience and thinking—which are more important as elements in the Hebrew contribution to the thinking of the world. It is necessary, also, to turn away from exclusive preoccupation with the external analysis of so-called "original" documents—E, J, P, D, and their numerous offspring—and ask ourselves what ideas, what attitudes to the external problems of the world and what esthetic forms in which to express these ideas and attitudes, do the books themselves, as they lie before us, contain? Original documents, for example, lie behind our Book of Genesis but for the meaning of that book as a mirror of the ideas of the Hebrews they may be disregarded. Rather, we have to ask, what did the artist mean who created our Book of Genesis as we have it? This is a commonplace in the study of literature, but is almost universally disregarded in dealing with the Old Testament. It is necessary, also, to take up an attitude definitely psychological and esthetic, as opposed to historical or critical. We must recognize that any rearranging of the literature of the Hebrews in strict order and any dating by years is far beyond us. We can see, sometimes, a sequence and development of ideas, but we are driven often, also, to recognize that it is of the very nature of great thinking and great literature to make great leaps forward, leaps which anticipate the slower thinking of centuries, and give still other centuries matter for thought. We ourselves are still assimilating the guesses of Plato and Aristotle. The doctrine of orderly development applies to the things of the spirit only with large accommodations. Nature may not go *per saltum*, but it is of the nature of the mind to leap. Nor is even language a sure guide. The untutored and colloquial freedom of the Hebrew style of the Books of Samuel is very different from the regularity of the Hebrew of the Books of Kings; but the Hebrew of Amos is already of classic regularity. Environment may easily overcome chronological sequence. Again, the very nature of this approach, minimizing for its own purposes history and chronology and laying all the stress on ideas and their esthetic forms of presentation, requires that the literature be viewed according to its types and kinds. We must begin with the literary form or the philosophical idea and classify the individual cases under that; thus the type and kind will explain the case. This, of course, runs in the teeth of the strictly analytic methods followed so far, but it has high advantages of its own. It is, in fact, the method of literature as opposed to that of physical science, the method of studying modes of expression rather than concrete facts. But it may be asked, How can those types and kinds be reached and defined before the individual cases in the Old Testament have been considered? Your method, that is, is unscientific. The answer is twofold. It is certainly not the method of natural science but it is the universal method of literature. When we come to consider a literature or an individual poet we have all got in our minds a system of classification which we apply, because we are dealing with universal ideas and not arbitrary facts. Lowth had his system derived from his Greek and Latin writers and his defect, if anywhere, was that he looked to find that scheme too narrowly exemplified in the poets of the Hebrews. Herder had the range of ideas which he had gained from his folklore studies in more primitive literatures. The modern student of "the Bible as literature" applies the categories of our modern literature and so falls into the absurdity of calling the Twenty-Third Psalm a sonnet, a complete misconception, even as a metaphor, of its literary form. But they all testify that the kind is primary and that the individual case falls under it. And, secondly, it so happens, as has been indicated above, that we do possess in the Arabic literature a complete set of types and kinds—a set of pigeonholes, in a word—in which, *mutatis mutandis*, the literature of the Hebrews can be tucked away. Lowth did not know it; Herder did not know it; our modern expounders of the Bible as literature know it still less. Michaelis and some few others who knew Arabic, have had glimpses of it, but it has only been of late years, through the development of folklore studies, including the more popular Arabic literatures, that this fact and consequent method have been fully brought home. All which means that the future expounders of the Old Testament must not only be folklorists but also Arabists. They will thus be able to begin with an accomplished synthesis and try it out on the surviving fragments of the literature of the Hebrews. For the Arabic literature, from the time of Mohammed, at least, has come to us practically entire and complete, while that of the Hebrews is only a gathering up of fragments—a collection, in many cases, of single, if magnificent specimens.

Finally, and most important of all, it is to be remembered that in such a consideration as this, we must read our Old Testament not for content—edifying or theological—nor for criticism—historical or textual—but purely for the effect of each passage upon ourselves. How do we *feel* them, respond esthetically to them? We must read, as it were, with a finger on the pulse of sympathy with beauty which throbs to the emotion which beauty excites, feeling for that leap which tells that the deepest springs of imagination have been touched. Let the student read in this spirit Judges v; Psalms xviii, xc and civ; Job xxviii, xxxviii-xxxix; Ezekiel xxvii-xxviii, xxxvii, 1-14, subduing all questionings as to where, when and why these things were written and taking them for granted as creations of sheer beauty by the eternal human spirit. Let him read them by preference in the King James Version, a very often faulty but always great romantic recasting of a mass of great romantic literature—one of the creative miracles of the English language. In his introduction to Canto II of *Marmion,* Scott has well expressed this self-abandoning absorption:

> ... ponder o'er some mystic lay,
> Till the wild tale had all its sway.
> And in the bittern's distant shriek,
> I heard unearthly voices speak.
> . . .   .
> Till from the task my brow I cleared,
> And smiled to think that I had feared.

If he does this he will know the difference between the always necessary but always deadening critical and historical analysis of details and the hearkening to the eternal spirit, "the spirit breathed by dead men to their kind." Our fathers knew this well, although they looked at it theologically and named it the witness of Scripture to itself. And that witness is true.

It is the suggestion, then, of this book that the Old Testament should be again approached on the side of literature, pure and simple, under the guidance of folklore in general and in particular of the literatures, ideas, and institutions kindred to it. Placed thus in the midst of the human race and of the peoples sister to the Hebrews, it will show both its general humanity and its unique character.

CHAPTER II

THE HEBREWS AND THEIR POETS

OUR study, then, is, first and last, of literature. And the Old Testament, first and last, is literature in the truest, broadest sense. In this it is to be distinguished from the New Testament, for the New Testament is primarily theology and what is theology in the first instance can only against the grain become literature. It is true that the New Testament contains some elements of literature; the Fourth Gospel and Luke's two treatises and some passages of Paul are literature of the first rank; the Apocalypse, too, has carried over some large utterances from its Hebrew originals. But the New Testament, throughout, is limited to the expression of the religion and theology of the earliest Christian Church and does not cover the whole life of any people. Its first three books are stated biographies of the Founder of Christianity and all the rest consists of meditation and theorizings on that primary fact and its consequences. All is religious and edifying, although often, in its theories, contradictory. The Old Testament, on the other hand, has been a puzzle to many excellent people, and an unholy joy to others not so excellent, because of its frank immoralities and perverted pieties. It covers the possibilities of life with the utmost liberality, and precisely because of that the expert sermonizer has found it invaluable. There are very few situations in the most modern life to which it does not hold up a mirror; its men and women, crude or sophisticated, walk the streets beside us and their most variegated adventures are told with whole-hearted enjoyment and complete simplicity. For while the Old Testament sometimes portrays sophisticated people, it does not belong to sophisticated literature. It was not produced as a whole by professional writers, but by all the people. We cannot think of its authors as sitting down to turn out "literature" or to write "works," as Buffon put on clean lace ruffles before he sat down to his desk. Rather the Hebrew people by the roadside, on the hillside, in the city, in the open country, expressed itself, individually, in story, in song, in meditation, in oration, just as it stood or sat there—in its shirt sleeves, as we would now say—and with little or no thought of anything but the spontaneous expression of their life and of the immediate situation. Their thinking and their words were an emotional and intellectual but thoroughly natural secretion. They produced it automatically and it expressed them—themselves. And yet it was no trivial "selves" that it expressed. It mirrored their whole history and development; showed how God had dealt with them and how they reacted to His dealings. There have been, and are, peoples whose sayings and doings, except as accidents and incidents in the stream of human life, are of no importance. But just as there have been individual men who count and amount in that stream of life, so there have been peoples. And the Hebrews were of these. It was not only that they produced a literature with elements of greatness in it. They did so, but the nations round them may have done the same. We do not know. But we do know that somehow, mysteriously, these Hebrews received, or found, a secret, entered into a relationship, which lifted them clear away from the ruck of those other nations. They believed, quite simply and undoubtingly, that they were in a special relation to the Unseen World and to a personality called Jehovah. They told a tale, reaching back into the times of legend, as to how this came about. This tale was perfectly clear and distinct, was solid history to the minds, for example, of Amos and the people to whom he talked, and only the extremest scepticism as to the truth of history can assert there was nothing to it; that nothing had happened to form a basis for their belief in this unique relationship. We may explain it all away as we please, but the fact remains that the Hebrews believed it and that it was the foundation of their national existence. All the expression of their existence in their literature turns round it and is related to it. This was much more than any philosophical discovery of henotheism or monotheism; it was a unique personal relationship to a unique personality and all their self-expression in their literature relates itself to that personality. So if there is any development at all in Hebrew thinking and in its expression in the Hebrew literature it is in the way, or ways, in which they thought of this personality. But the personality was given to them to begin with, and Amos in his time appeals confidently to the knowledge on that point, of the crowds whom he addressed. As to that, he could tell them nothing new; he could only remind them of their consequent duties. But the development lay in their views of the position of that personality in the Unseen World. On that, there will be much more hereafter.

All this being so, it follows that for the Hebrews, God was tremendously real and distinct—next in reality to their own selves. Their literature, therefore, being an expression of themselves, expressed Him too in the most direct fashion. They often were not at all what we would call pious, or regenerate, or religious-minded, but as to God they had no shadow of doubt. This explains the extreme simplicity with which, throughout, they accept Him and treat Him. He was so real to them that they were on familiar terms with Him and need stand on no circumstances with Him. They were the People of Jehovah. So real was this to them that it became a moral handicap. Jehovah would see them through whatever they might do or be. So we find in the Old Testament all manner of reactions to this fundamental idea; we find, that is, all the phases of the thinking and acting of the Hebrews. For the old Hebrews our secular and sacred were one. The supernatural and the natural were also one; the only difference there was of the invisible and the visible; and these two were equally real.

In looking, then, at the Old Testament as the literature of the Hebrews we must be sure of these points. (I) It was no artificial and unreal literature, the production of a professional class of authors; it came directly from all the people. (II) It was the spontaneous expression of their life, of their innermost and most essential character. (III) As such it mirrored their history and was dominated by the personality of Jehovah. But (IV) this personality was Jehovah as they saw Him and reacted to Him in all kinds of different and, to us, strange ways. Jehovah as He was in Himself we can only know, if at all, as we put all those different reactions together. But when we do that, even incompletely, a personality emerges that was quite unique, even as the Hebrews, on that Godward side of their thinking and emotions were quite unique. We often speak of "the Greek miracle"; from this point of view we are fully justified in speaking of "the Hebrew miracle." For their phenomenon was equally great, unique, and unexplained as that of the Greeks. And there is another resemblance between the Hebrew and the Greek miracles. Exactly as, from time to time, the world has seemed to forget the Greeks and their accomplishment, or, at least, to ignore them, and then has been compelled to return and again go to school with them; so, again and again, the world has thought that it could ignore the Hebrews and even make jest of that Jehovah whom they had expressed. We are now, more or less, in such a time. Yet there are ample signs that the necessity of explaining our thoughts and ourselves is driving us back to seek an explanation of the whole phenomenon of the Hebrews and of their faith in Jehovah. The fact of the personality of Jehovah is the secret of the Hebrews and they have kept it so far.

But our subject is not that ultimate Jehovah, whatever He was, or is, in Himself, but the Hebrews as they were in themselves and as they show themselves still in the pages of the Old Testament where they have recorded themselves. We have there the expression of their life, character, personality, as a people. In that personality, so mirrored in their literature, what is the most essential characteristic? All truly national, racial literatures have a characteristic and this characteristic comes out most clearly in the poetry, which is the soul of every literature and expresses the soul of the people that produced it. We recognize this when we look at all deeply into whatever national literatures we may really know. We know the difference of spirit between Homer and Virgil, between Aristophanes and Plautus, although we may find it hard to put that difference into an epigram. We know how far Catullus made himself into a Greek and how less far Horace. We know the strange spiritual gulf between Shakespeare and Goethe and the more easily understood chasm between Milton and Klopstock. We know how far English poetry in general, with its mist of imaginative possibilities in its expression, stands apart from the fine, thin clarity of French poetry with its exact precision. All these things we know if we cannot always fit them with precise words. But what of the Hebrews as to either their whole literature or more narrowly as to their poetry? What type of mind, working in the artistic medium of words, shows itself in them? This is not a question of form but of essence. The Hebrew poets had a form of their own, as we shall see hereafter, but they handled it very freely. Nor is it a question of poetic vocabulary; Hebrew poetry uses all the vocabulary of the language indifferently, ordinary and unusual. Nor is it the distinction of art against energy; Hebrew has both. And the Hebrew poet never objectified his work to himself enough to ask whether it expressed Aristotles' higher truth or was only Plato's noble lie. Our question is far more psychological and essential and goes to the depth of the Hebrew mind and to its reactions, emotional and esthetic, to the world round it. When the Hebrew looked at that world and at the things happening in it and was moved to put into words what came to him from it all; or when he looked within himself and found some things there which he had to express; what was more important to him, the ideas therein or the simple pictures and external facts? There cannot be doubt as to our answer here. Even in the brilliant, clear, many-colored external pictures of life in the One Hundred and Fourth Psalm or in Job xxxviii-xxxix or in Ezekiel xxvii-xxviii it is the idea—his own idea—which is most important for these poets; each of them gives the picture because it expresses himself and makes his point clear. The startling thing is that the apparent objectivity, so clean cut and bright, is only there to bring home an idea; that the idea is imposed upon the picture and is the primary and only real thing in it all. The Hebrew mind was ruled by ideas and what we call facts were for it secondary. And this screen of ideas came not only between it and nature; it affected also all the happenings of life. There is something remorseless in the way in which the Hebrew philosophized and theologized the supposed facts of life and history. It was so in idea, he held, therefore it must have been so in reality. And when the final, harsh, facts of life crushed the people in the Exile and in the last Destruction, the people became dreamers of dreams, of apocalyptic restorations. Even in ethical speculation the same attitude held. Jehovah is good; Jehovah rules the world; therefore be good and you will be prosperous. So runs the unflinching gospel of the Book of Proverbs although the facts of life shrieked at it. And in all these, in stories and history, in ethical teachings, just as in the pictures of nature, there is the same use of clear, objective, seemingly real, words and pictures to render what are only ideas. If it was the weakness of the Hebrew mind to be ridden by ideas, it was its strength to be able to express these so that they seemed as real and unshakable as the eternal hills. The essential characteristic of the

Hebrew mind was that it took itself thus seriously and took its ideas as the ultimate reality; the essential characteristic in a word was subjectivity. And the paradox in it was that it could be so concrete and objective in its statements of its subjectivities.

It may be said that this is a harsh judgment and makes the Hebrews the victims of their own baseless fancies and imaginations. That is pushing it too far. It really means that the Hebrews, so far as concerns even the cold workings of their minds, were Platonists rather than Aristotelians. As Plato in the *Timaeus* has been said to represent God as "geometrizing" in his forming of the world, producing everywhere in it philosophical ideas and geometric forms and ratios, while Aristotle looked at the myriads of concrete facts in the world and built up from these as uniform a scheme as he could; so the Hebrews, dominated by the idea of the creative, ruling, personality of Jehovah behind the world, felt compelled to accept that the world was an expression of that personality and of the ideas of that personality and that the world, therefore, was fundamentally rational, whether man could grasp these final reasons and ideas or not. It is significant, too, that for Plato the universe as a whole was modelled on an idea or pattern in the mind of God, while the only suggestion of "pattern" in the creation-ideas of the Hebrews is that man—not the universe—is formed on a pattern and that that pattern is God Himself. Man, in one Hebrew story of the origin of things, was formed in the image and likeness of God; without and within, God made him on the pattern of Himself. This was an expression of the belief of one school of their philosophers that the universe was created for man and that man could think the thoughts of God and so came also the assurance of the great mass of Hebrews that there could be giving and taking of kindly friendship, reciprocally, between God and man. The ideas of the Hebrews, then, by which they were so dominated, are no more to be condemned as philosophically empty and baseless than are the Ideas of Plato. Plato's geometrizing of the universe led him at times in the *Timaeus* into, for us and for Aristotle, strange vagaries of imaginative rationalizing, but the essentials of his vision in that book have led the thinking of half the world. The same can be said, and for the same reason, of the ideas of the Hebrews, running counter as they may to a good half of the evidence of life. They were ideas which had in themselves the very seeds and possibilities of future life. To put this in another way, the Hebrews viewing the bundle of contradictions of which life consists, felt that they, in their assured knowledge of Jehovah, could safely take and hold one side of these contradictions. What to Plato was a philosophical necessity was to them a necessity derived from the personality of Jehovah and their knowledge of it.

Subjective, then, on all sides of their lives the Hebrews assuredly were, whether for better or for worse. It was their strength and their handicap in their thinking and in the expression of their thoughts. But the subjective mind can be either calm in its working or swept by emotional storms. When it is calm, it reasons, narrates, describes—always subjectively—but when high emotion strikes it there is no room for anything but the self swept by its own feelings and rendering itself alone. This was the one essential difference between poetry among the Hebrews and all their other forms of literature. The Hebrew poet was the Hebrew under such strain of emotion; he was the Ἀοιδός, the inspired singer, possessed from within, under divine protection and uttering enchantments; he was not the ποιητής, the "maker" of a poem, separate, objective, as the sculptor with his block of marble. The wide consequences of this for Hebrew poetry can be put most simply in a series of propositions:

(i) The Hebrew poet felt and rendered his emotions; he did not think. Under emotion, quiet thought, the exercise of the logical faculty, was impossible to him.

(ii) Under this strain, he expressed himself. He could not express anything outside of himself.

(iii) He could not even understand anything, or any one, without taking that thing or person into himself, absorbing it and identifying it with himself.

(iv) He could not poetically, that is, emotionally, create without putting himself into the creation. His poetical creation had to be not only a product, but a record of his own emotion.

But all this was only when emotion entered; in prose—narrative, reflective, descriptive—there is not necessarily any emotion. The source and essence of Hebrew poetry was emotion. In this there is nothing new or strange. Primitive poetry everywhere passes through this as a stage; the early poet was everywhere inspired from the Unseen World and spoke by the dictation of a spirit which seized him and used him. He sang a song which came from the unconscious depths of himself, and he and his world ascribed it to divine possession. This phase of early poetry exists still in our convention of the muse and its dictation to the poet. Even amongst the Greeks with all their artistic control and objectivity we find this attitude persisting down to Pindar. Pindar was singer as well as poet, and his odes had a prophetic side. In his ethical utterances he still had a feeling of being inspired as though he were speaking at the shrine of an oracle. But the unique thing about Hebrew poetry is that it never passed beyond this stage or lost this attitude. And this attitude to the end—even through the inartistic absurdities of alphabetic psalms—controlled all Hebrew poetry. The convention of the muse for them had gone far deeper.

It is a singular and significant fact that in our extant Hebrew literature there is no specific word for "poet." There are possible words for "singer," several words for "prophet" on different sides of the prophetic function, words for "wise men" who may have expressed their wisdom in poetical form and metaphor, but none for poet in our or the Greek sense. This can hardly be accident. We shall see hereafter how closely the poet was connected with the prophet; the roots of both lay in a relationship to the Unseen World. The utterances of Wisdom, too, clothed themselves often in poetic form; the Book of Job is both poetry and philosophy. It is therefore probable that, for the Hebrew consciousness, the poet and his poetry had not separated themselves off as a category from the various garbs under which they showed themselves. The poet sang: he was a singer. He manifested from the Unseen World; he was a seer, a prophet. In his song he taught philosophic wisdom; he was a wise man. But the function of poetry, which lay behind them all, had not yet been abstracted. The old Arabs, however, had gone further and their general word for "poet" is deeply significant for the subjective emotionalism of the Hebrews. They called a poet *shā'ir*, a "feeler"—a perceiver, that is, by feeling. This expresses precisely the essence of the Hebrew poet. He "felt" and told in song what he felt. Herein lies the primitive and childlike side of Hebrew poetry. The poet was like a child, sitting and playing by himself; making a song about himself and himself the hero of all that happens in the song. As a child sings in his play of a moment, so the Hebrew race sang to itself, and its songs have remained and have gone round the world.

To put this in our terms of literary art, there is no Hebrew poetry but lyric poetry. Yet the Hebrews were face to face with life in all its multiplicity of suggestion and situation and their poetry, like all true poetry, had to be a criticism of life. So their lyric had, by one device or another, to fill all the functions filled in other literatures by the drama, the epic, and the didactic poem. The result was an immense extension of the possibilities of the lyric. They developed an epic lyric, a dramatic lyric, a didactic lyric, preserving in each the true singing, emotional, subjective note of the lyric. English poetry, being strongly lyric and strongly dramatic, has recognized and named the dramatic lyric in a series of poems by Browning and already in 1818 a little poem by Keats, "Hark, Hark!" contains the essence of the type. In it there is a dramatic situation, or a situation that normally would be developed dramatically, between agents reacting on each other, but which is put before us as seen and felt through the eyes and mind of one of the characters facing the situation, and he expresses it for us in monologue. Thus it comes to us through the interpretation of his emotions and colored by his subjective reactions. This is exactly what we have in the monologues of Job, as will be developed at length hereafter. The dramatic action is really in Job's mind, the conflict between his conception of the friendly God as he thought he had known him in the past and the hostile God who had now struck him down with ruin, grief, and disease. The skirmishing of his speeches with the Friends is not the action and only helps the action as it stimulates Job's mind to wider impressions and possibilities. Each of his speeches is in essence a conversation with himself, after he has brushed away the importunate Friend who has spoken last. The case is the same with the epic lyric. In Greek poetry it would be an Ode of Victory, but the Hebrew singer can put into it far more description and narrative than the Greek would have thought permissible. Yet the elements of description and narrative are all framed to carry the exulting emotion of the singer and the pictures and events in all their detail have no point or meaning apart from the singer. The great example of this in the surviving Hebrew literature is the Song of Deborah; and the song itself in the fifth chapter of Judges should be carefully contrasted with the plain historical narrative in the fourth chapter. Neither is made out of the other; they are independent ways of rendering one event. And the song has a wealth of detail that is not in the history, detail steeped in emotion and given only to develop emotion. The coming of Jehovah; the gathering of the clans; those that came not; the fight in the valley; the winding river of Kishon; blessed be Jael! the Mother of Sisera at her lattice; why lingers his chariot?—all render the exulting joy of the victorious singers. There is the material here for a Book of the Iliad, but Homer would have handled it with a clear objectivity, as an epic artist who stood outside his work and shaped it into form. Deborah and Barak sang and praised Jehovah out of the fullness of their joy and triumph. Yet there are moments in it of the most objective vividness; there is the sudden dramatizing of that scene between the Mother of Sisera and her ladies; she looked forth from her lattice and she still looks and listens—an abiding picture. Such flashes of drama the Hebrew could reach; for a moment, in an historic present, he could put himself into her at her lattice—but no more. The Mother of Sisera is not built up into the figure of tragic ignorance which Homer would have given to us.

This song is so significant that it will be well to translate it here:

Then sang Deborah and Barak, son of Abinoam, in that day, thus:
  In that the leaders led in Israel; in that the People gave itself willingly, bless ye Jehovah!
  Hear ye, O Kings; give ear, O Princes; I, to Jehovah, I, will sing; I will make melody to Jehovah, God of Israel.
  Jehovah! In Thy going forth from Seir, in Thy striding from the Field of Edom, the earth trembled; the sky, too, dripped, the clouds, too, dripped water. The mountains flowed down at the Countenance of Jehovah; Sinai, here, at the Countenance of Jehovah, God of Israel.
  In the days of Shamgar, the son of Anath, in the days of Jael, the caravan-roads ceased, and the road-goers were going their

way in winding bypaths. Ceased the dwellers in the open country; in Israel they ceased. Until that I, Deborah, arose; that I arose, a Mother in Israel, while they were seeking new gods! Then there was fighting at the city gates. Was shield or spear to be seen among forty thousand in Israel?

My inmost being goes out to the Governors of Israel, those that gave themselves freely in the People: Bless ye Jehovah!

Ye riders on white she-asses; ye sitters on widespread carpets; ye goers in the way—talk ye! As part of the noise of the dividers [of flocks] between the water-troughs, let them recite the loyal doings of Jehovah, the loyal doings of his open-country dwellers in Israel. Then did they go down to the gates—the People of Jehovah.

Arouse thee, arouse thee, Deborah; arouse thee, arouse thee, speak in song! Arise thou, Barak, and take thy captives, Son of Abinoam!

Then let a [mere] remnant of splendid men rule fully as a people, let it rule, Jehovah, for me among the mighty men. Out of Ephraim was their root in Amalek; "With thee as leader, O Benjamin!" [was their war cry] in Thy Peoples, [O Jehovah].

From Machir came down governors and from Zebulun they that wield the staff of the muster-master. And my Princes in Issachar were with Deborah, and as Issachar, so Barak; around him was Issachar sent forth in the Valley.

Among the watercourses of Reuben great were the resolves of heart. "Why satest thou among the sheepfolds? Was it to hear the pipings of the flocks?" At the watercourses of Reuben great were the searchings of heart.

Gilead, beyond Jordon, sat in peace. But Dan, why went he aside in alien ships? Asher dwelt on the shore of the seas and beside its anchorages sat in peace.

Zebulun was a people that scorned life unto death, and Naphtali [too] on the Heights of the Field.

The Kings came and fought; then fought the Kings of Canaan; in Taanach by the Waters of Megiddo; no rich plunder did they take.

From the skies there fought the stars; from their paths they fought with Sisera. The River Kishon in its crooks swept them away, that entangling river, the River Kishon.

Thou shalt tread, O my Soul, in strength!

Then hammered the hoofs of the horses from the charging, the charging of his heroes.

Curse ye Meroz, said the Messenger of Jehovah: curse ye its inhabitants—accursed! For they came not in to the aid of Jehovah, to the aid of Jehovah among the mighty men.

But blessed out of women is Jael, the wife of Heber, the Kenite—out of women in tent she is blessed.

Water he asked; milk she gave; in a splendid bowl she brought curdled milk.

Her hand—to the tent-peg she stretched it out and her right hand to the toilers' hammer. And she hammered Sisera; she pierced his head and split and went through his temple. Between her feet he bowed, he fell, he lay; between her feet he bowed, he fell; where he bowed, there he fell—destroyed.

Through the window she looked out and she cried out—the Mother of Sisera through the lattice: "Why disappoints us his chariot in coming; why linger the hoof-beats of his chariots?"

Her second-sighted ladies were answering her; yea she herself kept repeating her own words: "Were they not finding, dividing the spoil; a concubine or two for every man; spoil of dyed stuffs for Sisera; spoil of dyed stuffs, many colored, dyed and colored on both sides; carried on the shoulders of the spoil [themselves]."

May all Thy enemies perish, Jehovah! But those that love Him may they be like the going forth of the sun in its strength.

This song may seem to us disjointed, but it was not, is not so in reality. The links are unexpressed in the written words but they would be rendered by the voice and the dramatic gestures of the singer. And even in the words we can see a certain stately progress, broken by outbursts of emotion, by sharp addresses of praise and scorn and by still more sharply contrasted pictures. And the culminating contrast that closes it all is of high art, the contrast between Jael in her tent and the Mother of Sisera in her palace.

The case of the didactic lyric is much simpler. A great proportion of the Psalms fall into this class and we all know what their essence is. Impassioned self-confession, a record of personal experience, whether addressed to Jehovah in penitence, or to the Psalmist's soul in upbraiding, or to his fellow man in direct exhortation, is turned into moral arousing and guidance. The Psalmist has learned in suffering what he teaches in song, and so he pours out his emotional experience and his resultant ideas and reactions, and they go to form what is still the greatest manual for the personal religious life.

In all these cases we are face to face with an immediate individual singer, singing the song of a moment under the impulse of a moment. Hebrew poetry was all under impulse and the Hebrew poet could not rule and control his form. He could not think out and plan his poem and, then, work through it in detail, polishing line by line. Flashing phrases he could strike out, and brilliant pictures, "jewels six words long that on the stretched forefinger of all time sparkle forever," but it was not given to him to wield "the noblest measure ever moulded by the lips of man." There, strangely, the Arabs were his masters, for their great measure, *Tawil*, is the only verse that can hold its own with the Virgilian hexameter. The Hebrew poet was always improvising and he could never reach the great paradox and wonder of Pindar—otherwise so near him—in Greek poetry. Pindar could keep alive the emotion of the moment and yet use sedulously the file of form. Yet another contrast—perhaps clearer to us. It has been said that a sonnet is "a moment's monument." That is true. There is no great sonnet that does not embody a perception or conception, born of a flash of insight, or of a high emotional experience. And so far the Hebrew could have gone. But the sonnet, also, of all the fixed forms of literary art which have survived in living literature, is that which calls for the most rigid, slow, patient labor. No great sonnet was ever written straight off; and that holds of all its types. Its unity must be jealously preserved. In the Petrarchan form, the slow development of the pictures of the octave leads of necessity to the revelation of the sestet. And with the sestet all is said. Of that slow labor no Hebrew poet was ever capable; or ever dreamt. It is the culmination of the impossible for Hebrew verse.

CHAPTER III

THE BOOK OF JOB AS LYRIC

IF WE are to understand the Hebrew poet and the workings of his mind this complicated psychological relationship of the lyric, the drama and the epic will repay further consideration. It carries us back from the produced poems, in their marked types, to the poets who produced them, in their equally marked types. Looking at poetry from this viewpoint, it has been said that there are three classes of poets: the lyric, the semi-dramatic and the absolute dramatic. (i) The gift of the lyric poet is to sing himself and his own emotions. Some can do nothing else than this and have attempted nothing else. In American literature, Poe and Emerson, however little elsewhere they may meet, meet in this. Their poems, in the specific, limited sense, are all songs and songs of themselves, their own emotions and ideas. Poe made one attempt at a drama and, wisely, never printed it. But other, essentially lyric, poets have attempted more, and, at the most, have reached the semi-dramatic. Byron essayed both the tale in verse, in which, for the time, he beat Scott out of the field, and also the drama. But in both the only real personalities are reproductions of Byron himself. The other characters are class-types only. Browning, too, was an essential lyrist and handled the dramatic lyric with understanding and skill. But he could not tell a story in verse except obscurely through the mouths of the different characters, and in his specific dramas the characters run away with the action. (ii) The semi-dramatic poet can create class-types but not individuals. He is really a second-class dramatist, and a poor one at that, except when he can introduce a reproduction of himself. Then only does there appear a true, individual, personality on his stage. It is the lyric self-revealer surrounding himself with a dramatic action and shadowy fellow actors. (iii) The absolute dramatic poet is the only real dramatist and it does not matter whether he manifests his genius—in this case not himself —in what we call the epic or in what we call the drama. He puts before us an action and in the action there are several independent personalities, each a true self, and not the poet himself. The greatest examples of this in the world of literature are Homer and Shakespeare. When Priam approaches Achilles to beg for the body of Hector, each—Priam and Achilles—is a true personality, not simply types of an old man suppliant, a grief stricken father, and a young man, victorious, arrogant but magnanimous; they are Priam and Achilles and there are no others to put in their class. The dramatic genius of Homer has created two individuals and neither is Homer himself. He has gone outside of himself and produced another than himself. Shakespeare puts before us Hamlet and we have no doubt that this is Hamlet and not one of a class of Hamlets. His personality—in spite of all the expositors—remains as mysterious to us as that of any man we may meet in life, but it is as real, too, as that of any such man of flesh and blood. The figment of Shakespeare's imagination is a created fact, and it is not Shakespeare himself. In this case we can see, too, how it was only in the drama that his powers fully came to their own. When he told a story in verse or unlocked his heart with a sonnet-key it is plain how he was hampered and thwarted by the medium in which he worked. Only in dramatic action could he fully say what came to him and create his men and women. It would be possible and eminently suggestive to take other English poets—Milton, Keats, Scott, Tennyson—who have essayed those different types of poetic art and see how the psychological realities in each assert themselves and help and hinder, but the fact of the existence of the types—both in the poets and in their work—is probably now sufficiently brought out. It may seem to have carried us far away from the Hebrews and the Old Testament; in the reality of poetic art it lies very near.

Hebrew poets were of the first of these classes only. The character in a Hebrew poem must be the poet himself; the poet cannot create a character not himself. But distinctions and complications enter; the Hebrew artist is not simply a lyric poet, nor is lyric poetry in his mouth and brain of the simplicity of the modern song. The Hebrew literary artist had his prose and he had his poetry; he was a refined and creative artist in both and each was quite distinct from the other. Further, his range in prose was wider than in song; in prose he could put before us real persons who were not himself but who are as real as any in Homer or Shakespeare. He created

Abraham; he created Jonah; and these are individual persons. What, then, is the essential difference between Hebrew prose and Hebrew poetry? It is emotion and the emotion always goes with song. The sequence appears to be this: The Hebrew artist can tell a story straight and clear in prose; his brain is cold; he can think about his creation and develop it and shape it. It may be a creation of pathos or of terror, of repentance or of joy, but, so long as it is not the poet's pathos, repentance, terror, joy, he creates in prose and his creation is not himself. But should his brain be fired by the situation in which his character is and his own emotion roused; should he feel this situation as his own; then the thread of narrative breaks; he bursts into song; he and his character melt together and for that moment he can render only himself, how he felt and reacted to it all. It may be that after his outburst he will recover his self-possession and resume his narrative, but it will be in prose. This recovery and continuation of the story in prose is far more common in Arabic than in Hebrew. It is, indeed, the regular sequence in Arabic romances of adventure and chivalry. There all the story is told in prose. But, from time to time, the hero will burst into song, singing his love, his joy, his hatred, challenging an enemy or boasting over a fallen foe. While he thus sings, the story itself stops; then when he has fully expressed his feelings the story goes on in prose. In all Semitic song, which means all Semitic poetry, narrative is impossible. This does not mean that Semitic narrative cannot be artistic; the stories in the Old Testament are handled with consummate art. In truth, in Hebrew prose there is more art in the narrower sense of conscious handling and development of form than in Hebrew poetry, for the emotion of the poet—always a singer—prevents such calm elaboration.

But while the Hebrew poet is thus debarred from conscious mastery of his material on one side, on another, as already suggested, he has enormously expanded the bounds of the lyric. In a momentary effect he can strike out vivid, dramatic situations, as we have seen in the Song of Deborah, although he can never round and develop them. Suddenly he may thrust into the midst of his song a scrap of direct speech, as from the mouth of somone else, and produce with it a flash of dramatic creation. This device of direct speech is familiar to Arabic treatises on rhetoric but the

Hebrew already knew all about its practical use. Through description of nature, also, the Hebrew lyric artist has learned how to express himself. He has his eye on the object, simple or complex, but he stands between us and it, for we see it as it has passed through his mind, has affected him and has, in return, been colored by his emotion. The great range of the mountains of Moab walling the eastern horizon or the snowy peak of Hermon far in the north are brought out for us by a single touch, or the cataracts of the north country blowing their trumpets to the steeps; but we see them pictured not for their own sakes as beauty, but because the poet saw them and they meant thoughts to him. But perhaps the most striking use of this poetry of emotion is as an expression of philosophical thinking. Philosophy with the Hebrew went to his head; which means that it came from his heart and went to his heart. The ultimate problems of life stirred his emotions and he could not face them coldly and look at them on all sides. The great exception to this is Ecclesiastes and even Ecclesiastes breaks from time to time into a true lyric note of pathos. The pity of life overcomes him and he, because of this, cannot be fair to the God who is behind life. The other apparent exception to this is in the utilitarian philosophy of the Book of Proverbs that is so utilitarian that it can hardly be called philosophy at all. The real problems of living do not exist for these proverbial moralists; in their vision of the world there is no difficulty and, therefore, they have neither speculation nor emotion.

But in all Hebrew art, whether it is narrative or lyric, emotional expressions or philosophical grapplings with life, descriptions of natural scenes or scraps of momentary dramatization—all of them, except the narrative, under the domination of the emotions of the different authors, whoever they were—the great example is the Book of Job. Its external structure is highly compound; it proceeds undoubtedly from different authors and contains elements of narrative, poetry, and philosophy. But it will be well, as an illustration of the principles which have preceded, to consider it here as a whole. The figure of Job himself belongs to ancient Hebrew legend. Ezekiel (xiv, 14, 20) knew him, with Noah and Daniel, as a righteous man living in the midst of an unrighteous people and able to deliver only his own soul by his righteousness. That is still the Job of what is commonly called the Prologue (chapters i and ii) and the Epilogue (chapter xlii, 7-end) of our book. It is plain that the Prologue was taken from some prose story of Job by the poet of the Colloquies between Job and his Friends (chapters iii-xxxi) and used by him as an introduction. Whether he made any change in it and touched it up to suit his purposes we cannot be sure. It is an admirable piece of Hebrew prose, idiomatic and picturesque. The Adversary in it, as prosecuting attorney in the Court of Heaven, belongs to old Hebrew belief and is explicitly represented to have stirred Jehovah up against Job for no fault of Job's (ii, 3); Jehovah himself in His sweeping and amoral use of Job belongs to primitive Hebrew thought; he is the irresponsible oriental sovereign. Job, throughout, is entirely patient and submissive to the divine will and resists the temptation of his wife to end his misery by criticising God. This is plainly the Job that Ezekiel knew. But the poet of the Colloquies has his own opinion of it all. He has seen that the world is full of unmerited suffering—exactly as in Job's case. Here is a situation made to his hand. He will make Job open his mouth and speak his mind. Job will not only speak his mind but he will speak for the whole misery of the world, to which the pious Hebrews, as in the Book of Proverbs, shut their eyes and ears; he will show how the good may be oppressed and find no helper and how the wicked may be triumphant. He will confute all the answers and explanations which were brought, pious, philosophical, proverbial, in defense of the order of things and of the justice of God's government of the world. For it is plain that the world of the poet's time—and when that was we have no clue—was already faced by this problem and seeking an answer. To all appearances the poet himself had found no answer. And even if he had, the statement of the cause of Job's suffering in the Prologue and the picture given there of a morally indifferent God who heartlessly uses Job to make His point against the Adversary, would have effectually nullified it. In using the old story of Job as a starting point he tied his own hands. Probably he did not mind this; he had no answer by which to justify God as to the unmerited suffering in the world and sought only a mouthpiece for himself which had the prestige of old association. For he is Job and Job is he. This is no creation of a dramatic personality like Hamlet, distinct from his creator. Job has been absorbed by the poet and in everything speaks the poet's mind. So far, then, there is no dramatization at all save the externality of the use made of Job and his Friends. We have really a series of soliloquies by the poet on his great theme. These are of necessity philosophical moralizings; but they are really lyric philosophy and lyric moralizing, an expression of the experiences, the emotions and the conclusions of the tortured soul of the poet. That is when we view the Colloquies on the side of the specific argument itself. But there is another side, and here the dramatic lyric enters. Job himself could not have known of the scenes in the Court of Heaven; he could not know the God who is there so nakedly displayed. All he knew was what his own experience of God had been. And that divided sharply into two distinct parts, displaying God as of two personalities. In his old prosperous days Job had known a God of friendship who protected him and his and whom Job had learned to love and trust. Then all had changed and God was now apparently incalculable, not to be trusted and not to be loved. We have to remember that for Job, as for all Semites, there was this immediate personal cause of all events—God. As Job himself says, "If it is not He, then who is it?" Thus Job was faced by a problem that was peculiarly his own, the contrast between these two manifestations of God. Which manifestation was the true revelation of God? This was the problem of the Job whom the poet created, and not necessarily a problem of the poet himself, but the poet manages to create it for us. How the poet felt about this second problem we can only guess. The dramatic art with which he handles it in its lyric guise of an outpouring of Job's heart is very high, and he puts before us Job gradually steadying and calming himself through those very outpourings, until a personal reconciliation with God does not seem so utterly impossible as at the first. But the reconciliation will be no abject submission to God on Job's part; "as a prince I would draw near to him." "Behold my signature. Let Shaddai answer me and the book which my attorney [the poet] has written" (xxxi, 35, 36). And so that chapter fitly closes with, "The words of Job are ended." The ancient Hebrew was no Calvinist. He upheld the dignity of humanity even against its Creator; we shall see, hereafter, David in the Eighteenth Psalm dealing with Jehovah as one gentleman with another.

The words of the poet of the Colloquies are here truly ended. The book itself is not ended. Others had much and very different things to say on the problem which had been raised and what they said seems to have been pitchforked together in the remainder of our book. Just as the Book of the Isaiah of Jerusalem was used to gather up miscellaneously, and preserve safely, all kinds of odds and ends of prophecy, so our Book of Job became a receptacle for all manner of meditations and discussions on its eternal problem. But before looking at these it would be well to consider more exactly the structure of the Colloquies.

In chapter iii Job suddenly frees his soul in an outburst of magnificently sombre vituperation. The poet has definitely broken with the tradition of the patient Job; Job has now become the voice of humanity. It is as though the inhumanly patient Griselda in Chaucer's *Clarke's Tale* had suddenly arisen and spoken her mind of her husband. From this point the poet ignores Job's wife and the Adversary, but he sees the possibilities in the three Friends. In the original story they probably had played the same part as Job's wife and had urged him by disrespectful treatment of Jehovah to hasten his assured end. So at least we may gather from the condemnation of them by Jehovah in what has survived of the original story in the Epilogue (xlii, 7-9). But from being offerers of such acrid advice as was given by Job's wife, the poet turns them into representatives of the various defenses of Jehovah in his government of the world, that were current at the time. So Job in the original plan of the poet had to meet them, one after the other, in three rounds of speeches. A certain vague individuality is preserved to the three, especially as to Eliphaz who is really a dignified figure; but, broadly, they simply voice the arguments of the time and are, as it were, representative puppets for Job to overthrow. Job, on the other hand, is a person, because he is the poet.

Two rounds of these speeches are entire and complete. Twice each Friend assails Job's attitude with increasing bitterness and clearness of denunciation. It becomes gradually plain to them that what, at first, might have been pardoned as an impulsive cry, drawn from Job by his sudden and overwhelming sorrow and pains, was really calculated criticism of and rebellion against the Ruler of the world. Each of Job's speeches in reply divides into two parts: first he deals with the argument of the Friend who has just spoken and then he turns to his own soul's bitterness and soliloquizes on the inexplicable estrangement which has come between himself and God. The old, friendly God is gone and a Being has appeared who has smitten him down with blow after blow of hostile malignity. Which is the true Jehovah? Had he been mistaken all his life in the nature and character of Jehovah? The dealing with the Friends and their arguments is comparatively simple; the facts of life are against them and Job's eyes are now open to the facts. But the dealing with his own soul and its essential problem is not simple. Yet it is plain that he is gradually clearing his mind, as he frees it, and that possibilities are opening before him. These Colloquies have been criticized as too long, and the issues between Job and his Friends could certainly be put more shortly. But for Job's own development this slowness is necessary; he has to right his mind from the shocks of doom which have wrecked it. We have also to remember that while the poet is a moral philosopher he is besides that a literary artist. And no Semitic artist, working with words, can overcome the temptation to labor his point, over and over again, in beautiful figures and language. The Semitic artist has never known, as the Greek did, the beauty that lies in simplicity and economy of statement. His metaphors and pictures run away with his thought.

In the third round of speeches, however, there is a break. That the poet left it complete can hardly be doubted, for Job's final, careful apologia, in chapters xxix-xxxi, stands there as a close to the whole. But Bildad's last speech (xxv) is very short and Zophar has no speech at all unless it is chapter xxvii, 13-end, which in our text is put into Job's mouth. Also, before Job's final apologia there has been thrust into the text chapter xxviii, which has nothing to do with the argument at all. It is a separate little poem the point of which is that while man can find, extract, and use anything in the material world he cannot find absolute reason. That God alone has found—a very curious point—and has kept for Himself.

So, as we have seen, with the words (xxxi, 40), "The words of Job are ended" the work of the poet ends. What had he accomplished? Certainly no solution to the problem of unmerited suffering in the world, but a hard blow to the doctrine that all's well with the world. Also the poet has freed his mind on the facts in the case and has created a living, human Job in the place of the impossible Job of the folk-tale. Yet if the poet had freed his mind and had given the defendants of Jehovah their day in court, others were not satisfied. It is plain that the issue was a living one, and many felt that such an ending, that was no ending, was intolerable. Even the folk-tale was more satisfactory in its winding up of the action. In the chapters, then, that follow, we have at least two attempts at a solution of sorts. First, that of Elihu (xxxii-xxxvii). He is an entirely new character who had sat by listening and who finally could contain himself no longer. His elders had said their say and had failed to silence Job; so he would make his attempt. His argument adds nothing essential to what has before been said, except that more stress is laid on the educative value of adversity. We can easily imagine Job dealing with the educative advantages to his children in being killed. Also it is plain that whoever wrote the Elihu speech was not a poet nor an artist of the same class as the original poet. Job's last speech was the end of his words also.

But a poet was now to enter and take up the adventure who was at least equal as an artist to the original poet, but whose attitude on human life was entirely different. Among the Hebrews, as we shall see hereafter, there were two views as to man's place in the universe. According to the one, man was the crown of creation and the world had been created and now existed for the use of man. This is the view developed in Genesis i, in what is commonly called the First Creation Narrative. It is also the view implicit in the original poet's attitude. But there was another view and one probably more widely held. According to it man was simply a part of the world and had no special preeminence in it. God had created the whole world in the multiplicity of its parts for his own pleasure and the world was to him like a huge animated toy. This view is very plain in the One Hundred and Fourth Psalm where we have an elaborate description of the world as God sees it spread out before him. In that description man is only a part of this great toy with which God plays. The same conception rules the speech of the Lord in Job (xxxviii-xli). It is quite possible that we have here the work of more than one writer, for the speech is very disjointed and makes more than one fresh beginning. But the point of the whole is to put Job back in his place and make him feel how insignificant a part he has in the world. There is really no other argument behind the magnificent descriptions of animated nature. What is man in all this and, especially, what is any individual man? Of course it ignores all Job's arguments and pleas and the God who speaks here is not in the least the God whom Job had known in his earlier life. This is, it may be, the God of the Prologue, playing with human lives and their miseries. This God speaks out of storm as though in defiance of Job's petition (ix, 16, 17), "If I were to cry and he were to answer me I cannot feel secure that he would give ear to my voice. For in storm he would smite at me and would multiply my wounds without cause." That is literally what this God does to Job. And as this new poet had undoubtedly read the work of the poet of the Colloquies the point of his comment is plain. That, for him, is the way that God should meet such pleas as that of Job. It is for man to be silent and accept humbly whatever God does to him. The ideal, that is, of this new poet, is the patient Job of the Prologue. But he goes farther and uses in so many words (xl, 7*ff.*) the argument that he who has the greater strength has the right to use it as he pleases and the weak must submit. There is no moral law; might is all. He even uses the old argument that no one has a right to criticize how a thing is done unless he can do it better himself. Let Job try his hand at running the world and subduing the mighty creatures, Behemoth and Leviathan, in it. There is a certain sublimity in the impudence of this argument that because Job cannot hook and bind Leviathan he must not criticize the moral rule of the world. Job might have retorted that it was not his business to control Leviathan but that, most unhappily, it was his business to live in the world. This universal right of criticism on the part of the user and sufferer was once put in classical form by Dr. Johnson. Boswell came to him and told of a play, a very poor play, which he had seen. "But," added Boswell, "I have no right to criticize it for I could not write a better one myself." "You have every right, Sir, to criticize it," said Johnson. "It is not your business to make plays, but to enjoy them and know whether they are good or not. You could not make a table but you can tell whether a table is well made or not. It is not your business to make tables but it is your business to use them." Job had been put into a world in which he had to live and, though he could not make a better world, he had a full right to criticize the making and ruling of the world in which he was. So evidently thought the poet of the Colloquies, but the poet of the Speeches of the Lord thought otherwise. This is the most essential proof that those two poets, artistically on the same level, are separate and different. The poet of the Colloquies was more a dramatic lyrist; he saw deeply into Job's mind—that is, into his own mind—and put it before us. The poet of the Speeches of the Lord was a descriptive lyrist; he evidently cared little for Job's mind and its troubles. But he looked abroad into the living world and the pictures he saw there were full to him of the might and care of God for his creation; also he saw man as only a small, almost insignificant, part of that creation. "What is man that thou art mindful of him?" he might have said, except that he did not think that God was very mindful of man. God was more interested apparently in the green grass that springs in the wilderness where no man is and in the wild things that eat thereof. And so all his descriptions in their detail and beauty, are loaded with his conception of God. He enjoyed describing them, without doubt, but he did not describe them for their own sake as sheer beauty. Here there enters one of the great points of difference between the old Arab poets and any of the old Hebrew poets. The Arab poets of the desert were fond of just such descriptions as these; many have reached us in their surviving poems. They used them, just as did the Hebrews, to express their own emotions—the sense of solitude, the sense of the vanished past, memories and yearnings, things that often lie too deep for tears. Nature existed for the Arab poet and he knew its anodyne and the finger that it lays on the lips of care. But the Hebrew poet, and most especially this poet here in these Speeches of the Lord, went always from the scene before him back to Jehovah, the Maker and Ruler of it all. This sometimes reaches an almost pantheistic feeling for nature as the garment of God, as in the early verses of the One Hundred and Fourth Psalm, but here Jehovah is outside of the picture, looking at it and Himself telling about it. And for this poet to tell about it was a sufficient answer to Job or to any other critic. That gives exactly his standpoint—"See, realize, tremble!" This is not any displaying of the anodyne of Nature, as an Arab poet might have done. It is Jehovah, speaking out of the storm and hurling terrors.

Naturally, then, from the point of view of this poet, Job bows his head, lays his hand on his lips and submits. Twice he has to do this (xl, 3-5; xlii, 1-6), which may indicate that the Speech of the Lord is compound. But the poet of the Colloquies has already indicated in chapter ix that Job could never stand up before an angry God and has made Job entreat that God would appear on equal terms. If, then, the Speech of the Lord is by the poet of the Colloquies it must have been written in the most tremendous irony, only in this way, by terror, could God answer Job. But it has been already indicated that the whole philosophical attitude to the world and to man of the Speech of the Lord is different from that of the Colloquies.

There remains only a single question. How was xlii, 7-end, added to Job's submission? This is evidently the end of the prose folktale of the patient and righteous Job which Ezekiel knew. In it Job has held to his integrity throughout; so the Lord sets on his conduct the stamp of his approval; but the Lord does not approve of what the Friends have said about himself. They, it may be, have tempted Job as his wife has done. So, Job has to make entreaty and atoning sacrifice for them and their folly, that the wrath of God fall not on them. There follows, then, complete—for a folk-tale—restoration of Job's former prosperity and the names of his three brand new daughters are given with a quite feminist remark on their legal status. We seem here driven to the conclusion that the folk-tale went on to tell the further fortunes of those daughters. But that for us now is silence; the Hebrews assuredly had many good stories which, like the lost tales of Miletus, have not reached us. And we owe apparently even this mention of those heroines to the desire of some wooden-headed compiler to make a clear and prosperous finish. But it should be noticed that the finish is not that Job lived happily ever after but that, as in the stories of the *Arabian Nights,* he lived until he was visited by the terminator of delights and the destroyer of companionships.

So much may be said on the Book of Job as an example of the Hebrew use of the lyric to render all manner of emotional situations and attitudes. Hereafter it will have to be considered in its relation to the Hebrew story-telling genius and to the development of Hebrew philosophical ideas.

CHAPTER IV

THE HEBREWS IN JOYOUS SONG AND DANCING

THE term epic has sometimes been applied to certain parts of the Old Testament. This application has been based on a very loose and metaphorical use of the word and frequently also, on a misapprehension as to the purpose and meaning of those parts of the Old Testament to which it is so applied. An epic, whatever else it is, must be a narrative in verse and Semitic has never known verse-narratives. Such a way of telling a story seems to be more deeply alien to the Semitic mind than even the drama. In the neo-Arabic literature, just growing up, there is a distinct development toward the drama, but none whatever toward epic poetry. Shakespeare, Molière, Racine, have imitators in Arabic at the present day, but a translation of Homer which has been made, as a kind of *tour de force*, into Arabic verse has remained without effect. From what has been shown above of the emotional values of the dramatic lyric, it is therefore intelligible that a broader drama might thus in time be produced. But so long as prose stands ready and fully developed as a vehicle for the story, Semitic art sees no advantage in turning to the always emotional form of song. There are a very few cases in which approaches toward narrative verse have—always for distinct reasons—appeared in Arabic. There are no such cases in the Hebrew of the Old Testament.

Face to face, then, with this fact that for the Semite, poetry is still song, and only song, and that there has never been a narrative poem in Semitic, there is no profit in abstract consideration of the nature and origin and history of the epic. But it is of profit to consider the origin, so far as we know it, of the Greek drama and to put it beside the evidently cognate phenomena among the Hebrews. The Greek drama is said to have originated in the combination of two primitive elements in Greek life: (i) the dancing and song of the dithyrambic chorus at a village festival round the altar of Bacchus and (ii) the chanting of epic tales by a wandering ballad-singer. The dance and song of the chorus tended to be monotonous and the wandering rhapsode was called in to relieve that monotony. He addressed his recitation to the leader of the chorus, and dialogue followed between the two. The rhapsode, on his part, became an actor and threw himself into the part of each character in his tale. Thus the essentials of the Greek drama were provided; the epic theme; dialogue; choruses. Later a third speaker was added.

How much of this do we find among the Hebrews? Of the three elements, the joyous dance, the Bacchic song, the chanting of epic ballads, the Hebrews had the first two only. Their temperament, unlike the grave austerity of the desert Arabs, was evidently full of light laughter and song and it expressed itself naturally and automatically in more or less regulated dances and choruses. The influence of the land of Canaan with its corn and oil and wine, fruits and shady trees, had deeply affected them. The joy of life had struck in. It is true that the Rechabites, upon whom there will be more hereafter, kept up their protest of the superior sanctity of the nomadic life, but it is evident, also, that the protest had little effect. The land of Canaan remade this desert element of its population into its own likeness, as it has always done and still does. The prophets might protest as they pleased and preach a grimmer life and more serious faith, but the people went their way, and the prophetic teaching in this, as generally, was a failure. In the Old Testament narratives we can see what the people really were and did as opposed to the theorizing of theologians. And it is not only in the narratives that we find the joyous side of their religious life developed. In the eighth chapter of Proverbs, where the personified primeval Reason describes how she aided Jehovah Himself in the forming of the world, the culmination is the laughing joy of this Reason in His presence, as she regards it all. "Then was I beside Him as a skilled workman and I was in delight, day by day, laughing before Him for every occasion, laughing for His inhabited world and my delight was in the sons of human kind" (verses 30, 31). No Greek could have expressed more fully, or more naïvely the joy of the artist in his accomplished work. In the first chapter of Genesis, God Himself pronounces "good" each stage of His work until at last He rests from it all. Here we have an elaborate expression of the idea that the whole world is rational and that the world in itself everywhere proclaims Reason to man as the highest good. But that Reason is no austere deity, a stern daughter of the voice of God, but is a laughing, joyous spirit, pervading a joyous earth. The Greek Diké, who withdrew from amongst men as each age grew worse and who had strange points of similarity to this Hebrew Reason, was different here; judgment and not joy she brought; and she had no delight in humanity as it is.

But, to come to the narratives, they show us this joy breaking out in more or less ordered ways, communal and individual, in trained choirs answering each other and in orgiastic personal explosions, in marriage dance and song and solemn, if noisy, religious processions. Most fundamental of all as an expression of communal joy was the pilgrimage feast. We have allusions to this in Exodus v, 1; xxiii, 14; xxxii, 5, 6, 9. The word for the festival is always *hagg*, the same word as the Arabic *hajj*, used of the Muslim pilgrimage to Mecca. But the fundamental idea in both words is dancing round something and the essence of the Muslim *hajj* is a ceremonial dance by the pilgrims round the Ka'ba at Mecca. This has to be done with a certain ritual-step which is described as resembling dragging the feet in deep sand. Most curiously, there is an allusion to a similar ritual-step in the Old Testament. In the description of Elijah's contest with the priests of the Baal at Mount Carmel (1 Kings xviii) we are told that these priests "limped beside the altar which they had made" (verse 26). The word used here is the same as that used by Elijah himself in verse 21, "how long are ye limping between two ways?" We may be sure that the Hebrews themselves used similar ritual in the steps of their more solemn dances. But there was more to a *hagg* than such solemnities. In Exodus xxxii, 5, 6, a *hagg* is proclaimed to Jehovah. It began early in the morning; sacrifices were offered; "and the people sat down to eat and drink and rose up to play." The word "play" is used of laughing, sporting, mocking—evidently a joyous outburst after their feast. But the Hebrews also sang as they danced. Thus in Exodus xv, we have the song which Moses and the Sons of Israel sang to Jehovah after the overthrow of Pharaoh in the Red Sea. "And Miriam, the prophetess, the sister of Aaron, took a timbrel in her hand and all the women went forth after her with timbrels and with dances. And Miriam answered them, 'Sing ye to Jehovah'" (verses 20, 21). So, regularly, timbrels, dancing, and singing went together. Jephthah's daughter came to meet her father with timbrels and dances (Judges xi, 34); Laban reproached Jacob that he would not let him send him off "with mirth and songs, timbrel and harp" (Genesis xxxi, 27); Jeremiah prophesied of the restored people (xxxi, 4) "And I will build thee and thou shalt be built, O Virgin Israel; again thou shalt be adorned with thy timbrels and go out in the dance of those who laugh joyously." The word is the same that is used of Reason in Proverbs viii. In Psalm lxviii, 25, we have the description of a more solemn religious procession but it, too, has its maidens and timbrels and singing. "The singing-men went before, and thereafter the men playing on harps; in the midst were the maidens beating timbrels." Another more tumultuous and popular procession is described in Psalm xlii, 4, "how I passed on to the House of God with the sound of a shrill crying and praising, a noisy multitude keeping holiday." The last word of the description here is the same *hagg* above; the noisy multitude was a religious procession, dancing along. In 2 Samuel vi, there is a full description of a similar procession in which the solitary figure of David played the great part—a kind of *pas seul*. The description is very vivid of how he danced orgiastically, evidently regardless of all decorum, whirling and quivering in his rejoicing before the ark (verses 14, 16, 20). Another solitary dance but very different is described in the Song of Songs vi, 13*ff*. This is a description of the Dance of the Bride before the wedding guests, which is still a feature of a marriage festival among the Syrian peasantry. The local poet is called in to describe her in supposedly unpremeditated song as she dances before the throng.

From all this it will be evident that the Hebrews were amply equipped with the choral song and dance elements in the Greek drama. They knew fully how to express different emotions and to portray different situations by these means. But they had no singer of epic ballads to relieve the monotony of their dances and songs and to link all up into a unified action. From at least one reference —"like the dance of two bands" (Song of Songs vi, 13)—we know that the Hebrews had developed answering dances, like the answering choirs in the Twenty-fourth Psalm. And so, too, the women of Israel are described as dancing, singing joyously with timbrels and triangles, and "answering" one another in praise of

David (1 Samuel xviii, 7; xxi, 11; xxix, 5). But all this expression of joyous emotion, even by alternating choirs, is far indeed from the working out, on a stage, through the mouth of individuals, of a connected story:

> Presenting Thebes, or Pelops' line
> Or the tale of Troy divine.

That calls for the ability to put life before us in the round and not simply the flashing, as it were, on a screen, of separate pictures.

The childlike character, then, of Hebrew song persisted in all Hebrew poetry. The poet is a singer and he sings of himself like a child at play. We can turn, therefore, to some examples of Hebrew song, confident that in these we have Hebrew poetry in its ultimate range and possibilities. Early and primitive as the following scraps of song may be, all that followed them, however elaborate, was of the same essential type. To this, Hebrew poetry owes its constant freshness and universal appeal; it carried the dew of its childhood and youth to the end. We feel this still even in the stiffest and most mechanical acrostic psalms. When these are translated the acrostic element of necessity vanishes but the primitive charm remains. No other poetry stands so well a rendering into stately poetic prose, as that of the Old Testament in its transformation in the King James Version.

The Song of Deborah, a fragment of undoubted antiquity, has already been dealt with. Another fragment of, perhaps, even higher antiquity is the Sword Song of Lamech in Genesis iv, 23, 24. This is imbedded in the curious story about Lamech and his children, which tells how the arts and crafts were developed by the evil progeny of Cain. Cain is a wanderer in the earth by the sentence of Jehovah and lest, in the great open spaces, he should be slain, Jehovah has given him a sign by which he can be recognized and a promise of sevenfold vengeance on his slayer. So he goes out under the protection of the only law known to the desert nomad, the law of blood-vengeance. In the sixth generation from Cain comes Lamech. He had a son Tubal-Cain, a hammersman, the first of all artificers in brass and iron. With him is mentioned his sister Naamah—otherwise unknown. Of this girl, coming to us thus under the very shadow of the sword, the Hebrews must have had their tales, now lost to us. But for the godless mind of Lamech, these weapons of his son mean safety, and he breaks into song, addressed to his wives:

> Adah and Zillah, hear my speech;
> Wives of Lamech, give ear to my plea.
> For a man have I slain for my wound;
> A young man for my hurt.
> If sevenfold for Cain shall vengeance be taken,
> For Lamech it shall be seventy and sevenfold.

This scrap is a good example of early parallelism, for, of course, the "man" and the "young man" are the same. It is evidently quoted because it shows the godless mind of the House of Cain which found its protection in its own hand and sword, tenfold more than from Jehovah Himself. So in Job xii, 6, a godless man has his god in the sword in his hand. This, then, was a sword song, of which there are many in primitive literature. So, in the medieval Arabic romance of the desert hero Antarah, he finds a "thunderbolt" in the sand and takes it to a smith to be fashioned into a great sword for his own use. The smith forges and finishes the sword, mighty and heavy and long, and Antarah comes for it. "This," said the smith, wielding the sword, "is the sword, O Antarah, but where is the wielder of the sword?" "That is the sword, O Smith," said Antarah, snatching it from him, "and I, Antarah of Abs, am the wielder of the sword." And he smote the smith down where he stood. Then he breaks out into song in praise of his sword, Zami, the thirsty one. Everyone will remember a modern imitation in R. L. Stevenson's *Kidnapped*, where after the fight in the roundhouse of the brig, Alan Breck Stewart bursts out into praise of his sword and himself, "Thou sword in the hand of Alan!"

Another ancient and characteristic fragment is the Song of the Well in Numbers xxi, 17. It, too, is imbedded in a narrative, this time of the stages of the journeyings of the Sons of Israel through Moab. "And from there to Be'er [*well*]. It is the Be'er of which Jehovah said to Moses, 'Gather the people that I may give them water.' Then Israel was singing this song. 'Up! O Well [*be'er*] Sing ye to her! The well which the princes dug, the nobles of the people hollowed out, with the leader's rod, with their staves!" The point of this is that in old Arabia, and at the present day in the desert, the water of a spring is regarded as alive and must be encouraged to flow freely with songs sung to it, just as weary camels are encouraged with the special camel song. Above all, a newly found spring must be coaxed out of the ground by such songs.

But any real consideration of the song amongst the Hebrews must center round the personality of David. He, it is plain, put his stamp on all the later poetry and song, words and music, of his people, and to him a whole chapter must be given.

CHAPTER V

DAVID

IN ATTEMPTING to reach the real personality of David we face a very complicated problem. A sacrosanct figure was created by later Judaism and it is behind that figure that we must try to penetrate. For later Judaism "David" meant the Psalter; he meant the founder of the Davidic House and the prototype of the Messianic King; he meant the national existence as willed and guided by Jehovah. He meant, too, the organizer of the Temple worship, of its choirs of singers and musicians; he was, even, the inventor of their musical instruments. However we may regard this later development, it is plain from it that the influence of David had (i) been formative on the religious song of his people and (ii) that he and his house had come to be so identified with the Hebrew people as a religious community that a King of the House of David meant a Messianic ruler; such a King ruled by divine right.

How did all this come about? The first of these points, as dealing with literature, is more peculiarly our subject; but it cannot be considered without some reference to the second. The life of David and the songs of David are inextricably intertwined; the life produced the songs and the life was the starting point for the ideal conception of a divinely anointed, God-guided and protected, infallible head of the State. But the course in this development was a long one and must have moved slowly. The evidence of Amos here is significant. His one reference to David (for Amos ix, 11, is not Amos) is in Amos vi, 5, where he is describing the luxurious, heedless life of the wealthy in Jerusalem and Samaria: "Improvising to the sound of the harp; like David they invent for themselves instruments of song." The association here shows, at the least, that David was not yet for Amos a figure which must be kept clear of idle and profane suggestion. David meant for him an inventor of musical instruments which could be used in this useless life which he denounced and despised. This is very far from Ezekiel's vision (xxxiv, 23, 24; xxxvii, 24) of a future David, idyllic and idealized, who will be King and Shepherd of a restored and righteous people.

But what materials have we from which to reconstruct, if it be possible, the real David? Practically they are contained in the Books of Samuel which were evidently intended to give a life of David and a history of the founding of his house. With the Books of Kings, they form a history of the Hebrew people written from the viewpoint of the prophetic guilds and to the greater glory of the prophets in general. It is much as though the darwish fraternities of Islam had attempted a history of Islam from their point of view. On this there will be more hereafter. On another side, that of their original materials, these Books of Samuel, like the Book of Judges with which they connect, are a collection of traditional stories, strung together, practically without links or editing, but with a careless art which produces the happiest effect. For the same reason, they are the despair of the formal historian who takes these folk-tales seriously and tries to work out from them, often by violent "emendation," a consistent and smooth narrative. Fortunately, they have been transmitted to us just as the voice of the people passed them on to the original compilers and the vividness of the figures in them is undimmed by the efforts of rationalizers. He who would really understand and expound these stories in their living, picturesque, talking, Hebrew—a Hebrew very different from the ordered, literary language of the Books of Kings—should put himself to school for a time with the racy, popular stories which we have in such abundance in Arabic. Thereafter, he will not take too seriously their inconsistencies of statement and colloquial slipshod language.

And the style suits the theme. The ragged irregularity of the telling fits the ragged irregularity of the character of David. Plainly this is no simple shepherd. Doughty, who knew the desert on its seamy side so well, called him a scheming, climbing Bedawi. Our modern word for him on one side of his life, would be "racketeer." Blackmail is, perhaps, a more polite term, but it was really as a racketeer that Nabal knew him. And Abigail, plainly to her own content, became the Maid Marian of the Robin Hood. There were evidently many such in David's life. Yet he was no ordinary freebooter, but, with it all, a great soldier and a statesman. The prophetic compiler was within the truth when he put into the mouth of Jehovah: "And I have made thee a great name like unto the name of the great men that are in the earth" (2 Samuel vii, 9). So he climbed and accomplished and founded his house. The traditional stories of his life are given unsparingly and it would be easy from these to construct a most unedifying picture. The prophetic compiler has done his best with these materials. He has given the stories—they were too well known to be suppressed and he probably did not see them with our eyes—but he has also given with them pictures of David in his moments of repentance and more pious exaltation. The story of Bathsheba and of the rebuke of Nathan hangs together perfectly and may well be a straight, almost untouched, transcript of the popular story. The final turn of David's mind on the death of the child is no moralizing invention, but of a piece with David's keen sense of life. The ugly story, again, of Absalom, from beginning to end, with all its causes and development from lust to treason and tragedy, has recurred again and again in the annals of oriental royal houses. It is unflinchingly told and in one sense it culminates in the cursing of David, in his flight from Absalom, by Shimei, the kinsman of Saul (2 Samuel xvi, 5*ff.*)—a cutting to the quick of the earlier treason to Saul. And there is in it, too, the strange—indeed unique—speech to David of the Wise Woman of Tekoah: "For we must needs die and are as water spilt on the ground . . . yet doth God devise means that his banished be not expelled from him" (2 Samuel xiv, 14). Such were the tales and sayings that gathered round him.

All this gives a picture of David, and a picture which hangs together, but not a picture which explains his later influence either as shown in the Psalter or as shown in history. There is still a gulf between this David and the David of Ezekiel (xxxiv, 23, 24; xxxvii, 24, 25). Nor do the evidently later expansions and additions of the compilers help to bridge it. 2 Samuel vii, with all its pious phrases, is inexplicable in its context between the description of David dancing before the Ark and shocking Michal, and David smiting all the Kings round about. A proposal to build a permanent house for Jehovah there may well have been in the earlier story, but not these long speeches looking to Solomon and future Kings. Still less can we follow the chronicler (1 Chronicles xvi) in putting into David's mouth part of Psalm cv and all of Psalm xcvi. It is strange with how little psychological and historical insight these later redactors went about their work. Their great virtue is that they gave the stories so nearly untouched. Hereafter, we shall see what Hebrew story-tellers, who were artists, could do with the tales that their fathers had told them.

Where, then, besides these traditional stories, can we find David and the clue to his enormous influence? He was a poet, a singer, a musician—that is plain in the stories—and like all such, he must have left a collection of his songs. He was a many-sided man; a great lover—almost a romantic lover, a great warrior, a man of counsel and purposed plan, a man of wide experience in the adversities and successes of life, a man of close friendships, a man who slipped and fell and rose and went on, a great sinner and a great repenter. A man whose passions were strong and burned high; at times they swept him away and at times he held them in. He was a man, too, who could throw himself into the religious excitement and ecstasy of a great occasion, but, even in that, he had control and understanding; he knew what he was doing and, like Ecclesiastes in his experimenting (Ecclesiastes ii, 9), his reason stood by him. All this must have been expressed in his songs, for he was plainly of the type that must express itself. If there is any truth at all in the analogy, urged above and illustrated throughout this book, between the Hebrew and the Arab literary minds he must have had a *Diwan,* a collection of his poems, arranged and divided into books according to their subjects. And these would go out as songs in the ears and on the voices of the people and would be the models on which the singers of the future would shape their own songs. In the oldest extant Arabic literature there is a very close parallel to David on this side of his influence. About two generations before Mohammed there wandered, suffered, and sang in the desert a great heroic figure. This was Imr al-Qais, "the King Errant" as he was called, an exile from his kingdom, who sought aid, but to no purpose, here and there from the Kings of the desert and even as far, in the legend, as Byzantium itself. His life was that of a wanderer and everything that came to him of joy and sorrow, of bitter and sweet experience, of wisdom and folly, he turned into song. He was not, like David, a religious man; he was of lighter mind and, like most of the old singers of the desert, essentially materialistic. Nor was he, like David, an ultimately successful man; he was not of the kind to whom success comes. But he was in brain, blood and bone a singer and he left behind him his *Diwan,* poems which have been the norm for Arab verse ever since. His choice of subjects, his methods of approach and handling, his technique in verse and phrasing, down to the merest details, put fetters on the later poets. Unquestionably he was a great poet—the greatest of them all, thought Mohammed— and to him and to his influence that poetry of the desert owes much of its strength. He could feel and he could describe; he was intensely human and a line of his can still stir us, who are so far off, and bring tears to our eyes. It is recorded that on his way back from Byzantium, journeying in the desert, sick unto death and weary, he came to a mountain, called Aseeb, on the slope of which was a solitary tomb. He was told that it was the tomb of a certain king's daughter who, like himself, had come so far in her journeying and there had died. *A-Járataná,* he said—

> O Neighbor of mine, to whom the Fates have driven me,
> Here I abide so long as Aseeb abides—with thee!
> O Neighbor of mine, we are both of us strangers here,
> And one stranger to another is ever close and dear.

And there he died and at her side was buried and that was the end of his wanderings. So is the tale and all Arabia knows the lines. We have no exact knowledge as to where David lies buried, for the tombs of the Kings at Jerusalem have not yet yielded their secret. But it was not on the slope of any mountain in the desert nor by the side of any unknown Princess. David had made a success of his life and Imr al-Qais had not. Perhaps David, the poet, would have given all his gain to be sure that his songs, too, would live.

But of David, alas, we have no such *Diwan.* The later generations, jealous for the reputation of the sainted King, saw to that. We have the great mass of religious songs in the Psalter apocryphally ascribed to him and which tell us only that he—like Imr al-Qais on very different material—struck out an individual genre and fixed its law of content and phrasing. But fortunately, the compiler of our Books of Samuel has included some poems in which we can feel the real personality of David and find some clue to what his influence must have been. Possibly elsewhere, in the wide anonymity of the Old Testament, there are other fragments of his; his impress may even lie on that strange erotic jumble which we call the Song of Songs. The reputation of Solomon was given up by later Judaism as irretrievable, and songs really by his father may have passed under his name. That David's love-songs should have utterly perished is hard to believe.

The largest and the most important of the saved fragments in Samuel is the song which we commonly know as Psalm xviii. We thus have the poem in two recensions with slight variations of reading in almost every verse. This is as though we had two independent manuscripts from which to construct our text—a very rare advantage in the Old Testament. And the nature of the variations shows that the two recensions separated very far back and are virtually independent. The following translation is based upon both and its object is to bring out as vividly as possible the character of the singer, undoubtedly David himself. To do this it avoids as much as possible fixed religious language. These same words in the later Psalms plainly become stereotyped, but for David they were still fresh and must be rendered so as to bring out their freshness.

And David spoke to Jehovah the words of this song at the time when Jehovah had delivered him from the hand of all his enemies and from the hand of Saul: So he said:

I love Thee with kindred love, O Jehovah, my strength: Jehovah is my rocky peak and mountain fortress, my deliverer, my strong God, my great Rock in which I take refuge, my shield and my safe crag, my lofty protection. As to one greatly to be praised, do I cry unto Jehovah and from my enemies I am saved.

There encompassed me breaking waves of Death and deceitful watercourses were falling on me and terrifying me. Cords of the Grave surrounded me; snares of Death headed me off. In sore straits I would cry to Jehovah; unto my God I would cry for help. He would hear my voice from His palace and my cry for help before Him would enter in His ears.

Then trembled and quaked the earth and the foundations of the mountains were quivering; and they were all trembling as one, for He was in hot anger. There went up smoke at His nostrils and fire from His mouth was consuming; coals of fire devoured from Him. He put aside the sky and came down and deep darkness was under His feet. He rode on a Cherub and flew and swooped on the wings of the wind. He set darkness as His curtain; around Him His covert—clouds black with water, dustclouds. From the flashing before Him His clouds passed on —hailstones and coals of fire. And Jehovah thundered in the sky; the Most High uttered His voice—hailstones and coals of fire. Then He sent His arrows and scattered them and lightnings—many—and confounded them. The waterchannels appeared and the foundations of the world were uncovered; at Thy rebuke, Jehovah, at the blowing of the wind of Thine anger.

He would stretch from on high, taking me, drawing me from many waters, delivering me from mighty enemies, those that hated me; for they were stronger than I. They would head me off in my calamitous day, but Jehovah became a support to me and brought me out to a wide place, freeing me, because He has affection for me.

Jehovah requites me according to my loyalty; according to the cleanness of my hands He restoreth me; for I have kept the ways of Jehovah; I have not turned in wickedness from my God; for all His desires have been before me and His statutes I would not put aside from me. But I have been blameless with Him and have kept myself from my perverseness. So Jehovah has restored to me according to my loyalty, according to the cleanness of my hands before His eyes.

With a friendly man Thou showest Thyself friendly; with a blameless man Thou showest Thyself blameless; with a sincere man Thou showest Thyself sincere; but with a crook Thou showest Thyself harshly hard. For it is Thou a lowly folk that savest; but lofty eyes Thou bringest low.

For it is Thou that lightest my lamp; Jehovah, my God, flashes light on my darkness. For by Thee I burst through a troop, and by my God I leap a wall.

The mighty God!—blameless is His way; the saying of Jehovah is tried; a shield is He to all who take refuge with Him.

For who is a God apart from Jehovah and who is a Rock outside of our God? The mighty God!—He who girds me with might and who made my feet like the feet of hinds and on mine own heights He makes me stand fast; teaching my hands for battle and my arms alone bend down [i.e. string] the bow of bronze. He set for me the shield that saves me; Thy right hand supports me and Thy lowliness magnifies me; Thou lengthenest my steps under me and my ankles bend not.

So I can pursue my enemies unto overtaking them; I turn not back until I have finished them. I break them in pieces and they cannot arise; they fall under my feet. Thou didst gird me with might for battle, bringing low under me those that rise against me. Mine enemies, Thou hast turned their backs to me; and my haters I exterminate. They may cry for help, but there is none to save; even to Jehovah, but He answered not. So that I beat them fine like dust before the wind; like street mud I empty them out.

Thou deliverest me from the quarrellings of the people; Thou settest me as head of foreign peoples. A people with whom I had no intimacy serve me; at the mere hearing they show themselves obedient unto me; sons of strangers, they flatter me; sons of strangers, like withered leaves they quiver from their strong places. Jehovah lives, and blessed is my Rock, and lofty is my God that saves me; the mighty God who gives vengeances to me and drove the peoples under my feet; He delivers me from mine enemies, yea, from those that rise against me Thou settest me on high; from the man of violence Thou deliverest me. Therefore among the foreign nations I praise Thee, Jehovah, and to Thy name I make music.

For a theologian this song is the expression of a thoroughly unregenerate nature. There is no sense of sin—parenthetically it may be said here that the Hebrews were neither Puritans nor Calvinists—and the relation of the singer to Jehovah is of one gentleman to another. Jehovah is greatly more powerful; is, one might say, in a higher social class; but they are friends and as friends on an equal footing. Jehovah in his humility has stooped to David and thereby magnified David. So David is thoroughly assured of Jehovah's personal friendship for him. As to why this friendship exists we are given no clue; David accepts it as a primary fact just as Amos accepts his own relationship to Jehovah. But in David's case it is possible to conjecture that this relationship is like his own to Jonathan. In the same way—as shown in the story in Samuel, supported by David's lament for Jonathan—Jonathan had stooped in humility from his higher social rank and magnified David with his friendship. Again, the opening words of the song are significant. This relationship is like a blood-tie; the love between David and Jehovah is like that of kinship. This conception of Jehovah as of the kin of David is like the similar conception as to the People of Israel and the yet wider conception that the whole creation was a begetting on the part of God. It looks back to a time when this cosmic idea was not a metaphor and looks forward to the Christian doctrine of the universal Fatherhood of God. So, too, the humility of Jehovah towards David and His thus magnifying of David looks forward to the self-humiliation in the Messianic ideal and on the part of Christ the emptying of Himself and taking on Him the form of a creature (Philippians ii, 6, 7).

But, apart from such considerations which place the song in the broad current of Hebrew thought and religious attitude, the following connections with the later Psalm literature and differences from it should be noticed. The song is addressed to Jehovah, is based upon assurance of His intimate presence and is a record of intercourse with Him. In all these it is of the Psalm type. A Psalm is a didactic lyric; the singer has had experiences and he expresses these, addressing Jehovah, in a lyric outburst. But he does so with a didactic purpose; he has learned in suffering and now he would teach others in song. But in this Song of David there are differences. The psalmist, in the nature of the case, is humble towards his God; he has been disciplined and he knows it; it is his purpose to show it. David praises, thanks and glorifies Jehovah, but he is not in the least humble about it. It all goes very subtly to glorify David. Jehovah, it is true, has stooped to him and magnified him, but David has done his part. He has been loyal to Jehovah, blameless, clean of hands; he knows that and he tells Jehovah that. The two of them, Jehovah and David, are apart by themselves, holding together, almost one might say against the rest of the world. Jehovah meets people as they meet Him; he has done all these things for David, with David, because of David's attitude to Him. It is all so simple and naïve that we hardly notice the tremendous assurance of it. It is great religious poetry, but it is also utterly unregenerate. It holds possibilities for future development, but there is not a scrap of new-heart nonsense about David himself. He is a perfectly self-satisfied realist; with Jehovah he can meet the world. He has, in fact, so met it.

So much may be said for the spirit of the song. As to the language and form there are similar resemblances and differences. The Psalms tend to be abstract in expression, vague, even trite. When they use concrete words and phrases they are apt to give the impression that these are in a conventional language, are clichés. The words were alive once; now they are dead. We know exactly the same thing in the language of our hymns. But the words in the song of David are concrete throughout and alive throughout. It is as though he were using them in this way for the first time. Perhaps he was. But certainly he was putting on them the stamp of the great poet, making them look as though they were so used for the first time. And the same thing holds of the form, especially of the relation of the verses one to another. In that respect the Psalms are almost always formless; the verses do not link each with the other. If we were given the verses of a Psalm on separate slips of paper we could not possibly rearrange them in their original order. There are no links. But in this song of David's, verse with verse is linked; the verses can be paragraphed and the sequence of ideas traced and fixed.

So, at every point—spirit, language, structure—this song is original and the later Psalms show conventional imitation. And this leaves us with the question, Are there any other Davidic songs in the Psalter?—a question to which no absolute answer is possible. But it is quite safe to say that the only even approximate test must be this of reality, originality, vitality.

How, further, does this song fit in with the great songs of the desert Arabs in the old days, such as those of Imr al-Qais? There is the closest possible similarity in imagery and spirit with a single enormous difference. The description of the thunderstorm and cloudburst in the mountains, of the valleys and old watercourses filling up in flood and spate and coming roaring down, of the clouds, the thunderings, the lightnings, and of the peril of those in the midst of it all—that could be paralleled again and again in the old poetry of the desert. Again, the boasting, self-assured, confident attitude of David is that exactly of the old warriors and poets. They, too, called no man master; they journeyed, they fought, they sang, for their own hand. The Arab has always been an intense individualist and so he is still. He is also a braggart—conscious of his own worth and deeds and ready to tell of them. But there is also in this song a great difference. It is the reality and presence of Jehovah and the relation of David to Him. The thunderstorm is the coming of Jehovah to rescue David from his enemies; the boasting of David is of his assured standing with Jehovah, of his integrity in Jehovah's eyes. Of this—the fact of a Supreme Being behind and in nature—there is never a trace in the old Arab poetry. With the old Arabs the Unseen played a subordinate part. They had their equivalents for the nymphs and satyrs of our classical world; meetings with these in the desert and conflict with these occasionally touch the old poetry with the shudder of the supernatural. The different tribes had their different vague deities at different sanctuaries, but that was all. The desert does not seem to have known even such a mythological scheme as that of the Babylonian gods and goddesses. Their Fates were the ultimate haps of life—death in its different forms. And as for the widely spread belief with us that the people of the desert were naturally monotheistic, for that there is no basis at all. Monotheism came into the desert through Christian and Jewish influence. So David here, in his absolute assurance of Jehovah as his personal, intimate friend, has no relation to those old poets who were otherwise so closely of his kin. Whence he derived that assurance is part of the secret of the Hebrews. But the result is that we have here a most singular blend of the stark individualism and self-sufficiency of an old Arab singer and of that acceptance of the friendship, guidance, protection of a personal God which is the essence of the Psalms.

It may be worth while to give another song, found only in the Psalter, which meets the test of originality and reality. If Psalm xviii shows David as the wandering outlaw, escaping from his enemies in mountain warfare and crushing them under him; in his exile subduing alien peoples by his mere reputation and ruling over them, it is possible to conjecture that Psalm xxiii shows him in his dangerous isolation at the court of Saul and looking back on the old, quiet days when he was shepherd of his father's flocks. The thought throughout is of the protecting care of Jehovah and in the first part especially, where the sheep speaks, words are most skilfully used which represent at once physical appetites and needs and human feelings. In the following translation the physical needs are brought out:

Jehovah is my Shepherd; I cannot lack. In pastures of fresh, green grass He makes me lie down; beside restful waters He leads me slowly. My appetite He keeps restoring; He guides me in even paths, for the sake of His reputation. Even should I go my way in a ravine dark as the shadow of death I would not fear any evil thing; for Thou art with me; Thy club and Thy guiding staff are a comfort to me.

Thou spreadest before me a table in the presence of my enemies; Thou hast anointed with oil my head; my cup is overflowing. Only good and kindness will pursue me all the days of my life and my abiding will be in the House of Jehovah for long years.

If this is not David it is a deceptively skilful reproduction of what must often have been his thought.

In the stories in Samuel there occurs little which suggests that David was more than simply a poet-warrior and statesman; that the intimacy of his relationship to Jehovah had reached the point of prophecy. He had, of course, with him professional prophets—if we may use the term—such as Nathan and Gad who had joined their fortunes to him. As to the frequent mention of these it is well to reiterate that the story of his life, in the Books of Samuel, and the stories of the lives of his successors, in the Books of Kings, were very plainly compiled and written from the point of view of the prophetic guilds. How and when this was done we do not know, but the guiding influence on these books was certainly of those guilds and not of the priestly organizations. In these books the prophetic guilds have put up a solemn and sometimes sanctimonious bluff. This appears most strongly in their use of Samuel as against Saul, but also in their treatment of the figure of David. This is not a criticism of the great prophets, who were personalities, but of the organized prophetry of which Amos, for example, had no high opinion. Further, it is impossible to escape the impression that in the stories themselves references to David as a prophet have been suppressed and that he has been represented as dependent on the guidance of professional prophets and priests. The quite naïvely primitive ideas of the Hebrews as to the nature of prophecy and its near relation to the inspiration of the poet will be taken up hereafter. But from David himself we have his own testimony preserved for us in that singular fragment in 2 Samuel xxiii, 1-7, and entitled there: "These are the last words of David." Whether they were his last words or not, they are a clear claim that he was a spokesman of Jehovah and their style is of a singular, weighty, oracular impressiveness, closely compacted of words loaded with meaning and pictures, very hard fully to translate, in the same way that the old Arab poetry almost defies complete rendering:

> The utterance of David the son of Jesse, the utterance of the man who was set up on high, the anointed of the God of Jacob and the maker for Israel of pleasant songs. The Spirit of Jehovah spoke in me and His Word was on my tongue; the God of Israel said to me; the Rock of Israel spoke: "He that ruleth over mankind must be just, a ruler in the fear of God. As at the light of morning, the sun shining out, whether a morning without clouds or a flashing of light out of rain, soft green grass comes from the earth." Surely is not thus my house with the mighty God? For an abiding covenant He hath appointed for me, equipped with everything and guarded. For all my help and every desire will He not cause to spring up like grass? But worthlessness is like thorns, thrust away, all of them. Not with the [bare] hand can they be taken; but who would touch unto them must guard his hand with iron and a spear-shaft, and with fire they must be utterly consumed where they lie.

If this is of David—and there seems no reason to doubt it—then to him already had come the assurance that his house was to be a ruling house, founded in righteousness and godly fear, a house of an eternal covenant with God, based on such usefulness as has the tender green grass, contrasted with thorns fit only for burning.

Yet another side of David has been preserved for us and one strangely different. The old poetry of the desert is full of laments for the dead. Both in form and in spirit these are singularly fixed. The dead man is gone; the gap he has left is bitterly felt; he is described as he was. But his house is now the grave, an eternal abode from which there is no return. He *is* there, but hopelessly there; his abiding is like that of the eternal, lifeless mountains; he is "blown about the desert dust, or sealed within the iron hills." Above all, for the old Arab, with death there was no religious association. The Fates had struck, "as a blind camel at random treads"; and a man had died. Whatever tribal gods there might be had nothing to do with the dead and little with the living. Much of this reappears amongst the old Hebrews and it will be dealt with hereafter in considering their sense of the weird. But with David, and his intense feeling of the reality and closeness of Jehovah as a friend, a deliverer, a hearer of prayer, we might look for something else. In the Palace of Jehovah might there not be a place for the heroic dead? David's lament for Saul and Jonathan (2 Samuel i, 17-27) answers that question.

And David made this lament for Saul and for Jonathan, his son, and he commanded to teach the Sons of Israel "Bow" [apparently a melody]; it is written in *The Book of the Upright*.

The Glory [of the land], O Israel, on thy heights lies slain. How are the heroes fallen!

Tell not in Gath; give not this good tidings in the streets of Askelon; lest the daughters of the Philistines be glad; lest the daughters of the uncircumcised exult.

Ye Mountains in Gilboa, let not dew, nor rain, be upon you—ye treacherous fields; for there the shield of the heroes was cast away, the shield of Saul, unanointed with oil. From the blood of the slain, from the best of the heroes the bow of Jonathan never drew back; the sword of Saul was not wont to return empty.

Saul and Jonathan! The beloved, the kind in their lives; in their death they were not divided; than eagles swift, than lions strong.

Daughters of Israel, weep for Saul who clothed you in scarlet with loveliness, who put on your garments golden jewels.

How are the heroes fallen in the midst of the battle! Jonathan on thy heights lies slain.

Anguish is mine for thee, O my brother, Jonathan; thou wast very kind to me, wonderful was thy love for me, passing woman's love.

How are the heroes fallen, the weapons of warfare lost!

No old Arab poet could have voiced a more hopeless sorrow. There is not a word about Jehovah whose anointed Saul had been and before whom David and Jonathan had made eternal covenant. David does not look even to any shadowy, lifeless existence in a Sheol, or Hades, like that from which in the legend Samuel had been raised to confront Saul. This is like an end in the desert; at the best such eternal rest as Imr al-Qais sought beside his chance-found, dead, Princess. There is not even a word of the consolations of Jehovah for David; grief goes behind all that. He can only take comfort in the pale anodyne of nature, in adjuring the hills, as so many in sorrow, greater or lesser, have done. The mountains of the desert for the Arab poets were always the eternal and abiding verities of life; they remain though the generations of men pass away. To them these poets lifted up their eyes, not from any sense of a God of strength and comfort behind them, but simply because they remain and are calm however the generations of men may grieve and despair as they go their way. So in Micah (vi, 1, 2) Jehovah calls on his people to present their plea to the mountains and hills, the unchanging foundations of the earth, that they may judge how loyal and righteous he has been. Our memories go back to Byron's heart-cry, "Hills of Annesley, bleak and barren!" Why, then, in face of human loss and grief did all thought of Jehovah thus drop away? There is no answer. For David at least, Jehovah was God of the living and not of the dead. There will be more on this hereafter.

In 2 Samuel iii, 33, 34, there is a scrap of another lament by David, one for Abner, which shows, at least, that in his *Diwan,* if he had one, there would be a book of such poems. The scrap is so broken as to be hardly translatable: "As a fool dieth was Abner's dying? Thy hands were not bound nor thy feet struck in brazen fetters; like falling before wicked men didst thou fall?" The point is evidently an allusion to Abner's trustfulness and Joab's treachery. Abner had been no such grudging, obstinate churl as Nabal—

the word here for "fool" is the same—or he might have lived. But it is recorded that the people, at this lament, were swept away into tears. For Absalom David himself wept, but we have no record of a song of lament.

It may be well, finally, to renew a question raised above. Do those more or less assured songs give us any clue as to Davidic elements in the Psalter? It is quite certain that no attention can or need be paid to the "of David" in the headings of so many psalms. Is there, then, any evidence from style or spirit? For individual cases there seems to be nothing that goes beyond possibility. Reading the Hebrew—for through no translation can those things show—we may say: Here is freshness, originality, greatness; this is a great poet and no mere writer of hymns or religious verse. But that does not carry us to David. It is true that in the Psalter it is highly probable that there are snatches of song by David, scraps of his religious expression of himself. But that does not carry us very far. And the problem is complicated by two elements in it that are perfectly certain. The Hebrew poet, like the Arab poet, pushed imitation to the farthest extreme; for him it was a form of literary art. Sometimes it was conscious parody, a touch of ridicule aimed at some well known verses and their ideas. But much oftener it was admiring imitation; a later poet trying to do exactly the same thing that an earlier poet had done consummately well. In Arabic this went so far that there was a proverb: "The merit belongs to the precedent." Imitation was easy once the way was shown; in Tennyson's words, "All can raise the flower now, For all have got the seed." The seed of the Davidic style in religious song was scattered widely among the Hebrew people. The Hebrew people knew that, and so they called the Psalter "David." The second complicating element lay in the adjusting of songs of personal experience to communal singing. From this many poems in our hymn-books have suffered and the Psalter is a hymn-book. It is not difficult in it to distinguish conventional phrases and lines plainly added for their value in the mouth of temple or synagogue singers. But completely to purge the text of these is quite another matter.

There is another danger which the investigator of this problem of David may run and has run. We have to beware of saying at any point, David, being what we know he was, living where he lived and when, could not have said that—whatever it may be. In the first place we do not know what David was with any such surety. We know that he was a great poet, and a great poet is capable of anything. He does not belong to his own place or time; he belongs to the whole earth and to all time. In Psalm xviii we have already seen him reaching out in thoughts, germinal thoughts, which had in them the universal Fatherhood of God and the conquering humility of Christ. There was no clear theological thinking in those thoughts of his; they were simply flashes from his experience as poet and prophet and friend. In Psalm xlii there are similar upbursts of emotional insight, joined to a picture-making power like that of Wordsworth when he heard "the cataracts blow their trumpets from the steep." This song comes very close to meeting the artistic and spiritual test of David. As David reached out to Christian theology, so he reached out to the conceptions of nature followed by Wordsworth and his school. Farther than this we can hardly get, for our materials are too scanty. But at least the following elements in David stand out clearly. He was a great poet, of the old Arab type and a musician who put his definite mark on the future music of the Hebrews. He felt himself in the closest personal relationship to Jehovah and under Jehovah's peculiar protection. He had so strong a feeling of the immediacy with which his religious song came upon his lips that he believed himself to be a prophet commissioned to pass on the words of Jehovah. He was capable, too, of such orgiastic acts of devotion as the professional prophets practised. This personal prophetship of his was minimized by the later prophetic writers of his biography. Nor, even, do these writers bring out clearly his position in the history of Hebrew literature as the fixer to type of the psalm; consciousness of that seems to have grown up later. As a result of his personal relationship to Jehovah he felt assured that he was founding a royal dynasty under divine protection. Yet with all this he could produce laments which conformed closely to the old Arab type and had no religious element in them. Only so far, and in such contradictory fashion, does the original David show himself to us. So it is with a sense of comparative failure that we turn from our attempt to reach him. There can be no question of the depth and width of his influence on the mind of his people and on their literature. But there can be no question, also, that the two pictures which commonly represent David for us, that of the crowned psalmist with a harp and that of the shepherd called from his flocks to the kingdom, are totally inadequate and even positively misleading. His was one of the great and dominant personalities of Israel and he must have given Israel models and leadings for much more than the psalm. These, probably, lie hidden in the later literature of his people but the clues have vanished.

CHAPTER VI

HEBREW POETRY AS ROMANTIC SONG

THE foregoing study of the personality and work of David has been a break in the method of this book. We are concerned primarily with the types and broad forms of Hebrew literature and only in a secondary degree with the individuals who produced it. But it is so plain that David was a type in himself and that he fixed a type in the songs of his people, that he calls for separate and personal treatment. With no other Old Testament author do we seem so to get back to an absolute beginning as with him. "Absolute," of course, is too strong a word even here—there are no absolute beginnings in literature—but some such word is needed to bring out the degree of his originality and the weight of his personal influence. For he is a personal figure, too, and thus stands clearly out in the crowd of Old Testament writers who are either entirely nameless, or else only names. We know in a certain outline who David was, but who was "Ecclesiastes," who the author of the Colloquies in Job, who the philosopher-artist who gave form and meaning to our Book of Genesis? They are among the greatest literary creators of the world, but they have not even a name.

David calls himself "the maker for Israel of pleasant songs." That stood for him on equality with his prophetic gift and the anointing and divine destiny of himself and of his house. He had been a conspicuous and accepted maker of the songs of the people; for the Hebrew expression here is of far wider meaning than "the sweet psalmist" of our version. What were those songs of the people? They have vanished like the great mass of the songs of David himself. We have allusions in the Old Testament to collections of popular songs. The lament for Saul and Jonathan is said to have been written in a certain *Book of the Upright*. From this same book there is a quotation also in Joshua x, 12, 13, and that is all we know about it. It was probably somewhat like that book of well known songs in Arabic literature known as *The Book of Hardihood (al-hamása)*. Another collection of songs, with historical reference, was called *The Book of the Wars of Jehovah*. We know it only from a quotation in Numbers xxi, 14. In the same chapter, verses 27-30, there is quoted another fragment of verse with historical and geographical reference. It is introduced with "Therefore the *Móshelim* say . . ." and the *Móshelim* were apparently the producers and singers of songs with a biting, personal application which made them didactic, like a *mashal*, a proverb, parable, wise saying. Balaam's utterances in Numbers xxiii-xxv will be considered under prophecy.

But it is evident from all this that the Hebrew people were a singing people. If they could not produce the narrative ballads of other peoples in their simple objectivity, and thus rise to the literary epic, they could in their songs voice the popular emotion at given moments of crisis in their national life. It may well be, too, that the series of stations in the wilderness wanderings was held in memory with rough verses sung and passed from generation to generation. Parallels for such memory-verses could be found in the history of the Arab tribes. Song seems always to come before Story in literary development. Under Story it will hereafter be suggested that the Exodus narratives go back to a tangle of popular prose romances with historical basis; and that basis may well have been such scraps of song, but longer and more detailed, as are preserved for us here in Numbers. Similarly, the Arthurian romances passed at one of their stages from verse to prose, and prose, too, through which the original verses still glimmer.

What is the essential in song which distinguishes it from other poetry? It is music in the singing voice. The words and the melody must go together and neither really exists without the other. Songs without words are a late sophistication and words without music may be poetry but are not song. Further, the combination of the two—words and melody—produces a third thing which is neither, but a new thing in itself. As Browning's Abt Vogler framed "out of three sounds, not a fourth sound, but a star." The words may be commonplace, the music trivial, but the combination will search the heart. Thomas Moore used himself to sing his *Irish Melodies,* and it was well said by his hearers that only then was he perfecting them as poems. All know how flatly they read. Robert Burns has left on record in a letter [printed in the *Times Literary Supplement,* October 25, 1928, p. 783] that he began his songs always from a melody, going over and over the air until the song itself came into being. Having such a beginning his songs can have a perfect rendering only in the singing voice. Tennyson used to chant his poems, striking a mean between song and prose speech. Children invariably chant or sing verses unless the pedantry of their elders prevents. So, too, the ancients always; recital of verse to imitate prose is late and essentially artificial. Thus in all early poetry, song meant the emotion of the singer and of the poet if he were himself the singer. And in all Semitic poetry song and therefore emotion—or emotion and therefore song—was its *differentia* from prose. The Semitic poet, as has been said above, was a "feeler," not a "maker"; man feels before he thinks. So the combination in David of music—harp and voice—and of poetry was fundamental for all Hebrews.

With this combines the Hebrew weakness as to sense of form. The song struck out by the emotion of the moment may be staccato in structure, a series of sharp cries, or it may be rambling in structure, wandering in meditation from one phase to another of feeling. But from its very nature it cannot be of complicated concatenation. There can be in it no dark inwoven harmonies, no linked premeditated sweetness. The music of the fugue and the structure of the sonnet are alike impossible for it. Its metaphors will be a series of separate pictures which may stretch out indefinitely. Hebrew is full of rhymes, assonances, alliterations, but none of them is regular, coming with inexorable return. A poet could rhyme or not, as he pleased; and in the same poem will occur blocks of rhymes and then unrhymed gaps. Arabic poetry always rhymes and its long odes are bound to one rhyme throughout. Hebrew poetry shows signs of being on the way to such bondage, but the goal is far off and only subconsciously felt. The Hebrew poet plainly liked such rhymes, but felt in no way bound to them and was careless of them. If they came, well and good; otherwise he sang on. In consequence of all this, when Hebrew verses were written to a structure it was a mechanical structure. We have acrostic psalms and poems, working through the letters of the alphabet. These, of course, point to a time when there was an alphabet of definite order and to writing, not singing, of verses. They lie outside of the spontaneous and real workings of the Hebrew literary genius.

All the above goes to demonstrate that Hebrew literature is romantic, not classical. These two words are often used with many different implications and have become battle-grounds for theories, not simply of literature but of life and of fundamental attitudes to life. But in the present case they can be used, and exactly used, of a precise contrast in literary attitude and method. That this contrast meant, too, an attitude to life may be left at present on one side. A classical literature, then, means a literature governed by a sense of artistic form, a literature which has standards to which it must adhere. These standards may be explicit and universally accepted; in that case the literature in question is already moving down from the peaks of achievement. Or they may be implicit in the mind of the artist, something to which by his own nature he must conform and by which he must shape his work. But there must be a norm or rule implicit or explicit. Romantic literature, on the other hand, knows, in its essence, no rule; its source is impulse, the creative impulse of the moment in the soul of the artist. This, by its nature, brings with it freshness and overwhelming, instantaneous reality. And its freshness is the freshness of the strange—the seen, or shown, or realized for the first time. This distinction holds not simply for literature but for all the arts and each kind has its own strength and value. The appeal of all romantic art is immediate and unescapable. A new thing stands before you with a strange, fresh beauty that meets you like a blow. The effect may be only momentary and may die out; or it may last and renew itself. All that depends upon the degree of reality in the art. The romantic beauty of one age is too often not that of another; it may become grotesque and ugly to a following age. Similarly the poetry of sentiment may pass rapidly into the sentimental and absurd. But truly great romantic art is as permanent in its effect as any classical art, just as true sentiment maintains its pathetic reality for every age. The opposite of all this is classical art. It has no immediate knockdown effect, except perhaps for the trained student of art. For most of us the effect of a product of classical art is slow in coming. But when it does come, as it will come with patience, if the art is true and not simply wooden, the effect is permanent. It may take time to find the beauty of *Lycidas,* while the effect of *Il Penseroso* is immediate. But the beauty of *Lycidas*—in spite of Dr. Johnson and Milton's evident bad temper and dislike of his time—abides, once we have caught it. Of course, there is so-called classical art, which keeps all the rules and is worthless, just as there is the pretty product of a romantic movement which never outlasts the movement.

To pursue this further, it may be said that there are three stages of the romantic. There is the primitive romantic and to that the Hebrew artistic mind belonged and of that the Hebrew artistic mind is perhaps the best representative. For while that mind attained the highest artistic perfection it never ceased to be primitive and romantic. There is, second, a later romantic, not at all primitive, coming in waves of revival, cleansing and revitalizing old and fossilized literatures. It is genuine, because it springs from the inexhaustible youth of the race, touching again as it were the life-giving earth and bursting the bands of pseudo-classical rules. Such was the Romantic Awakening from which the present study of Hebrew literature begins. It was perfectly true and genuine and its great works retain their value as great poetry to this day. But, third, there was and is, a sophisticated romantic which tries to produce its effect by mechanical means such as vocabulary and strained grotesqueness of metaphor and structure. If the best representative of the second stage of romantic in our literature is Walter Scott in his carelessness, the best representative of the third, for all he was a true poet, was Dante Gabriel Rossetti with his search for "stunning words" and picturesque situations.

Finally, to bring all this home and link it up with our Hebrews, hear Robert Louis Stevenson sum up Scott, "a great romantic, a playing child," and Goethe sum up Byron, "when he thinks he is a child" and hear the dictum of Francis Bacon, a romanticist, if a queer one, "there is no excellent Beauty, that hath not some Strangenesse in the Proportion" (Essay xliii). So were the Hebrews: great artists; playing children, incapable of thought when they sang; moulding in their language forms of new, strange beauty. They were primitive and they were modern, more modern than any of the men and women of either Greece or Rome. Their singers, story-tellers, speakers, seers, were like our own, for we, heart and soul, are irrepressibly romantic still. Our thought may be Greek; our poetry springs from our soil.

Again, and because of all this, the clue to the Old Testament as literature is not to be found in our professedly religious poetry, but in our poetry at large. When our poetry tries to be religious, as in hymns, or when it tries to deal directly with Old Testament figures, as in Browning's *Saul*, sophistication enters, the picture is blurred and we get theological speculation and not the religious attitude which was the natural life of the Hebrews. But take Palgrave's *Golden Treasury* or take Wordsworth almost anywhere—but especially his great *Immortality Ode*—as books to keep beside the Old Testament, and to read with it, and their music will ring as one and their thoughts will mingle as one. That is the marvel of that literature of the Hebrews that it, sprung from the Syrian and Arabian soil, should be so closely akin to our northern and western life and thinking.

CHAPTER VII

ORIGIN AND METHODS OF THE HEBREW PROPHETS

BUT there is yet another side to Hebrew song which must be worked out in at least some of its more neglected aspects: it is as important a side of Hebrew song nationally as is the individual phenomenon of David. This is the racial phenomenon of the prophet. But to approach it, although poetry and prophecy are closely akin and have in fact their origin in the same world of the Unseen, a fresh beginning must be made. In what here follows little attempt is made to deal with prophecy on its spiritual and intellectual sides. To these, in recent times, so much attention has been paid as to throw out of proportion our picture of the literature and thinking of the Hebrews. The impression has been produced that the prophets were the great, and almost the only, contribution of the Hebrews to the spiritual life and progress of the world. The following pages are not an attempt, in our modern vulgarity, to "debunk" the prophets but are an attempt to place them, if shortly, in the broader scheme of Hebrew literature, beside Hebrew poetry and philosophy, and, especially, to give the sources from which prophetism sprang and the machinery and apparatus which the prophets inherited and used. They attempt to answer such questions as these: How did the prophets look to the people round about them? What did these people think of them and where did they place them? How did the prophets fit into the broad picture of their times and with what usages and institutions were they most closely associated? Again, does our modern psychology, in its investigation of automatisms and psychical phenomena in general, throw any light on the obscurities of the prophetic phenomena among the Hebrews? All these are questions which have been too little considered and to which we now turn.

All literature, everywhere, divides into two classes, the dynamic and the static, the literature which changes nothing but merely recounts and the literature which brings to bear a force and impulse and which results in something new and different. With the static literature of the Hebrews we have nothing here to do. It occupies a great part of the Old Testament with describing, narrating, enumerating,—all simply to describe, narrate, enumerate the past. But the dynamic literature of the Hebrews was another matter; in it was life, force, feeling, thought—and the future. It may be divided under three significant heads: Poetry, Philosophy, Prophecy. These three are distinguishable according to the ultimate source from which they proceed and which impels them to go forth and produce their effect. As we have seen above abundantly, the ultimate source of poetry is the emotional experience of the poet; he feels and he sings what he feels and therefore the commonest Arabic word for "poet" means "the feeler," "the perceiver." The results of philosophy are reached by and from conscious thought; the thinker wittingly and of purpose applies his reason and reaches his result. Hereafter we shall have to look in detail at this whole question of reason—our versions call it wisdom—in Hebrew literature. The distinctive source of the third, prophecy, is different from both of these. The prophet finds something in his mind or words on his tongue which he has not, for his own consciousness, reached by reason or through emotion. Something is given to him, or laid upon him, and he is quite sure that it has come from the Unseen World and that, for a prophet, means Jehovah. We shall see hereafter in how many ways and forms this unknown something may come. But in them all it is an immediate influence and gift from the Unseen World and the prophet himself has nothing to do with its coming. These three, then, are primarily separate and distinct in their sources, which are personal emotion and experience, personal conscious thinking, a direct unconditioned impact from the Unseen. That is the primary, simple, situation; but recorded prophecies, as we have them, are always mixed. There is the prophet's emotion and experience which work upon and color the flash of intuition which has come to him. There is also the prophet's conscious thinking which moulds that flash, develops it and applies it. But without that first flash and gift from the Unseen there would not be prophecy. It is the element which makes the difference between prophecy and philosophy. In a word, with no Unseen to throw its light into the prophet's mind there would be no prophecy. In consequence, the frequent modern attempts to rationalize and desupernaturalize the operations of the prophet's mind run in the teeth of the whole attitude and psychological experience of the Hebrew world and make unintelligible these phenomena. The Hebrew prophets themselves knew perfectly well that they were essentially channels for influence from the Unseen World of spirits; that is, from Jehovah.

This brings us face to face with the whole matter of the reality of the Unseen for the Hebrews. They lived in contact with two worlds and they were completely assured of the reality of both. There was this material world in which they lived and which was a creation of Jehovah. There was the world of spirits, separated from the material world by a shell as to the nature of which they apparently did not speculate. They seem to have been afraid of speculation about it, lest it should lead them back into the heathen mythology from which Jehovah had delivered them. This will be dealt with at length under the relation of the Hebrews to the Weird. But they were very sure that this shell between the two worlds was constantly being broken through from the spirit side, and that in ways which were partly legitimate and partly illegitimate. The legitimacy consisted in the method of contact being approved by Jehovah and carried out in His name. It was then licit; otherwise it was illicit. For just as this world was the abode of a race of rational beings, the Sons of Adam, so the spirit world was the abode of another race of rational beings, called the Sons of God, or of Elohim. These, to begin with, were of the same nature as Jehovah and Jehovah was simply their head and ruler. But this conception naturally opened the way to indefinite mythology and even polytheism, and the Hebrews, when we know them, were bending every effort to prevent such retrogression. Jehovah had delivered them from all that and they clung to the uniqueness of His dominant personality. The "spirits" in that Unseen World belonged to His court and were under His rule. And just as there were good and bad men, truthful and lying men, so there were good and bad, truthful and lying, spirits. But Jehovah controlled them all and they all stood in His presence. The result of this is a curiously, for us, mixed and contradictory picture of that Unseen World. The masses of the Hebrews, if we may judge from the narratives in Samuel and Kings, do not seem to have had difficulty with it. Yet there was, also, a tendency to simplify and unify this spirit world. Amos, for example, although he uses pictures which go back to the old Semitic mythology, has cut down the whole Unseen World to Jehovah Himself, eliminating even His angel messengers. For Amos, all happenings of every kind in this world are carried out by the immediate and personal action of Jehovah.

So, whether this Unseen World was an elaborate world of spirits good and bad, but all dominated by Jehovah, or was simply Jehovah Himself alone, the Hebrews had no question as to its reality and as to its frequent influence on the material world in which they lived. And this influence was not simply in ways that we would recognize as supernatural. This Unseen World was the source not only of prophecy and soothsaying but also a source of poetry. In fact one of the reasons why the Hebrews did not distinguish the poet as such and give him a name derived from his craft may have been that he was still confused with the prophet. For the Hebrews, just as for the Arabs and for primitive peoples in general, poetry was a form of inspiration from the spirit world. For the desert Arabs a poet had his own particular attendant spirit, a comrade belonging to the Unseen World, and his verses were dictated to him in one way or another by this spirit. This was regarded as different from the oracles which came through diviners, for these oracles were in a very elementary form of rhymed but not exactly metrical speech. But the poems which came through poets were in the fixed meters of ordinary Arabic verse. This rhymed language of the diviners was recognized as the specific form of oracles from the Unseen and the whole of the Koran is in this form of speech. But still it was influence from the spirit world that lay behind both poems and oracles. We have ourselves two contacts with this idea, one artificial and the other belonging to what is vaguely called the occult. The artificial is the convention of invoking the muse which even Milton followed. The other is the singular and psychologically quite unexplained phenomenon of the subconscious production of verses. In our literature the most outstanding example of this is the *Kubla Khan* of Coleridge. But it has appeared again and again in the case of the most different individuals, some of whom were quite incapable of producing verses at all in their conscious and waking moments. It cannot be doubted that this perfectly certain although, as yet, unexplained phenomenon is the basis of the fixed belief of the Hebrews, Arabs, and primitive peoples in general that poetry is a form of inspiration from the Unseen.

When we look, then, at prophecy among the Hebrews we find it connected with three things, for us widely separated:

A. Poetry
B. Soothsaying
C. Ecstatic Religious Emotion

For A and B, consider the following cases. In Numbers xxii-xxiv we have the oracles of Balaam. They are poetry—song—and they are soothsaying. Further, they are blessing and cursing of friends and enemies, derived from a supernatural sanction; the utterances of Balaam are dictated from the Unseen and he is powerless to change them. They are couched, too, in a hieratic language. In exactly the same way among the heathen Arabs, before Mohammed and, as a survival, in his time and immediately after his time, the poet of a tribe was its soothsayer and its supernaturally guided leader; it was his business also on battle day to ride out before the tribe and solemnly to curse the enemies of his tribe. He could do that and his curses went home because his voice and words were from the Unseen. That was what being a poet meant. His inspiration might be used in one way or another. Again, we have already found this same combination of poet and prophet in the Last Words of David. And broadly it may be said that all Hebrew prophecy, in its vital period, was delivered in the language of poetry and was sung or chanted.

To work out the associations of prophecy with B, soothsaying, is much more complicated, but also leads us much nearer to the center of the problem and to the machinery and usages of the prophets. Soothsaying among the Hebrews, as we have seen, was of two kinds, legitimate and illegitimate. The difference between the two apparently was that the first came from contact with Jehovah specifically, and with His spirit, and the second was a result of contact with the spirit world through primitive methods. These were the methods of folklore magic which seem to have been —and to be—common to all races. This can be best brought out by examples. Of legitimate soothsaying a good example is the story (1 Samuel ix, 6*ff.*) of how Saul went to inquire of Samuel about his father's stray asses. If the story is read carefully—and it should be, for it is very significant—it will be seen that Samuel is treated simply as a village clairvoyant. There are all the details, even to the necessary piece of silver; yet Samuel was a prophet of Jehovah and a man highly respected in his community. The vocabulary used in the story should be specifically noticed. In our English version Samuel is called a "man of God." That inevitably suggests to us a godly man, but such is not the idea in the Hebrew phrase. It means simply a man in contact with the spirit world, that world of Elohim, "gods," described above. The Hebrew word Elohim had many usages, but they all go back to the conception "spirit-beings" as opposed to material beings. It is in form a plural and mostly a plural in usage. So it can mean "ghosts"—as of Samuel brought back by the Witch of Endor; "spirits" of all kinds—as of the "sons of God" who had intercourse with the "daughters of men"; the "gods" of the heathen nations; and, in various phrases, "the supernatural." It is thus used often in an almost impersonal way. Very strangely, and still in the plural form, it is used of Jehovah, i.e. our "God" with a capital. "Man of Elohim" in this story is one of the cases of its vaguer use, for Samuel was a man who had to do with the Unseen. He is called also a "seer," and that is an exact translation of the Hebrew word used and means our "clairvoyant." In verse 9 we are told that seer was an old word and that the seer was "now" called prophet. The Hebrew word here —*nabhī'*—is that translated "prophet" throughout the whole Old Testament. From it a verb has been derived, and is translated throughout "to prophesy," although it is plain that it is used in different ways, some not in the least our idea of "prophesying." There is not at present any generally accepted derivation for the noun—and the verb is evidently derived from the noun—but a guess may be attempted. In Hebrew the root of noun and verb has no independent existence, but in Arabic that root is quite common and has the fixed meaning, "to give information." It seems, therefore, quite probable that the noun *nabhī'*, meaning "a giver of information" or "a recipient of information," i.e. as to the Unseen World, came from Arabic into Hebrew and that then the Hebrew verb forms were derived from it. This would fit with the remark in Samuel as to its use "now" instead of the older "seer." Very much later, in post-Christian times, this same word returned to the desert with its acquired Jewish meaning. Thus *nabī* is now the regular word in Arabic for a prophet and purists distinguish between it and the original *nabī'*. Further, it will be well here to notice that there is still a third word used in Hebrew for "prophet" which means literally "gazer," one who looks intently at anything. These three words, apparently, had different applications and suggested different ideas. One of many puzzling and tantalizing references to the older, and lost, books of the Hebrews is in 1 Chronicles xxix, 29. There for the details of David's reign we are referred to three books: the Book of Samuel, the Seer—probably our Book of Samuel; the Book of Nathan, the Prophet—the word is *nabhī'*; the Book of Gad, the Gazer. The phrase translated here "book of" is "according to the words of" but the meaning is probably just "book." Unless "the words" of Nathan and Gad have been incorporated in our Books of Samuel their books have been lost. But it is tolerably plain from this reference that the terms "seer," "prophet," "gazer," were not exactly synonymous. It is plain, too, that the "gazer" was the equivalent of our "scryer" or "crystal gazer," whatever were the material of the smooth, shining surface at which the Hebrew gazer looked in order to make contact with the Unseen. As to the methods of the "prophet" and the "seer" we can only guess; but there is good evidence, as will appear hereafter, for what is called now in abnormal psychology "automatic speech." The rest of this story of Saul and Samuel deals with our division C—ecstatic religious emotion—when "the spirit of Jehovah" leaps—the word is used elsewhere of the leaping of fire from one thing to another—upon Saul and compels him to "prophesy." But in the first part the position of Samuel as a paid consultant in ordinary and trivial human affairs, in virtue of his relation to the Unseen World, is quite clear. With him such a business is legitimate, because it is done in the name of Jehovah.

The case of the Witch of Endor is quite different, and her story also should be read with care. She (1 Samuel xxviii) was a practitioner of ancient magic, a "possessor of an *'ōbh*," which our version translates, "having a familiar spirit." Literally an *'ōbh* means a water-skin (Job xxxii, 19). This is its only occurrence in the Old Testament in that primary, concrete sense, but it recurs repeatedly in connection with illegitimate soothsayers and necromancers. The best description of the nature of its manifestations in this sense is in Isaiah xxix, 4, where a faint, low voice whispering from the dust of the ground is compared with an *'ōbh*. It may be that those ghostly sounds suggested the gurglings and murmurings of an emptying water-skin; but it may be also that a water-skin was simply part of the apparatus of a witch, used in some unknown way. There was evidently no doubt that such a woman as this could reach the world of the departed and bring up a dead man to undergo questions. So Samuel came up out of the earth, in obedience to her call, "an old man covered with a mantle." The woman, who apparently was the only one who saw him and who had to describe him to Saul, says that she sees *Elohim*, spirits, ghosts, coming up. But when Samuel speaks Saul hears his words. We are not told by what method the witch evoked Samuel; probably everyone knew. But Samuel came up—had to come up, is implied in the story—from some vague subterranean world of the dead, out of which he was "shaken" and "disturbed." With him, in that world of the dead, Saul and his sons would be on the morrow. We are told no more.

Between this witch using her primitive ritual and the honored figure of Samuel with his recognized status before Jehovah anyone could distinguish. But apparently there were also equivocal figures, calling themselves prophets, perhaps believing themselves to be prophets, whom it was harder to distinguish. It might be said that these were "false prophets," but how could that be known? There are stories in the Books of Kings which show how puzzling the distinction might be. Twice in Deuteronomy an attempt is made to give a solution. In xiii, 1-5, the test is to be the message itself which is brought. Even though the prophet offers a sign or wonder, that shall mean nothing. Does he teach to follow Jehovah? That is everything. Similarly in the New Testament (1 Corinthians xii, 3; 1 John iv, 2, 3) the test for those "speaking in the spirit" is whether they acknowledge Jesus as Lord and as come in the flesh. But in Deuteronomy xviii, 15-22, the test in the case apparently of the otherwise accredited prophet is to be the fulfilment of his prophecy. All this evidently is later and theoretical consideration of what must have been for the Kings of Judah and Israel a practical and immediate problem.

But how, apart from such theorizing, did the Hebrews think of a prophet; how did he look to them when he was actually about his business of prophesying? There have been preserved for us some very curious stories from the earliest times, connected with Moses. These represent Jehovah in the most physical and anthropomorphic fashion, but they undoubtedly give us the ideas of the masses of the people as to the relationship between Jehovah and His prophets. One of the most curious is the story of the family quarrel and the jealousy of Miriam and Aaron against Moses about the Ethiopian woman (Numbers xii). The upshot of it is a declaration by Jehovah Himself, that while He communicates with prophets in general by dreams and in ways that call for interpretation and guessing of obscure sayings, to Moses He speaks mouth to mouth and Moses looks at His very shape. Again, in Exodus iv, 10-16 and vii, 1, 2, Moses pleads to Jehovah his lack of eloquence and Jehovah permits him to use his brother Aaron as a spokesman to the people and to Pharaoh. The relationship, it is explicitly said, will be that of God and a prophet; a prophet is a spokesman—literally a mouth—for God. This at once suggests to us the perfectly assured psychical phenomenon which is called "automatic speech." This phenomenon is not at all as common as "automatic writing," which is the commonest of all the automatisms, but it occurs often enough to have been carefully observed. We have, then, to think of a Hebrew prophet, on some occasions at least, as standing before his audience and pouring forth words over which he has himself no control and which do not proceed from his own conscious thinking. For him and for them he is a mouthpiece used by Jehovah to convey His will to His people.

But this conception of the prophet, as a mechanical mouthpiece, would, of necessity, as the prophetic office gained in dignity and importance, develop into a more spiritual and conscious instrumentality. Balaam might pour forth a torrent of oracles under stress from the Unseen, but Amos, Hosea, and Isaiah would know what they were saying and why they were saying it. So with Amos (iii, 7; cf. ii, 11, 12) we find explicitly expressed an entirely different conception of the prophetic office. In this conception, while the prophet may still be a mouthpiece, he is above all the interpreter to the people of the actions of Jehovah. The prophets are in the secret counsel of Jehovah and he tells them why he is doing this and that. For everything that happens is the immediate doing of Jehovah and He has His own reasons for everything that He does. This leads with Amos to a clear magnifying of his office. He, as an individual, is in a peculiarly personal contact with Jehovah; he can intercede with Jehovah; his intercession is heard; and he tells the people so. He is an extreme case of the mystic—the man in immediate contact with God—who is also a politician. In consequence, it is quite evident and intelligible that he and his kind were a nuisance to all established rule and government, priestly and regal. He went behind them to the presence and rule of Jehovah Himself. So far as changed conditions would permit he took up again the position and attitude of Moses who had spoken with Jehovah face to face. But no one could possibly call Amos "very meek, above all men" (Numbers xii, 3). This will at once suggest to us the political preacher of our own days, but the resemblance is still closer to darwish preachers, moralists, politicians, and rebels of Islam. They, too, claimed, and claim, immediate divine insight and guidance which put them above all obedience to human government. If they are successful they found new States, governments and dynasties; if they are unsuccessful the government they have opposed deals shortly with them. Amos apparently —for we know next to nothing about him—was content to say his say and depart. As a producer of literature he was an inspirational preacher, who addressed the people in open-air orations wherever he could get an audience. His fundamental ideas had come to him in subconscious meditation; his words came to him in poetic outburst face to face with his hearers. Several times, under emotional stress, his self-control breaks and his words melt away in doxologies of the glory of Jehovah. All the time he must have been trembling on the brink of such emotional collapse. So, throughout his utterances, we feel that he is holding himself in difficult but strict restraint, dominated by the conceptions he had reached and urged on by the infection of the hearers before him. As an inspirational preacher he wrote nothing himself, but fragments from his speeches were remembered and recorded by his disciples and collected into what we call his book. But his place in the history of prophecy is his explicit claim to be the interpreter of God's actions, rather than the transmitter of God's words.

Another significant description of the prophet, belonging to much the same time, is in Hosea ix, 7, when the judgment of the masses on prophets in general is expressed, "the prophet is a fool (the obstinate, pig-headed fool); the man of the spirit is insane." To the word translated here "insane" (*meshugga‘*) it will be necessary to return hereafter more than once. It means exactly "insane" in our modern sense and is still used in that meaning in Yiddish and among Jews generally. It goes with our significant little tap on the forehead. "Man of the spirit" must not be understood, as in the King James Version, as "spiritual man." It means a man who is in contact with spirits—a spiritist. The passage shows that for the masses of the people the prophet was either a pig-headed fool or mentally lacking.

But the passage brings us also to the question, essential for this whole subject: What did the Hebrews understand by "spirit" and "spirits"? It would be possible to write the history of all philosophy round the word "spirit," but that is not necessary here. The Hebrews were not metaphysically minded and spirits for them were simply the inhabitants of that other, unseen, world, beyond a veil, where Jehovah peculiarly was. These were, as has been said above, good and bad, truthful and lying, just like men; but they were all in the presence of Jehovah and controlled by him. Some illustrations from stories in the Old Testament will make this clear. That Jehovah in these stories is a very human King shows how genuine and untouched they are. Let 1 Kings xxii, 5-28 be read in the King James Version; it is in general translated there excellently. Nothing could be more vivid than the picture of the four hundred prophets "prophesying" with one accord in the presence of the two Kings sitting enthroned in their robes before the gate of Samaria. And there is the touch of humorous color in the picture of Zedekiah who held to his brow a piece of iron like horns and butted his fellows with it to show how Jehovah would butt the Syrians. With such clowning the baser sort of the prophets—and there must have been many kinds among four hundred—held their audiences. In exactly the same way modern darwishes mingle clowning and testimony. But Micaiah, when he appears, is of a different kind from Zedekiah and Jehoshaphat sees plainly that he is putting him off. From a passage which will be quoted shortly it is clear that when a prophet was really acting as the mouthpiece of Jehovah there were on him certain evident signs—hypnotic signs we would probably phrase it—that he was under spirit control. So there are traditions in Islam which tell that the Companions of Mohammed could always distinguish, from his appearance, when he was speaking as a prophet and when he was only preaching.

Then Micaiah (verses 19-23) gives one of the great descriptions of Jehovah enthroned in His court, a heavenly counterpart of the earthly scene in which he himself had part: "Therefore hear thou the word of Jehovah. I saw Jehovah sitting upon His throne and all the host of the heavens standing beside Him on His right and on His left. And Jehovah said, 'Who will befool Ahab so that he may go up and fall in Ramoth-gilead?' One said thus and another was saying thus. But there came out a certain spirit and stood before Jehovah and said, 'I will befool him,' and Jehovah said unto him, 'Wherewith?' And he said, 'I will go out and become a lying spirit in the mouth of all his prophets.' And He [Jehovah] said, 'Thou wilt befool and also prevail; go out and do thus.' And, now, behold; Jehovah hath put a lying spirit in the mouth of all these thy prophets; but Jehovah hath spoken against thee a calamity." With this description of a scene in the court of Jehovah should be compared Isaiah vi and Job i, ii; this scene and that in Job are distinctly popular and humorous and belong to folklore. That in Isaiah is touched with a higher literary finish and loftier spirit. Even in the English version it opens as with a solemn roll of drums: "In the year when King Uzziah died. . . ." Then it goes on with the picture of the Lord, high and lifted up, and the skirts of His robe filling the temple. So Isaiah had seen King Uzziah solemnly enthroned with his court around him and so Jehoshaphat and Ahab had sat on their thrones in their royal robes and looked out over the mob of four hundred frantic prophets "prophesying." But Isaiah's scene is in the Temple with the altar and its live coals and culminates in a solemn purification and dedication. Yet the scenes all spring from similar memories of a royal court.

Another significant passage is in 1 Kings xx, where the whole story from verse 31 should be read. The important passage for our purpose is in verses 35-37. "But a certain man of the prophetic guild said to his fellow in the word [or affair, business] of Jehovah, 'Smite me, pray' and the man refused to smite him. Then he said to him, 'Because thou hast not listened to the voice of Jehovah, behold, while you are going your way from with me, a lion will smite thee.' And he went his way from beside him and a lion found him and smote him. But he [the first prophet] found another man and said, 'Smite me, pray,' and the man smote him with a blow that wounded him." It is evident that the comrade called upon to smite should have recognized by the signs on the speaker that he was speaking "in the word," or "business" (Hebrew will stand either rendering) of Jehovah. Another point is that this story is exactly like stories told of Muslim darwishes, even to the intervention of the lion. Lions in these stories are frequent and are called, in consequence, "the dogs of Allah."

Another group of significant stories is that connected with the possession of Saul by an evil spirit and the driving of it away through the harp playing of David. The two passages 1 Samuel xvi, 14-end, and xviii, 5-xix, 10, should be read carefully. "But the spirit of Jehovah had turned aside from Saul and an evil spirit from Jehovah was wont to fall upon him and terrify him. And the servants of Saul said unto him, 'See, now, a divine evil spirit [literally, an evil spirit of Elohim] is falling upon thee and terrifying thee. Let our Lord command, pray, thy servants who are before thee, they should seek a man well acquainted with playing on the harp. And it will happen when the divine evil spirit is come upon thee that he will harp with his hand and then thou wilt be well.'" The story goes on with the introduction of David and the good effect of his playing upon Saul. "And it used to happen, when the divine spirit came unto Saul, that David would take the harp and harp with his hand and Saul would be refreshed and well, and the evil spirit would turn aside from being upon him."

The perfect simplicity and directness of the story are plain; the spirits, good and bad, come from the same world and belong to

Jehovah. No one has any doubt as to what Saul's ailment was and as to the proper method of treatment. It is a breaking in upon Saul from that Unseen World—the abode of all manner of spirits—and music can deal with it. This may have been known from experience or there may be some subtle connection which we are not given. That music—instrumental and vocal—played its part in contacts with the Unseen World we know otherwise; it does so to this day in the religious services of the Muslim darwishes. In strictness this belongs to connection C of prophecy, that with ecstatic religious emotion. That is made clear by xxviii, 10: "And it happened on the morrow that a divine evil spirit leaped upon Saul and he prophesied in the midst of the house." The phrase here describing the assault of the evil spirit upon Saul is exactly that used for the first coming of the spirit of God upon him when he was anointed (1 Samuel x, 6, 10). And as a result of this psychic invasion he prophesies, running about, apparently, through the house. What does "prophesy" here mean? It can only mean showing the external signs in physical action and speech that go with invasion and possession by a spirit. For us it would mean the senseless actions and talk of a lunatic. It is, then, to be noticed that for such actions and talk could be used the word "prophesy." Probably in all simple, automatic prophesying there was a dash of the same kind.

A still stranger story is told in Numbers xi, a story so strange that it found its way into Hebrew folklore and produced a book by itself in later Hebrew literature, the Book of Eldad and Medad. The story, which should be read in full, tells how a body of seventy elders were set aside to bear the burden of the people along with Moses. That is, seventy were chosen and their names were written down but only sixty-eight went out to the Tent of Assembly to be ordained by Jehovah for this task; two of them, Eldad and Medad, by some accident, remaining within the camp. In verse 25 the story goes on: "And Jehovah came down in the Cloud and spoke unto him [Moses] and put aside some of the spirit which was upon him and placed it upon the seventy elders; and it happened, when the spirit rested upon them, that they prophesied and ceased not. But two men were left in the camp, Eldad and Medad by name, and the spirit rested upon them— they had been amongst those written, but they had not gone out to the Tent—and they prophesied in the camp." Then there follows the attempt to silence those two who were prophesying thus irregularly and the great saying of Moses, for which it may be our story was preserved, "Would that all the people of Jehovah were prophets; that Jehovah would put his spirit upon them!"

The "spirit" here is not a personality which proceeded from its own world and "leaped" on its recipient as in the case of Saul, but a divisible thing which can be taken from Moses and distributed among seventy others. Its effects are evidently religious ecstasy of a violent, observable kind; they are the outward and visible sign of the inward and spiritual equipment to be the assistants of Moses. It will be noticed also that it was the writing down of the names which governed and produced this, not the physical presence at the Tent. Of Eldad and Medad the Old Testament tells us nothing more.

It has been said above that the inhabitants of the Unseen World were for the Hebrews good and bad, like men, but all under the absolute rule of Jehovah. The traces which remain of mythological adversaries of Jehovah, whom He has crushed, are only poetical survivals, much as English poets of the seventeenth and eighteenth centuries still talked about Jove. But what was the attitude of the Hebrews as to such spirits as we call devils? The answer is very simple. They knew no devils. It was unthinkable to them that there could be any spirit not under the rule of Jehovah. The name Satan occurs a certain number of times in our English version, but only once in the Hebrew is this word possibly used as a proper name. Even there (1 Chronicles xxi, 1) it can be quite well translated "an adversary" as everywhere else. In the New Testament, of course, Satan is clearly a proper name and so occurs thirty-six times, but the doctrine of spirits in the New Testament is entirely different from that in the Old. *Satan*, then, in Hebrew is a common noun meaning an "adversary" of any kind, man or spirit. The especial spirit-adversary who appears in Job i, ii and in Zechariah iii, 1, as an officiating figure in the Court of Heaven, may be described as that Spirit of Jehovah whose business it was to bring accusations, a prosecuting attorney. Naturally, he was not personally liked and so he was depicted as entering with too great zeal, even enjoyment, into the duties of his office and as making trouble

ORIGIN AND METHODS OF THE HEBREW PROPHETS

in that way between Jehovah and men. This is plain in both Job and Zechariah. The people also found it possible in time to pass on to him and impute to his initiative dubious actions of Jehovah which a simpler and more naïve generation accepted without cavil. Thus the sin of the numbering of the people by David, which in 2 Samuel iv, 1, is ascribed to the motion of Jehovah Himself, is in 1 Chronicles xxi, 1, ascribed to the incitement of Satan, or an unnamed spirit-adversary. This is all the progress that the Hebrews of themselves made toward a doctrine of an evil personality in the world, opposing and endeavoring to thwart the will of Jehovah.

Reference has already been made to the very curious fact that for the masses of the Hebrews a prophet in the exercising of his function suggested a madman. The associations of this are much more complicated and difficult than would appear at first. The passage in Hosea ix, 7, has already been cited and the word used there for an insane man given, *meshugga'*. There is another significant passage in 2 Kings ix. In it, the story is that Elisha gives a box of ointment to a young prophet and sends him to Ramoth-gilead to anoint Jehu as King. He is to take Jehu apart into an inner chamber, anoint him King, then open the door and flee for his life. The picture is quite vivid of this young prophet coming on his dangerous errand and finding Jehu sitting with the captains of the host. When he has done his task and fled and Jehu goes out again to his companions they want to know: "Is it all right? Why came this *meshugga'* to thee?" He tries to gain time and pass the affair off, "You know quite well that kind of man and what his talk would be." To which they, "Lies! tell us!" Then he tells them exactly and they publicly proclaim him King. The story shows what Jehu and his like thought of prophets in general, but also that a messenger from Elisha was significant and meant business. Again, in Jeremiah xxix, 26, this same word *meshugga'* is given to every man who poses as a prophet. Further, the word primarily meant for the Hebrews what we would call "a jabbering lunatic," and that of the most disgusting, offensive kind, for it is used of David when he played madness at the court of Achish, King of Gath (1 Samuel xxi, 13-15). But has the word any other associations? That is where the puzzle comes in. The root in Hebrew is used not only of madness and mad behavior but, also, as we have seen, this particular word from it is used for the apparently mad behavior of prophets. Exactly the same root in Arabic is never used of madness, but it is regularly used of the speech of prophets. Primarily it means in Arabic the cooing of pigeons and the prolonged groaning of a she-camel. But metaphorically it was the name of the kind of language used fixedly by diviners in giving communications from the spirit world. In this kind of language—short, rhythmical but not metrical, clauses, all rhyming together—the whole Koran is composed. What is the same expression as to root meant in Hebrew the speech of a lunatic and in Arabic the speech of a diviner. That the Arabic usage is the more fundamental and original seems proved by the fact that it is traced back to natural phenomena like the cooing of pigeons and the groaning of she-camels. The Hebrew usages never get behind madness and madmen. But how did the transfer take place and why the change? We know the answer as little as we know why the Arabic word for "diviner" is exactly the Hebrew word for "priest." But the evidence seems to be that the word *meshugga'* was first applied to the cooing, groaning, murmuring language of a diviner among the Arabs, then transferred in that sense to the Hebrews and among them came to describe an insane man because of the diviners' apparently senseless behavior and talk. All this is, of course, conjecture, but it is not conjecture that a prophet to the masses of the Hebrews suggested an insane man.

The description above of the external appearance of prophets in their prophesyings and of the impression which they so made on the masses of the people leads naturally to the consideration of connection C—prophecy as ecstatic religious emotion. Cases have occurred above and to these the following should be added. There are, first, the two cases of "Saul among the prophets" (1 Samuel x, 5-12; xix, 18-24). In the first of these Saul, after he has been anointed by Samuel, meets a company of prophets coming down from a high place with harps and pipe and tom-tom before them and they are "prophesying" as they go. And the spirit of Jehovah leapt upon him and he "prophesied" with them and was turned into another man. This means, apparently, that he was swept away by religious emotion and so completely transformed that no one would

ORIGIN AND METHODS OF THE HEBREW PROPHETS

have recognized him as the same. In the second passage David has escaped and has taken refuge with Samuel. "And Saul sent messengers to take David. And they saw the company of the prophets prophesying and Samuel standing, stationed over them, and a divine spirit came upon the messengers of Saul and they too prophesied." The same thing happens to a second and third band of messengers sent by Saul and at last he goes himself. "And he went on his way thither to Naioth in Ramah, and a divine spirit came upon him too; so he went on his way, going and prophesying, until he entered Naioth in Ramah. And he too stripped off his clothes and he too prophesied before Samuel and fell down naked, all that day and all the night."

The scene here of the prophets prophesying and Samuel standing over them, directing them, is exactly the same as at a zikr of darwishes seen by the present writer in Egypt. And there can be no question as to the hypnotic influence and drawing power of such a scene and performance. To that, too, the present writer can testify. Our religious camp meetings have seen much of the same kind. But as to darwish zikrs a sharp distinction must be made. There are those which are genuine fosterings and expressions of religious emotion and their nearest equivalents are our prayer meetings. These may be dull and monotonous but they are real and meet a need. But there are also zikrs which are purely ceremonial and perfunctory and as remote from genuine and automatic religious emotion as the performances of a paid choir. The present writer has seen both kinds and the point of the reference to the professional choir will appear shortly.

There may be a question whether David's dancing before the Ark in 2 Samuel vi, to which reference has already been made, comes under this rubric, for the word "prophesy" is not used in describing it. Yet that it was an expression of orgiastic religious emotion there can be no question, and the prophetic compiler of the Books of Samuel regards it with evident approval. Yet, from the comment of Michal it is evident that more conventional people thought differently. David had emphatically placed himself on the side of the emotional religious expression, which characterized the prophets in the wide sense.

Reference has already been made to Elijah's sacrifice at Mount Carmel and to the ritual dancing, with limping step, of the priests of the Baal round their altar there (1 Kings xviii). This performance is specifically called "prophesying" (verse 29). And, afterwards, when Elijah ran before the chariot of Ahab to the entrance to Jezreel he did it because "the hand of Jehovah" had come upon him (verse 46).

We come now to the significant way in which this spontaneous and individual expression of religious emotion ran out in professionalism. Similarly, we have all, ourselves, seen congregational praise turning into a placid listening by the congregation to the performance of a paid choir. In Cairo the present writer, himself, observed at a professional and public darwish performance, one of the actors pausing in his supposed crisis of religious enthusiasm to look at his watch.—How much longer had he to keep this up?— In the Old Testament the chronicler has given us very elaborate descriptions of the final and detailed organization of the Temple worship. This is given, with whatever historicity, as of the times of David and of Hezekiah. We may take the details for what they are worth; they are probably an attempt to find sanction in the past for later organizations. But, throughout, both songs and religious instruments are connected with David, and in 1 Chronicles xxv, 1, 2, 3, certain sons of Asaph and Jeduthun are described as "prophesying" with harps and other instruments to give thanks and praise to Jehovah.

Thus the tumultuous and orgiastic religious services over which we have seen Samuel presiding developed eventually into the formal performances of the Temple choirs. But the original type must also have persisted, just as it still does in Islam. Illuminating parallels, therefore, for this whole subject can be sought in two very different directions. The references in the New Testament to tongues, prophets, gifts of different kinds show that there was a religious background then of exactly the same nature as with the older Hebrews. The phenomena are the same if the historical links of connection have vanished. And, still later, these same phenomena reappear in all their details in the world of Islam. For that the present writer can only refer to his *Aspects of Islam* throughout; also to his *Religious Attitude and Life in Islam*, especially Chapter I, and to his various articles bearing on the subject in the Leyden *Encyclopaedia of Islam*. The curious political activities of the prophetic guilds and of individual prophets, which are unmistakable in Samuel and Kings, suggest another parallel. It is with the Greek oracles. From stories told by Herodotus we are led to gather that at the shrines of the oracles there were organizations with definite political plans. Thus, as was natural in the expanding Greek world with overseas ambitions, the Oracle of Apollo at Delphi guided Greek colonization. The Hebrew prophetic organizations seem rather to have been concerned with defending the religious unity of their people under the headship of Jehovah against any scattering of that kind. But the source of their authority and the methods by which they worked were strikingly like those of the Greek oracles. This holds even to the oracles being couched in verse of a kind. That Pindar regarded himself as, more or less, an heir of these organizations has already been said.

CHAPTER VIII

THE BEGINNING AND END OF PROPHECY

IN THE preceding long chapter an attempt has been made to deal with the side of the prophetic activity which is too often obscured; that is, to deal with the soil from which Hebrew prophetism, as it is commonly regarded, sprang; to see in detail its background of ideas and its machinery; in a word, its more external institutes. That soil, background of ideas, and machinery are found in a certain degree and sense everywhere. In the Old Testament, however, they are found with something and producing something which is not found everywhere. The Hebrews, in the case of some outstanding minds, combined those common human phenomena with a certain great moral earnestness and a certain definite object. The seeing of their great seers was not limited to trivialities, but widened into the great purposes of God. It is there that the difference in the case of the Hebrews lies. The activity of their seers was part of the great revelation of His personality by Jehovah, that mysterious self-revelation which the Hebrews accepted so simply. And it had its wide consequences. "With you only," said Jehovah to Israel through Amos (Amos iii, 2), "have I been on intimate personal terms, out of all the families of the earth; therefore upon you will I visit all your iniquities." Instead of a vague and non-moral Unseen World, the seer of the Hebrews was in contact with the personality of Jehovah.

But it is to be held clearly that, in all this, the Hebrew prophet was still the seer of the Unseen. That was the rock from which he was hewn; the soil from which he sprang. And he himself never forgot it or obscured it. Our rationalizing interpreters may portray the Hebrew prophets as only statesmen of insight and moral energy; but their insight as statesmen is open to grave doubt, and their moral energy often wavered. Yet they never forgot that they were seers of the Unseen, and when prophecy came to its long decline and fall it ended in that ghastly and mechanical travesty of foreseeing—apocalyptic. Foreseeing, therefore, true or false, was the very essence of prophecy from beginning to end. The Hebrew prophets, whether as mouthpieces of Jehovah or as interpreters and justifiers of his ways to men, were foretellers.

In this connection also it is well, and again as a corrective to widespread views as to the prophets and to common applications of their attitudes to modern times, to remember that by the very logic of their situation the prophets were what we now call "defeatists." This held in politics and, also, one may even say, in morals. Their peculiar mission was to convict the people and their Kings of sin. The sin might be towards Jehovah or on the part of men to their neighbors. But in either case they had to denounce punishment, the anger of Jehovah for His broken law. When they spoke, then, in a political atmosphere, as so often, that meant announcing defeat. Jehovah, the God of all the earth, would use other peoples to punish His own people. In consequence, the prophets overwhelmingly prophesied ill-fortune. That they were thus a great political nuisance to the governments of the time, who were responsible for the continued existence and prosperity of the people, is very intelligible. The panic-monger and woe-predictor can always find good moral reasons for his position. But there come crises in a people's history when such a position is a crime against the people itself. The prophets were so full of a consciousness of their divine mission that they seldom saw this. Occasionally there was a "good" King from the prophetic point of view whose hands were upheld in his goodness; and, towards the end especially, the people were so utterly broken and afflicted that nothing but the preaching of hope and comfort was possible. The prophet might even labor with Jehovah out of compassion for a crushed and dwindling people. But in politics the defeatist attitude was logical and dominant. The moral defeatism of the prophets is more difficult and obscure. It is quite plain that they did not succeed and that, later, the preaching of the Law did. And there hangs over their moral teachings a pathetic, melancholy and hopeless tone. It is very different from the positive hopefulness and assurance of the teachings of our Lord and of the early Christian Church. That Church knew in whom they had trusted and felt secure; they looked beyond the nations of the earth to spiritual realities. The prophets knew and trusted Jehovah but they were completely entangled, even in their moral attitudes, in the national destinies, and these were hopeless. We are left with a conjecture of the persistence, in an underground fashion, through all the period of dominance of the Law, of the prophetic organizations with their religious attitudes, equipment and methods of worship, until they burst out into a renewed and more completely spiritual life in the life and usages of the Christian Church.

But this is an issue somewhat apart, and we return to the prophets as foretellers. Is there any such thing as true foreseeing and foretelling? A generation ago, or less, there could have been only one answer to that question. Only reactionary theologians and such people as took their Bibles quite literally believed in the possibility of true foretelling. Now the case is very different, even for philosophy and physical science. This may be put from two points of view. First, our conceptions of the nature of time and of its place in the universe are changing. Philosophy always knew that "time" was practically indefinable. So we did not really get beyond the celebrated answer of Augustine when he was asked what "time" was: "I know when you don't ask me." And now the fixity of our three-dimensional universe with a non-existent past and an unknowable future has vanished, although we do not yet see where all this uncertainty is going to come out. Physicists have turned metaphysicians and, to the old-fashioned metaphysicians who have been through the exact training of the schools, seem often to be talking very wildly. The three-foot rule no longer exists; it may be any length, according as it is turned. Mathematicians used to admit that some solutions of their equations were irrational if others were rational; now all the solutions are being tried out on our physical universe. The square root of -1 used to be a mathematical diversion; now it seems to be turning into the basis for existence. What will be the upshot of this no one knows, but there is one certain negative result. Time has no longer, for our thinking, that fixed nature which forbade us to accept the possibility of any foreseeing and foretelling.

But, second, there has gradually accumulated a mass of evidence that foreseeing and foretelling actually take place. In the old days this evidence would have been laughed out of court. Such things don't happen, said our fathers, and that was an end of it. But this short way with abnormal facts is no longer possible. All facts, however unusual, have to be faced and they are being faced. The result is that for open-minded people, who are not ridden by *a priori* ideas and theories, it is becoming assured that certain human beings, under certain conditions, in certain ways, and from time to time, have flashes of pre-cognition. These come mostly through the different "automatisms" and most of all, apparently, through crystal gazing. They are of the most multifarious character, come unexpectedly, mixed with non-veridical matter; a door opens and shuts, and that is all. There seems no purpose to them; no mind behind them. That is, of course, because we do not yet know enough about them. They are irrational in a sense, but there seems no escaping it that they precede their events in our world of space and time. This should be carefully distinguished from the whole range of beliefs which are called Spiritualism. Spiritualism is one of the theories in explanation of these and other similar abnormal facts. But the fact of pre-cognition has been widely accepted among those who reject all connection with Spiritualism and disavow its creeds. Among these are even some frank materialists. Thus the largest collection of evidence on the subject is given by Professor Charles Richet, the eminent French physiologist, in his *Traité de Métapsychique,* Chapter VII. The title of the English translation is *Thirty Years of Psychical Research.* With it should be taken the long review by Sir Oliver Lodge, a confessed spiritualist, in the *Proceedings of the Society for Psychical Research,* Vol. XXXIV, pp. 70-106. Many years ago a similar collection of evidence was brought together by Andrew Lang in his *Making of Religion,* Chapters IV and V, and the appendices to these.

It may be taken, then, that the old-fashioned position as to an *a priori* impossibility of prevision must now be abandoned. This means that we can, not irrationally, conceive of the Hebrew prophets as having had *in flashes* pre-cognition of events still to come. This would be in flashes only, and probably, on modern analogies, in pictures. We may see such a flash and such a picture in Micaiah's vision (1 Kings xxii, 17), "I saw all Israel scattered upon the mountains like flocks which have no shepherd; and Jehovah said, 'These have no lord; let them return each man to his home in peace.' "

It does not lie in the design of this book to deal in detail with the prophets; there are many books devoted specifically to that purpose. The present object is rather to bring out some aspects of the prophets and certain sides of their relation to the literary genius of the Hebrews which are too often obscured. Some of these have now been given; one still remains. Have we any light as to how the utterances of the prophets, verbal always at first by their very nature, came to be written down and to form part of the literature of the Hebrews? That leads to a still wider question. The literature of the Hebrews, as we have it in the Old Testament, is plainly a collection of fragments, gathered up and saved. That the loss has been enormous is also plain; we have seen already how scanty are the surviving fragments of the songs of David, although probably, in that case, there was purpose as well as accident in their destruction. How, then, for the saved remnants, did the gathering up and saving take place?

In the case of what we call the Book of Amos it is possible to show one of the ways in which this writing down and gathering up came about, and thus to suggest possibilities, at least, for other cases. The title of the book runs truly "the words of Amos," for the book is exactly and only his words. We have no life or acts of Amos and what little we know about him must be gathered from his words. Of earlier prophets we have lives and doings and only incidental words. The contrast is thus very great between the evidence for Amos and the evidence for his nearest predecessor Elisha. Elisha died about 798 B.C. and the *floruit* of Amos was rather more than a generation later, about 760-740. Why, then, the difference in the ways in which the activities of the two men have reached us? This knot used to be cut by saying that a non-writing age had passed into a writing age. We know now that that explanation is impossible. For centuries the Hebrews had been living in a writing age. There is monumental evidence that an alphabetic system of writing was widely spread from northern Syria to the Sinai peninsula, taking in Moab on its way, from the thirteenth century at least. Elisha, a statesman and courtier, was certainly in daily contact with writing and yet we have no "words" from him, only tales about his life and doings. From Amos, the herdsman, a generation later, we have only "words" and no tales. It is plain that there must be some other explanation. Is the explanation again in the accidents of the destruction and preservation of the Hebrew literature, rather than in its being recorded or not? Have such folklore tales as those about Elijah and Elisha been saved for us by being incorporated, as history, in our Books of Kings, just as the legend of Job was saved, in part, by being incorporated in our Book of Job? Whatever collections of the "words" of Elijah or Elisha may have existed might then have perished as of lesser popular interest. Or a time may have come when a prophet was more a preacher and less a doer. We cannot tell; all these are as guesses only, however possible.

But it is possible to see very clearly how the words of Amos came to be recorded and turned into a book. Throughout those words Amos is always a speaker. We can always see him, out in the open air, standing before a crowd and talking to them; only as we hold that picture of him can we really follow and grasp his utterances. Again, these are plainly fragmentary. The fragments are of very varying lengths and some are of a verse or two only. His first discourse alone (i, 2-ii, 13) seems to be a complete and ordered sermon with a long introduction leading up to a surprising and devastating application. Or, rather, it is not entirely complete, for the application was so devastating that it was probably cut short by a shower of stones from the audience. Verses 14-16— which were probably also words of Amos on some other occasion —have been pressed into service as a conclusion. How were these fragments recorded and saved? The problem is the same as that of the recording and saving of the discourses of our Lord. They, too, are fragmentary and disconnected, but we know that they must have been saved either in the memories or in the notes of our Lord's disciples. This situation is universal in the East. The wandering teacher is always attended by one or more pupils who are his recorders and who preserve his weightier utterances. But how are these made into a book? We know how great a puzzle the arrangement of the discourses of Christ in Luke has proved. For Amos's book the analogy of the structure of the Koran is very close. When Mohammed died he left a jumble of separately recorded "revelations," long and short. The editors of the Koran had to make a book of them. By putting bits together which seemed, more or less, to belong to each other in subject, style or rhyme they built up a certain number of chapters of very different lengths. These, then, they arranged in order of length, beginning with the longest and diminishing to the last of a few verses only. The result was a purely mechanical arrangement in which the oldest parts come at the end. It is demonstrable that our Book of Amos, however short in length as compared with the Koran, has been put together out of fragments of varying lengths in the same mechanical fashion. That demonstration, however, would not be in place here. Oriental literature, when it is not inspirational, is very apt to be mechanical. And this method of recording, saving, and compiling probably applies to much more of the Old Testament than the Book of Amos. The fact of the compilation of our Old Testament out of separate and originally distinct fragments has now come to be widely recognized. Sometimes these fragments emanated from one speaker or writer. Thus in our Book of Amos there is very little that does not bear the distinct mark of Amos's personality. But our Book of Isaiah, to take an extremely different case, is evidently of the most heterogeneous origin. Fragments of many authors, widely separate in date, place and ideas, have been saved for us by being incorporated in a collection guarded by the name of the great pre-Exilic prophet and statesman. And this does not apply only to what used to be called the Deutero-Isaiah, for Isaiah ii, 2-4, is exactly the same as Micah iv, 1-3. And of the Book of Micah it may be said that it is composed of the most multifarious fragments. This is not the place to enter upon details, and so much has been said here, only to show a stage in the recording and preserving of prophetic utterances and to show, also, the consequent hindrances which meet us in forming conceptions of the literary workings of the Hebrew people.

It can hardly be doubted that the Isaiah of Jerusalem himself put into writing his sermons to the people. For they bear the marks of written sermons, whether written before delivery or after. That is, there is in them the peculiar combination of spoken address to an audience and of literary care in composition which is the essence of the sermon. There is also, certainly, a full persuasion that it is the will of Jehovah which is being proclaimed. Sometimes this is put as in the direct words of Jehovah; at other times it is from the prophet addressing his audience, but always as in the spirit of Jehovah. It must have been exceedingly difficult for the prophet, and for his audience, to distinguish between those two. So, even in the Koran, although it formally consists of the direct words of Allah addressed to Mohammed, there are some little passages which suggest that they are from sermons of Mohammed slipped in by chance among the words of inspiration.

When we reach Jeremiah the writing down becomes explicit. We have the story (Jeremiah xxxvi) how, by divine command, he dictated all his utterances, from his first mission in the days of Josiah, to Baruch his amanuensis. The written roll thus produced was sent and read to the people; it was read again in the presence of King Jehoiakim who destroyed it. But all its contents were redictated by Jeremiah to Baruch in another roll with many additions. The prophet, then, retained in his memory the words of his messages; he could dictate them and redictate them and it was impossible for any earthly power to destroy them. This impossibility seems to be the point of the story.

But it is plain that careful artistic writing gradually took the place of inspirational and emotional speech. The thoughtful theologian appeared who was also a conscious artist in language. There is a great gulf between Amos and the producer of the Cyrus prophecies in the Book of Isaiah. Some of these are so elaborate in their structure as to suggest the preciosity of a sonnet sequence. Foretelling, too, has become conscious, and the prophet appeals for a hearing to his previous successors. Amos had trusted to the inherent witness of the word of Jehovah to itself in his mouth. The end was in sight.

It came in two forms. One of them was the tract. No one can read, in the Hebrew, Amos and Joel together without realizing that while Amos necessitates an actual audience listening to his words, Joel is a man sitting quietly by himself and writing. He is producing a tract in the exact sense, a short didactic treatise with a moral which is illustrated by anecdotes. It is a good tract; its anecdotes are full of realistic truth and the moral is well driven home; but it is a tract.

The other form is apocalyptic. It is the *reductio ad absurdum* of foretelling and is represented for us in the Old Testament only in the latter part of the Book of Daniel. Jewish literature, attempting to keep up the national courage, produced crowds of similar apocalypses, until the Jewish people, in the disgust of repeated disappointment, disowned the whole kind. Most of them have perished in their original Hebrew or Aramaic form and have survived only in Christian translations, read in isolated Christian communities as a second class of apocrypha. One, the Apocalypse of Ezra, a document contemporary with Paul, shares with him his perverted exegesis of the Garden Story in Genesis.

The wheel thus came full circle, and prophecy returned to foretelling in a crude and mendacious form. But throughout its whole development the six elements were present to one degree or another: the foreteller; the mouthpiece of Jehovah; the interpreter of the actions of Jehovah; the conscious theologian and theorizer; the moral tractarian; the apocalyptic foreteller.

CHAPTER IX

THE BOOK OF GENESIS

THAT the Semites were, and are, a story-telling people is a commonplace. The *Arabian Nights,* whatever its ultimate origins, is a demonstration of that fact for the Arabic-speaking peoples and the Old Testament for the Hebrews. But all primitive peoples, at all times, have told stories; the records of folklore are full of such stories. Yet no one will doubt that both the Arabic and the Hebrew literatures are rich in stories which have a difference, a peculiar appeal, because they are of a peculiar humanity. Their stories go home to us all in a way quite different from the common, bare, folklore tale. They are like the fairy stories of Hans Andersen as contrasted with the folk-tales collected by the Brothers Grimm. Folk-tales tend to be mere outlines of events, and characterization in them is rare. But in Arabic and in Hebrew the figures in the stories are alive; we know them and have met them often. In that the Semitic subjectivity shows itself. The author tells his tale with a personal enjoyment and delights to suggest, and even to work out, the hidden motives in his characters. They not only do certain things but they do them in a way to show of what kind they themselves are. For the Hebrew—and the Semite in general—if he was no metaphysician, was an acute psychologist and, what is rare among psychologists, he could make characteristics plain through actions; he did not need to involve himself in explanations of the why and how of these actions. That is, his subjectivity expressed itself through acts and events, just as Hebrew song breaks through and out, from time to time, into scraps of dramatically objective personification. The Hebrew artist was subjective in prose as in verse, but in prose he kept his head cool, his emotion under, and worked out his ideas in the persons of other people. But the ideas are there; there are always ideas behind a Hebrew story.

When, then, we attempt a classification of these Hebrew stories the only possible method is to arrange them according to the uses made of them by the teller; that is, according to the types of ideas in which he, as an artist, is dealing. For, as has been said above, the teller of a Hebrew story is much more a conscious artist than is the spontaneous singer of himself, in a Hebrew song.

It is unnecessary here to enter upon the curious and involved distinction between Story and History. We are concerned at present only with the Story although we shall come in time to History as a subdivision developing from Story. So the Greek epics passed into Greek history; they were all the history the Greeks had before the age of Herodotus and Hecataeus.

We must begin, then, with the great reservoir of folklore tales as it lay in the memories of the Hebrew people. These stories came blown to them on all the winds of their own origins: out of the desert; from the Euphrates Valley; from northern Syria; from the Forest of Lebanon; from Egypt; from the Great Sea; but, above all, out of the desert. The desert has always been full of such tales: stories of tribal migration with broken and again reunited ties of kinship; stories of love and family strife; stories of great warriors, their deeds and their deaths; stories of long-deserted and forgotten cities; stories of journeyings in the desert solitudes and of contact, friendly and hostile, with beings of the spirit world—the primitive inhabitants of the wilds; stories of tribal feuds in all their age-long bitterness and abiding memories. Out of such stories, collected and written down, the later Arabs built up the history of Arabia. And from these the still later Arabs, down into Muslim times, drew plots and motifs for their more artistically developed and imagined tales.

So, too, it was with the Hebrews. They, too, had their accumulations of stories, preserved in the memories of the race, told round the campfires and beside the domestic hearths, by men among themselves and women among themselves, by fathers to sons and by mothers to children. So the memories were passed on and the later historians, philosophers, poets and prose artists drew on these for their materials. As a consequence of this later reworking, there is very little in the Old Testament that has been preserved for us, in an untouched form, as it came from the lips of the people; and we have no real assurance as to what that little is. Nor is it for our purposes of much importance. Our subject is the literature of the Hebrews rather than their legends and folklore; our interest is in the ultimate forms which these legends assumed when handled by literary artists. For example, it is possible, to a certain degree, to separate out in the Book of Judges stories which look like primitive legends and which are certainly primitive enough from our point of view. But it cannot escape us that the whole Book of Judges has been adjusted to a scheme which is really a philosophy of history. In the appearance, career, success and ending of each judge there is a certain fixed sequence. Jehovah starts His people on the path on which they should go; they fall away from it; Jehovah delivers them into the hands of their enemies as a punishment; they repent and cry to Jehovah for help; He raises up a deliverer and for a time, after their deliverance, they go as Jehovah would have them. Then the cycle begins anew and so it goes on. This scheme of philosophized history was evidently congenial to the Semitic mind, for it continued among the Muslims. There is a class of Arabic theologized histories—called generically the Stories of the Prophets—which is constructed exactly according to this scheme. It will be plain, then, how uncertain we must be as to what the original folktale legend of, for example, Samson or Gideon had been.

Again, we have, as we have seen, in the Books of Samuel the popular stories about David, a far more conspicuous and well known national figure than any in Judges. But can we from these at all clearly separate out David as he had lived in the memories of the people? We cannot but doubt it. The religious forces which suppressed the great mass of David's songs, which suppressed his activity as a prophet in his own right and which did their best to create out of him a sacrosanct and royal Messianic figure, have been too strong for us. The editors of the prophetic guilds gave their material largely untouched but they gave it to suit themselves and their purposes.

The stories of Elijah and Elisha in the Books of Kings stand by themselves. No one can read through those books in Hebrew without being conscious that these stories of prophets have been taken over from some source and incorporated solidly by the historian in his work. This result is not an impression derived from an analysis of details but is of a broad literary character. But have they been taken over unchanged or have they been adjusted to the context of the history? As to that we can have no assurance, for the style is much more literary and smooth than that of the stories of David in Samuel. It is a possible conjecture—perhaps too daring—that these stories come from an older literary collection of stories of the lives of the prophets. There is no evidence for this except the way in which they there occur in the Books of Kings and the fact that such a collection would be in agreement with Arabic analogies. The same thing suggests itself as to the origin of the story of Job as used by the poet in our Book of Job.

But let us turn to more evidently and completely sophisticated forms. Our Book of Genesis stands in the whole Old Testament by itself. It produces on us the effect of a single, great work of genius, complete and rounded and contrasting sharply with the chaotically jumbled stories of its professed continuation, Exodus. In the beginning of Exodus there are the materials of good stories, but they are far from being well told; they have not passed through the brain of a real story-teller. And Genesis stands thus apart not only in the literature of the Hebrews but in the entire literature of the world. It is safe to say that there is no other book which combines as it does a philosophical study of the fundamental institutes of human life, a psychological study of a family of marked characteristics, developing into a people equally marked, and a political and economic study of that people over against the rest of the world, personified in the great figure of an adventurer of their race; the whole told in clear, objective stories which can be the delight of children, yet with a depth of sheer thought behind them which has stirred and led the thinking of the world more deeply than have the speculations of Plato. Behind the book there are, of course, the documents—E, J, P, and the rest—of our documentary analysts; we are not concerned with these. Still further behind the book is a wealth of folklore tradition and story of the most multifarious origins; we are not concerned with it. But we are concerned with the phenomenon of the book as it stands there on the opening pages of our Old Testament, a single, unified, great literary phenomenon postulating a great literary creator. As to who he was we have absolutely no clue; as to when he lived we can only make guesses. But as to his greatness as artist and philosopher there can be no shadow of doubt; nor as to the depth of his influence on the thinking of the world from Ecclesiastes to our own day. He is the greatest Unknown of Hebrew literature, which has so many unknown or only partially revealed figures.

What can we really say, with assurance, of him? First, that in his philosophy the fundamental fact was the great fact of Life, Life as a reality, living, growing, developing. He does not begin, as do most philosophers, with Reason, or Thinking, but with living beings and the scheme to which they belong. Others may say, "I think, therefore I am," and take that as their unassailable point of departure. He felt the life that is in the whole structure of the world, and especially in man, and made that the basal and irreducible thing in existence. This has probably gone to obscuring the fact that he is a philosopher; yet a biologist may be a philosopher as well as any metaphysician. But had he reached this consciously? The mystery of the *élan vital* in existence lies behind the Book of Genesis, but did it exist, even as a mystery, in the mind of the creator of that book? There is no explicit sign in that book, but that mystery did explicitly exist in the kindred mind of Ecclesiastes. Second, that he took what we may, for convenience, call a proto-Genesis, containing roughly the material in our present Genesis, worked over it, as artist and philosopher, and made it into what we now read. Third, that this was probably done comparatively late in the course of Hebrew literature. We are so apt to think of Genesis as the first book of the Bible, that we have difficulty in realizing that the first clear trace of its existence is in the use made of it in the quite late Book of Ecclesiastes. The other, earlier, allusions, scattered in the Bible, are to the original legends and not to our book. These stories the Hebrews knew from the beginning, but the distinctive ideas of our book do not reappear until we read Ecclesiastes. That author had been deeply affected by these ideas and in his book reacts to them. To bring this out it will be necessary to go through the Book of Genesis in some detail and, also, as a whole. The book, therefore, has to be put for our treatment in some class or other and it seems most convenient to put it under

Story. On the surface it is plainly a book of stories and its author, though for very different reasons, is as definite a personality as David. Yet, just as the Book of Job, it consists not only of stories but of stories which are philosophical in basis, treatment and object, and, therefore, it could almost equally well be held over until we come to Philosophy. The stories, however, are the most outstanding and immediate characteristic. Every child knows them, even although the ideas which they were meant to convey have no existence for him. For his elders these stories have often meant history, but it has always been history with meaning in it; of that they have been sure. For us, looking at them from our present standpoint, they are philosophical stories in the telling of which the writer has tried to express the most fundamental things for him in life.

These were three. First, life itself; its foundations and institutes. Second, the People of Israel in its character; a psychoanalysis of Abraham and his family. Third, the People of Israel against the world; Joseph, the Hebrew adventurer, going out into the wide world making his fortune there. This last may, perhaps, suggest, if very broadly, the time of the writer. He is not thinking of Israel as a conquering nation; his are not the ideals of the kingdom of David and Solomon. He is not thinking of Israel, either, as a separate, hermit nation, keeping itself apart behind the fence of the Law and holding the world at arm's length. But he is thinking of Israel as a people of influence which must send its sons out into the world to hold their own in that world by sheer character. The old expositors were not so far wrong when they saw in Joseph a type of Christ. Because it is evident that, for this philosopher-artist, Joseph typified the mission of Israel, in its peaceful penetration of the heathen world, and as bearing the name and stamp of Jehovah. The time of the philosopher-artist must have been one when such a conception of the mission of Israel was possible—if only for him. But to fix that time is a more hazardous problem.

The first of these three divisions comes in Genesis i-xi; the second in Genesis xii-xxxvi; and the third in Genesis xxxvii-end. It will be noticed that these divisions have nothing whatever to do with the current division into documents. In so far as the documentary hypothesis is sound—and it seems to be so, broadly—the book had been put together from these documents before the time of this philosopher-artist and so lay before him. It is that book which he used as his basis. He may have made considerable insertions in it; he certainly made a large number of little insertions. And, throughout, he was limited in his handling by the fact that the stories in the old forms were all well known to the people. In consequence, there are elements in them which he was compelled to leave untouched however repugnant they may have been to his religious or philosophical feeling. One of these, for example, is the fear of man on the part of Jehovah, lest man should encroach still further (Genesis iii, 22).

In the first part, then, the first story and the first foundation laid for life is in i, 1-ii, 4a, down to the word "created." The second story begins with ii, 4b, "In the day. . . ." The first story is commonly called the First Creation Narrative as contrasted with the Second in chapter ii. Why are there two entirely different stories as to how God made the world? If the narrator is telling about the Creation as an historical event his method is evidently contradictory and absurd. But he is really taking two apparently already existing and certainly separate narratives of that event and retelling them; not as history, but because they enable him to convey, through them, some ideas which for him were of the first importance for the understanding of life. Incidentally, by thus giving to us two quite different stories of Creation he shows that neither of them for him was historical fact. They afforded him a very subtle way of insinuating ideas into the popular mind. And it has been a very successful way, for many generations of theologians and philosophers have fed upon those ideas. The first idea is as to the place of man in the world and the narrative begins: "In the beginning of God's forming the sky and the earth, while the earth was (*or* had become) waste and empty, and while darkness was upon the surface of the abyss, and while a (*or* the) divine spirit was brooding upon the surface of the waters, then God said, 'Let light come into existence,' and light came into existence." This seems to mean that there was a watery abyss, or chaos, with darkness on its face but that a divine spirit was brooding upon it, literally brooding as a bird on its eggs, and that the first act in forming our world was that God said, "Let light come into existence." This, as to light, was an absolute creation out of nothing, but the rest of the making of our world was a process of forming out of materials. There are three Hebrew words used here for the divine making of the world. One of them is this "causing to come into existence." It occurs here in this sense only of light. The second word, translated commonly "create" means primarily "cut, shape" and in the great majority of its occurrences it is used of God's creative "shaping" out of something. The third is the common word meaning "to make." The translation "While the earth had become" is possible and, in fact, more in accordance with classical Hebrew. It would imply that there had been a previous cosmos to which this chaos had succeeded. The word translated abyss is really a proper name, borrowed from Babylonian mythology, but it here evidently means chaos. The first words of the Fourth Gospel, "In the beginning," are an allusion to this narrative, and that Prologue of the Fourth Gospel continues the allusion by saying of the Divine Reason (Logos) that he was not only life but the light of men, shining in the darkness (verses 4, 5). This combination is an expansion of Proverbs viii on which the Prologue is otherwise constructed. Did the author of the Fourth Gospel connect the "Reason" of Proverbs with the Divine Spirit here? Another, and a very different allusion to this passage is in Wordsworth's *Ode on the Intimations of Immortality*:

The eternal deep, haunted forever by the eternal mind.

The words in Genesis are evidently of the kind that stir thoughts. That Light, for the Hebrews, was a separate entity, apart from the luminaries in the sky, is plain through the whole Old Testament.

The narrative goes on to describe, stage by stage, and evidently according to an accepted scientific scheme, the construction of our world. It culminates in the making of man, male and female, "in our image according to our likeness." The word "image" is quite concrete and means the external appearance; "likeness" is more abstract and covers the whole being. Within and without, man is to be "like" God. And to man is given dominion over everything previously formed; the world, in all its multiplicity of beings and parts, has been created as a habitat for man. Further, the world in all its parts is "good" in God's eyes; is under His blessing and approval.

All this shows a definite philosophical position. This narrative is much more thoughtful and scientific throughout than anything which follows. And it gives one of the two answers by the Hebrews to a question which, perhaps, they never explicitly put to themselves, Why did God create the world? Yet we must posit the question if we are really to reach clearness as to Hebrew thinking. The answer here approves of the physical universe and asserts that it exists in order that man may exist. The other Hebrew answer to this question was that the world, in all the multiplicity of its parts, and including man as one only of the parts, existed for the pleasure of God who looks at it like a child before an elaborate toy. This is expressed most clearly in Psalm civ and in the speeches of the Lord in Job. Further consideration of this will come under Nature and Philosophy. But the view here expressed only leads to another question, Why did God wish to create man? And to that question the Old Testament gives no direct answer, although there are suggestions in some of the more personally mystical psalms. But even in this narrative there is a curious hint. What is the full implication of man's being in God's image and according to His likeness? If it had been merely "image" it might have been possible to say that this is nothing but another anthropomorphism reversed. Man had thought of God as in man's image; therefore, when he thought of God forming man, it was in God's image man was formed. But the point is labored and emphasized with "according to His likeness." We cannot help feeling that there is here the same groping as in Plato, for whom the world was formed according to a divine pattern. Here it is not the world that is so formed but man and the pattern is not an idea in the divine thinking but the divine personality itself. The personality of Jehovah for the Hebrews was more than His thinking; they were quite ready to accept that Jehovah could make a mistake and regret it; thinking and ideas might err but personality was another matter. Personality for them was always a more fundamental thing than thought and thus they were primarily religious and not philosophical. But in this narrative the word throughout is not Jehovah but God (Elohim) for the relation which it considers is that between the whole human race and the Divine Being. How close was that relation felt to be? Is there in that "likeness" of the human race to God a suggestion of the essential attitude of the mystic that he can immediately and personally know God and be taught by Him? That there is no unlikeness as a barrier between them? That every man is his own prophet in virtue of his human nature? This, in the more daring flights of the mystic, reaches the position that if man has need of God and is restless until he rests in Him, God also has need of man; that therefore God in His timeless loneliness created man for His own companionship and comfort. Their likeness means that they are complementary and supplementary one to the other. To this, when it works itself out to the end, the craving of the mystic normally comes. It is the antithesis, for theology, of the conception of God as standing in no need of anything outside His own existence. Both conceptions worked themselves out fully in Islam and we are left with the question as to how far the Hebrews had moved, consciously or unconsciously, down those paths. Some passages in Job and Psalms, dealing with the personal relationship of men to God and with a continuation of that relationship after death will be dealt with hereafter; they are full, at the least, of far-reaching surmises as to that possibility and are all based on the feeling that the soul which has once known God can never be separated from Him. Man is "like" God in a way that is true of nothing else in the world.

It is significant that this first of all the stories in Genesis should be so well constructed and should cut so deeply into philosophy, theology, and the cosmology which we call natural science. The Hebrew literary artist always depended greatly on his first impression upon his reader and so worked out carefully the opening of his book. Thereafter he tended to become careless and often very careless. Then, at the end, when his book really reached an end, he redoubled his care again. The Book of Ecclesiastes, as we shall see, is a good example of that sequence of care, lack of care and, again, care. In the case of this Book of Genesis the care is evident, and suggests that this whole first narrative may be either new or a complete recasting of some more primitive story.

Between the two narratives of creation there comes a mysterious phrase having no apparent connection with either. Translated exactly it runs: "These are the begettings of the sky and the earth when they were formed." The word "generations" in our versions obscures the exact meaning, for the word refers precisely to physical begetting. Further the Old Testament shows in a few passages (Genesis ii, 4; Psalms xc, 2; Proverbs viii, 24, 25) that among the Hebrews, as among many primitive peoples, the conception of the production of the world as an act of begetting on the part of God had survived. Even among the Greeks the same conception continued to exist and Plato in the *Timaeus* (34 B; 37 C, D) called Zeus "the begetting father" of the cosmos. But neither of the present two narratives of creation shows any sign of this conception. In both God is simply a "former," a "maker." Is it too rash a conjecture to suggest that this phrase is all that is left of a creation narrative describing the process as a begetting? Was it cut away as unusable by the philosopher because of its crudeness and was the present first narrative, a statement of his own scientific and philosophical position, put in its place?

But the second story, which may be called for convenience the Garden Story, is an almost pure folk-tale. Yet it, too, through discreet insertions, has been made to bear a weight of meaning. The grotesque details in it belong to the folk-tale; the meanings and essential philosophy are from the artist; he had to take the story as people knew it and keep it as untouched as possible. It begins: "When Jehovah (that is, God) made earth and sky, while no plant of the field was yet come in the earth and no herb of the field was yet sprouting, because Jehovah (that is, God) had not caused rain to fall upon the earth and there was present no mankind to till the soil, only an *'ēdh* used to go up from the earth and used to water all the surface of the soil, then Jehovah (that is, God) shaped mankind of some dust taken from the soil and blew into his nostrils living wind; so mankind became a living person." Grammatically, the structure of this long sentence—time clause, circumstantial clauses, principal statement—is exactly that of the first sentence in the first story. But the vocabulary, the ideas, and the scene depicted are entirely different. Further, the time clause is impossible, for "earth and sky" were evidently in existence at the time of the circumstantial clauses. The text at the beginning of the sentence has evidently suffered, but the broad meaning is plain. Again, the narrative ran originally only in the name of Jehovah, but a later editor has thought it necessary to explain with every occurrence that Jehovah is the same as "God" in the first narrative. Further, we have no clue as to the meaning of the Hebrew word '$\bar{e}dh$; it occurs only once elsewhere (Job xxxvi, 27) and that passage does not help. Man as first created in this story is male only; the providing of a mate for him is an afterthought; in that is the essential point of the story. The story goes on to describe the planting of a garden in Eden—Eden is evidently a known place. This is a fairy garden with two special trees, a tree of life and a tree which gives the knowledge of good and evil, what we would call conscience. The garden also is the center of the world and from it the four great rivers of the world go out. This is a folk-tale bit of the story and no use is made of this by the philosopher. Plainly the garden in Eden would not be that garden without those rivers, known geographical rivers. In this garden man is set after he has been made and he is forbidden to touch the Tree of Conscience; he is told that he will assuredly die if he eats of it, which is not true as the story shows. Then man's need of a "help corresponding to him" is recognized and all the beasts are formed from the soil in the same way that man had been formed; they are brought to man and he gives them their names. But none of them did he recognize as a "help corresponding to him." (In a Babylonian mythological story man had intercourse with the animals before woman was made for him.) So man is cast into a deep sleep; a rib is taken from him and is built up into a woman. She is brought to him, as the animals had previously been brought, and he says, "This one, this time, is one of my bones and some of my flesh; this one shall be called woman because this one was taken from man." So the "help corresponding to him" has been found and the teller of the story adds, "Therefore does a man leave his father and his mother and stick to his wife and they become one flesh." The expression, "stick," is used of any kind of temporary or permanent sticking together, even of soldering.

The story is used to explain that fundamental fact and mystery of life, the attraction of sex. The explanation is essentially the same as that which Plato gives in the *Symposium* (189C *ff.*). In Plato's myth Zeus created man a four-armed, four-legged creature, both sexes in one. But this creature was too formidable, so he separated it into two sexes—there are grotesque details in Plato—and ever since they have tried to become rejoined each to the other half. Between the two stories there can be no question that the Genesis philosophical myth is the more beautiful and true.

Then comes the second part of the Garden Story and it begins with a characteristic Hebrew pun. "They were both naked, man and his wife, and they were not ashamed. But the Serpent was more 'naked' than all the wild things of the field which Jehovah (that is, God) had made." It is impossible to represent in English the play here upon the two meanings of the Hebrew word, "naked" and "crafty." The play is used by the story-teller to introduce with effect the personality of the Serpent. The Serpent was just a serpent but all serpents are wise and knowing. The word here used of the Serpent, may mean wisdom or craftiness, good or bad. The implication is that the Serpent knew too much and made malicious use of his knowledge. But he undoubtedly spoke the truth when he told the woman what really would be the effect of their eating the fruit of the tree of conscience. So they ate it and there happened what happened. It is characteristic for the Hebrew mind that the first working of the acquired conscience was no great moral unveiling, but that they recognized that their nakedness was unseemly. A keener feeling for propriety is one of the differences between the Hebrew and the Arab minds and also between the Hebrews and both the Greeks and the Latins. There are straight up-and-down and coarse expressions in the Old Testament, but far less than in any similar body of primitive literature. So this first recognition of "sin" is shock at an impropriety. Again, human kind before this eating was simply a superior kind of lower animal; man is lumped in with the lower animals in the earlier part of the story. The point, then, is that their eating of the tree of conscience was a step up and made the essential difference between man and all other animals. Man alone possesses a conscience. Incidentally Jehovah had lied; they did not die on eating the fruit of that tree. The philosopher could not help himself here; he had to follow the story and his interest was human nature and not the nature of God. Then came the punishments and in these are found the explanations of a collection of observed facts in life and the world, trivial and deep. (The strange things about the serpent in which he is different from all other creatures: how he can move swiftly without legs [cf. Proverbs xxx, 19, where it is one of four wonderful things]; his apparent eating of the dust; and the instinctive antagonism between him and men.) Was it because of this observed hostility that he was chosen to figure in this story? The root of the Hebrew word here for serpent occurs often in connection with soothsaying and the cognate root in Arabic indicates bad luck. In the original folklore myth it may be that the serpent was a mythological serpent, but for the philosopher the punishment shows that he was only the serpent of ordinary life. We have no real clue and the basis may be the curious separation which exists everywhere between serpents and all other creatures. So in verse 14, "cursed art thou with a curse that separates thee from all" other creatures, is the true rendering. Much deeper are the observed facts as to woman. "Unto the woman he said, 'I will make very great thy laborious pregnancy; in labor thou shalt bear sons; and unto thy husband is thy desire but he shall rule over thee.'" Pregnancy, childbirth, yearning towards the husband and submission to him—these are woman's destiny for the philosopher. But the last expressions are ambiguous and the philosopher may have been speaking in naïve simplicity or cynically. The word translated "desire" occurs only three times in the Old Testament: here, Genesis iv, 7, and Song of Songs vii, 10. In the last passage it is evidently erotic desire, but in the passage iv, 7—probably also due to the philosopher—it is used of Sin, personified as a wild beast, desiring to overcome Cain, while Cain should rule over and subdue Sin. The verbal parallel here is very close and would mean that woman's desire is to control her husband, but that he should control her. She *had* controlled him in eating from the tree.

Even more momentous are the consequences for man and the whole human race: "Because thou hast listened to the voice of thy wife and hast eaten from the tree as to which I commanded thee, saying, 'Thou shalt not eat from it,' cursed is the soil on thy account; in toil thou shalt eat from it all the days of thy life; thorn and thistle it shall make to sprout for thee and thou shalt eat the herb of the field. By the sweat of thy face thou shalt eat bread until thou returnest unto the soil, for from it thou wast taken; for thou art dust and unto dust thou wilt return." There is no special reference to grainstuffs in the word "bread," for in Hebrew idiom "to eat bread" means simply "to eat" and the words might be used of a great banquet. But the reference in the whole is to the abiding fact that a man must work if he is to eat. From this time on it will be the nature of the soil to produce useless and noxious things rather than its kindly fruits. For these man must sweat himself in labor. This is the observed fact of the innate depravity of the soil which every farmer recognizes and in this way it came about. And the end will be the return of man to the soil from which he was taken; that is inevitable, sooner or later. Man is simply dust and his end is in the dust again. It seems unescapable that these words are an emphatic denial of an assertion in the author's time that man was more than dust; that there was in him a spiritual something and a destiny beyond the dust. In that belief the philosopher had no part; death for him ended all.

But he had still this story on his hands. Man had become of the Elohim, so far as being able to distinguish for himself between good and evil; in that degree he was separate from all the other creatures made from the dust. It is deeply significant that this new endowment, possessing a conscience, was the essential differentia between man and the lower animals. The difference was moral and not intellectual. There are many implications in this but they must be left for consideration in connection with the Hebrew philosophy. Here it need only be said that there is no word in Hebrew for "conscience" and this philosopher had to invent the phrase, "knowing good and evil."

Then comes the philosopher's last and best development of this old tale; a flash of humane and creative insight. "So He [Jehovah] drove out man and He placed in front of the Garden of Eden the

Cherubim and the flaming sword which keeps turning over, to guard the way to the tree of life. But Man knew Eve his wife, and she conceived and bare. . . . " Man was cut off from the garden in which he had lived the life of a fairy-tale; there was no possibility that by eating of the tree of life he might defy God and live forever; only an existence of daily toil lay before him until the end in the inevitable dust of the grave. "But," and there is a depth of meaning in that "but," the human family is well and truly founded and the real human life begins. If a man cannot live forever the human race can and does, through the human family with all that it implies.

But what has this to do with the Fall and whence comes our doctrine of the Fall? Here there is no fall and in this story, if anything, man acquires a new power of moral discrimination which separates him, once for all, from all other animals. He is on his way upwards towards the Sons of the Elohim. The Muslim theologians have been so puzzled by the accepted fact that the name for this event is "the Fall," that they have taken the word literally. The Garden was on a mountain summit and Adam and Eve, on their expulsion, fell down from the mountain. But the origin of the Fall taught by our theologians is to be found in the position of a Jewish school, of about the Christian era, which followed, or devised, a very perverted exegesis of this story. We have two pieces of evidence for the existence of that school. One of these is the Apostle Paul himself who taught the inheritance in man of a taint of sin from Adam's sin; that Adam acquired a sinful tendency by this first disobedience and that his offspring inherit it from him. Except as in Paul, it may be said most absolutely that neither our Old Testament nor our New Testament knows anything of this position. But it is found also in a Jewish apocalypse, the writer of which was probably a contemporary of Paul. This is the Apocalypse of Ezra, 2 Esdras of our Apocrypha, and the doctrine will be found there in iii, 7, 21; vii, 11, 15, 116-118. There are some other references to the Garden Story in our Apocrypha, whether to the original legend or to the story as told by the philosopher, but none of them understands it in this way. They are mostly occupied with abusing Eve. That Paul took up the position of this Jewish school and passed it on to the entire Christian world is about the most unlucky bit of theological mischief ever perpetrated. Yet the whole Christian world did not receive it with equal favor. There is no trace of it, outside of Paul, in the New Testament, nor in the early creeds, and it may have been one of the Pauline teachings "hard to be understood, which the ignorant and unsteadfast wrest" (2 Peter iii, 16). The Oriental Church has laid little stress upon it, and the Roman Church has modified, as far as possible, the position of Augustine on it. It was left to the Protestant Churches to emphasize it in various ways and make it fundamental to their theologies. But all this has nothing to do with the literature of the Hebrews, who never dreamed of such a position, and is dealt with here only to avoid misunderstanding. The genuinely Hebrew development will be seen when we come to Ecclesiastes.

As we look at the whole series of these early stories as retold and adjusted by the philosopher for his own purposes we cannot help noticing that the so-called First Creation Narrative (i, 1-ii, 4a) belongs as a whole to his scheme and is not simply made to express his ideas by little insertions. On the other hand, the Second Creation Narrative is as a whole a piece of folklore and there are elements in it which were of no use or meaning for the philosopher. He had, however, to leave them standing because everyone knew them.

That is not at all the case with the first narrative. It is a combination of natural science and philosophy. The science is a statement of the structure of the world from its beginning out of a chaos down to the appearance of man in it. Its science is not modern science but its method is the method of all science, not the dreams and imagination of folklore.

And, again, with this scientific statement of the facts of the structure of the whole there is combined a philosophical statement of the purpose of the whole. This elaborate structure was made that it might furnish a habitat for man; man is, therefore, the final cause of the world. May we, then, conjecture that this is a preface constructed by the philosopher and prefixed by him to his Book of Genesis, the book in which he proposed to lay down his fundamental philosophy of man and lead up to the mission of the Hebrew race among men? If this conjecture be at all possible we should, then, notice further that the singularly elaborate sentence with which the narrative begins is an imitation of the structure of the first sentence in the second narrative, while the sense is entirely different.

The next story is that of Cain and Abel and in it, too, an ethical twist has been given to a story originally of little ethical point. Cain is a tiller of the soil and Abel a pasturer of flocks. The two classes have always and everywhere been at odds. But for the Hebrews the difference became a question of theology, and it has remained so for the entire Near East. The Hebrews came into Palestine as nomads, sheep and cattle men, and they were only gradually assimilated to the native population of farmers. Some were never so assimilated. There was the tribe of Rechabites, especially, who clung to ancient ways and to ancestral teaching, refusing to build houses, to sow seed or plant vineyards—broadly, to become fixed on the soil. On them see in detail in Jeremiah xxxv. In 2 Kings x, 15, we find Jehu enlisting their aid in his war against the House of Ahab which had gone over to the worship of the Baals, the native gods of Palestine and essentially vegetation deities. Put theologically and reduced to a principle the question came to be, Which is the most God-pleasing life, that of the shepherd with his flocks, moving about as he seeks pasture, or that of the farmer, fixed to the soil and its ancient sanctuaries with their ritual of worship, dedicating corn and oil and wine to the Spirit and Lord of the soil who gave them? For Baal means "owner" and the Baal of a country was its divine landlord, the owner of the soil and protector and fosterer of those who lived on it. This belief that there are certain occupations which, for one reason or another, are peculiarly God-pleasing appears regularly in religious-minded communities and with religious-minded individuals even among ourselves. Through the history of the Muslim peoples it has showed itself again and again and especially in the exact form of what was probably the original story here in Genesis, a glorification of the life of the shepherd who, nourishing himself from his flock and with a mind free from worldly cares, could give himself entirely to the worship of God. But the philosopher was very well aware that there was no such easy, occupational road to the pleasing of God and the avoiding of sin. Sin was a reality in itself, and he saw Sin everywhere waiting for its victim, like a wild beast crouched. This universal presence and possibility of Sin was for him, though with a difference, our "wolf at the door." So Jehovah said to Cain, "Why art thou wroth and why is thy countenance fallen?" (There had appeared plainly on him the signs of the dominance of some evil principle.) "Is it not true that if thou doest well it will show in an uplifted countenance? And if thou doest not well, at the door Sin is lying crouched and unto thee is its desire but thou shouldest rule over it." The matter lay with Cain himself, not in any difference of offerings. The wild beast Sin is trying to dominate him, but it is for him to subdue Sin. It cannot be accident—however cynical it may sound—that the same words are used here as of the relation of man and wife in iii, 16. And then, to bring home still more clearly that it was not Abel's being a shepherd which made his offering pleasing to God, Cain is driven out into the nomadic shepherd life from the cultivable soil on which his life hitherto had been. Nor is this meant as a means of salvation for him; in that life as a wanderer in the wilderness he will be hidden from the very face of Jehovah. The nomad, simply as a nomad, is no specially God-pleasing person and does not live in the presence of God.

In this narrative, too, there is a curious link with the Book of Ecclesiastes, a link which, so far as Ecclesiastes is concerned can hardly be accidental. And it is only just conceivable that it may point to a philosophical attitude common to both the philosopher of Genesis and to Ecclesiastes. The names Cain and Abel have both significance as used in their story. "Cain" is a play on the words used by Eve, "I have come into possession"; Cain was a possession which had come to her from Jehovah. Apparently there lies in it a recognition that Jehovah had given her something to make up for her exclusion from the Garden. Abel, on the other hand, is the Hebrew word (*hével*) for a mere "breath of wind," and then, metaphorically, for "transitoriness" and "emptiness." But this is the word used repeatedly by Ecclesiastes in his book in the first of these senses and which is falsely translated in our version "vanity." "Oh, how transitory; all things are transitory," the book begins and with the same words it ends. Abel's brief life is the life of Everyman.

The story goes on to give the record of the Godless House of Cain. With the Sword Song of Lamech, the fifth from Cain, we have already dealt. His son Tubal-cain was the forger of his sword and, in the story, the first of all workers in metal. But the whole family was noteworthy; each was the first to be or do something. What exactly Jabel did as an initiator is uncertain; it had something to do with tents but the text is corrupt. His brother Jubal first produced musical instruments and Tubal-cain had a full sister of whom we are told only that her name was Naamah, "Pleasant." Of her, too, tales must have been told, as of the three daughters in Job's second family. Similarly, Arabic literature is fond of lists of people or things that were Firsts. It will be observed that this puts the arts and crafts, the means and instruments of civilized life, in this evil family. There is undoubtedly a widely spread feeling in the East to this day that elaboration and sophistication of the means of living are destructive of the true life of the soul. It is not only the intellectual materialism of the West against which the East protests but the very comforts and refinements of its life. The Eastern case against Main Street would be not simply that Main Street did not think, but that it thought in terms of bathtubs and plumbing. How deeply this went in the Hebrew mind may be seen by reading chapter vii of the Book of Enoch which is an expansion of this passage. That may be taken as quite certainly the popular, folklore, attitude here. But how did the philosopher regard it? He has shown clearly his belief that sin is a mental attitude and that God does not account different modes of life sin or virtue. Is instrumental music, are cutting instruments of brass or iron, hurtful to the soul? He does not say; he only leaves standing this sequel to the story of Cain and Abel.

The next story on which the philosopher had clearly left his mark is the legend of the Flood. Between comes chapter v with genealogies in which he may have been interested or not. But at the beginning of chapter vi, just before the story of Noah, there is a bit of Semitic mythology which has had the widest influence in literature and on what we call, roughly, superstitions. The Jewish rabbis made much of it; early Islam and even the Koran itself made still more of it, until it flowered in Thomas Moore's *Loves of the Angels* and even continues in semi-occultist novels of our own day and in the reveries of half-baked theologians. For the Hebrews it was an explanation of the giant races of ancient Palestine (Numbers xiii, 33); for the folklorist it is the Hebrew parallel to the Greek stories of demigods and heroes. As to what it meant for the philosopher we have no clue, but one expression in it meant a great deal for Ecclesiastes (Ecclesiastes vi, 10) and so it is well to translate the whole passage here. "And it happened, when mankind had begun to multiply upon the surface of the soil and daughters had been born to them, that the Sons of Elohim saw that the daughters of mankind were very beautiful and they took to them wives of all whom they preferred. And Jehovah said, 'My Spirit will not contend in mankind forever, because he is also flesh; so his days shall be a hundred and twenty years.' The Nephilim [so in Numbers xiii, 33] were in the earth in those days and also thereafter, for the Sons of the Elohim kept going in to the daughters of mankind and they kept bearing to them; those were the heroes who were of old, men of renown."

The Hebrew belief as to the two races of intelligent beings, the Sons of Mankind and the Sons of the Elohim, has already been brought out. This shows that for the primitive Hebrews, at least, intercourse between the two races was possible and was their explanation for the existence of certain human races. The explanation must be very old for we have no clue as to the origin of the name "Nephilim." What Jehovah says is an interruption and seems to be an insertion, possibly by the philosopher. The point is that in man there are two principles, the flesh with its instincts, derived from the dust, and spirit, here said to belong to Jehovah. These so combined in man are in perpetual conflict, but, hereafter, the conflict will last only one hundred and twenty years in each individual, for that will be the measure of human life. There is nothing here as to what becomes of this divine spirit after death. Man's flesh as we have seen (iii, 19) returns to the dust and that is an end of it. But what of this "spirit"? Ecclesiastes carries the matter a step farther. The "spirit," meaning evidently the life-principle, returns to God who gave it (Ecclesiastes xii, 7) and is reabsorbed in God. Also there is no difference between that "spirit" in man and in the lower animals (Ecclesiastes iii, 19-21). If this remark is an insertion by the philosopher he tucked it away here as a convenient place to register his position. He must often have had difficulty in finding such suitable places.

Next is the legend of the Flood, told in long detail from the folk-story. But the point of it all for the philosopher is put in viii. 21, 22, and ix, 12*ff*. "And Jehovah smelled the satisfying odor and Jehovah said in his mind, 'I will not ever again curse the soil on account of mankind for the shape of the mind of man is evil from his youth, and I will not ever again smite all living as I have done. While the earth remaineth, seedtime and harvest, cold and heat, summer and winter, day and night, shall not rest.' " This begins with a bit of the crudest anthropomorphism derived from the ritual language of the altar and it ends in an elaborate expression of the stability of nature and that man can depend upon that hereafter. From this time on the cycle of nature is assured; there are to be no more catastrophies. The farmer may know that, just as the sequence of day and night, so, perhaps a few days earlier or later, the year will make its round. He can plant his seed and know that he will reap the harvest. As for "the shape of the mind of man" being evil, that is part of a certain hopeless attitude which the Hebrews took towards human nature. Man is bound to go astray; he was made that way, of unclean dust taken from the ground. No Fall was needed for man; that was his created nature. Compare with this the defeatism of the prophets brought out above. This reference, also, to the fixed cycle of the years is the nearest that the Hebrews came to our conception of nature and this nature in things, it will be noticed, is assigned and guaranteed by Jehovah. This is done, as is worked out in the next chapter, by a covenant between Jehovah and all the living creatures of the earth. In the earlier verses of that chapter the position of man's supremacy over the whole earth and all life in it, is repeated and emphasized. That is the blessing and gift of God to Noah and his sons. But in the latter part the covenant is with all: "And God said, 'This is the sign of the covenant which I am putting between Me and you and all living beings which are with you for perpetual generations. My bow I put in cloud and it will become a sign of a covenant between Me and the earth. And it will happen, when I bring a cloud upon the earth, that the bow will be seen in the cloud and I will remember My covenant which is between Me and you and all living beings, consisting of all flesh, and the waters shall not again become a deluge to destroy all flesh. When the bow comes in the cloud I will remember, on seeing it, a perpetual covenant which is between God and all living beings, consisting of all flesh, which are upon the earth.'" The bow here is the rainbow but the word used for it shows that God in some early mythology was pictured, like Apollo, with a bow from which he showers the arrows of the lightnings. Compare his arrows in Psalm xviii, 14.

So far, then, we have had to do with the institutes of human life as they apply to the earth as a whole and to all mankind. But mankind is broken up by various divisions of race, of language, of soil and of nationality. The same classes of division exist with us to this day and the philosopher, when he looked out upon his known world, saw them there. There had come to him in his proto-Genesis a genealogical table of the descendants of Noah through his three sons. How could he adjust this probably very primitive table to the observable facts under his eyes and under the eyes of his readers? What adjustments in detail he made we cannot tell and almost certainly shall never be able to tell. But one broad adjustment was to turn it from a purely genealogical scheme, with all its uncertainties and equivocations, into a picture of the whole known human race in all its relations and divisions. Acceptedly they came from Noah and therefore they had to be joined up with the scheme of Noah's descendants, but the present and evident facts about them were another matter. He met this paradox in the simplest way by inserting three times in chapter x (verses 5, 20, 31) a formula with little variations, "according to their families, according to their tongues, in their countries, according to their nations." By this he meant that this classification of peoples was not purely genealogical but had cross-divisions; it was racial, linguistic, geographical and national. We know that there are no pure races; that all races have crossed and mixed one with another and with many others. We know that a race can completely change its language for that of another race. We know that races move on the face of the earth and have at one time one soil as a habitat and another at another. And we know, the most surprising fact of all, that there is a thing called "nationality," leading to a national feeling of unity and separateness, which seems to be independent of race, language, religion and all the other marks of kind, belonging to people living together on the same territory. In the United States that shows itself very strongly even in isolated communities, peopled from one race, country and language. With it all they feel that they have part in the nationality of the United States of America. A still stronger example from the old world is in the story told by Robert Louis Stevenson of a certain Roman Catholic regiment from the Highlands of Scotland. They had been quartered in Ireland among a population of the same race, language and religion as themselves, but when they were brought back to Scotland and landed in Galloway, in a population of alien blood and language and of the dourest covenanting Presbyterianism, they fell down and kissed the soil. It was the soil of Scotland and they were of Scottish nationality. Now all this the philosopher of Genesis knew as well as we do, and when he looked out on the world of his day he distinguished these four—race, language, soil, and nationality. Can we, looking at this table, tell what world that was at which he was looking with his eyes? Can we thus reach his time and place? Unhappily it does not seem to be possible. Whatever he may have done to details, the basis of the table was too genealogically and primitively archaic for that. We must be content with noting that he knew well what were the divisions among men, and that he saw those divisions quite as clearly as did Herodotus.

The next chapter begins with the story of the Tower of Babel, a pure folk-tale and a step backward in time. There is no trace in it of the keen sociological insight of our philosopher; he gave it because he was given it. But it explains the scattering of the peoples in the way that folklore has always liked, by tracing it to a catastrophe. So the scattering of the Arab tribes was traced in Arabian legend to the bursting of the dam of Ma'rib—an historical event like the building of the great tower temple at Babylon—and the Arabic historians and geographers give exact details of how the different tribes were sent in this direction and that and Arabia was peopled.

The philosopher has now reached Abram, the Father of the Faithful, and he, hereafter, gives all his attention to him and to his descendants, the Chosen People. But his first task is solidly done:

he has shown the place of man in the world; he has shown the essential difference between man and the lower animals; he has shown the essential nature of the relation of man and woman in its details and the fixed facts as to the life and death of man; he has founded the human family with all its possibilities; he has defined well and truly the nature of sin; he has fixed and explained the fact of the stability of nature and its basis; he has looked at the world of his time and distinguished the different kinds of division there. The way is cleared for what was the greatest fact of the world for him, the fact of the People of Israel. And it is significant that he accepts that fact, as a given fact, like all the other facts in the world; he makes no attempt to explain why Jehovah chose Abram and his descendants to be his peculiar people. In this and in everything he was a realist and pragmatist; the fact was so and the fact of the People of Israel is so.

But how was this fact to be handled? So far there has been no interest in individuals except Lamech and he was given by the folk-tale and in his sword song. Even Cain is only a type and Abel is the shadow of a shade. But now the characters were to be everything; he had always been more interested in ideas than in concrete things; all the facts so far—given and observed—have been really ideas; now his interest is to be in characters rather than events. He is embarking on a psychological study of a family and of the individuals in it—from Abram and to the Sons of Jacob; that is the patriarchal history for him. A comparison has often been made between the great trek of Abram across the desert from Ur of the Chaldees to Palestine and the voyage of Aeneas and the Trojans through the Mediterranean from Troy to Latium, and, therefore, between the Aeneid and this part of Genesis. But they have very little in common and the treatment is essentially different. Virgil was possessed by the idea of the founding of the Roman State and his characters meant little to him; they were carried on upon a flood of destiny. But in this story of Abram the Hebrew subjectivity had full play and used what events there were to bring out the characters which were everything. And the psychological material in those characters every preacher knows, or used to know. Yet that material is not given to us directly. There are no characteristics of Abraham rehearsed to us in an analysis of him; we are only told some stories about him and he stands there before us. So, and perhaps still more, Sarah stands and talks. Beside her we have the figure of Hagar—Arabia's mother—who does not talk; but we get her nevertheless, in her story of suffering and eternal pity. And there we see another strange thing in those stories—how the women stand out, separate and clear, Sarah, Rebekah, Rachel and all their kind and rivals besides. We hear much of the suppression and nonentity of oriental women from those who do not know either the East or their Bibles. These women are the equals of the men and, for better or for worse, are their rulers. And how distinct the men, too, are; take the three, Jacob, Esau, Laban. With what zest and interest this keen psychologist works each out. He does not take sides as the modern preacher does; he is an artist and likes them all equally well and knows them all from the inside out. He liked Rebekah and even Jacob as Thackeray liked Becky Sharpe and as Galsworthy liked all the multitude of figures in his *Forsyte Saga*. Just so this philosopher-artist balances and rounds all his characters. Consider that perfect bit of characterization not only personal but racial, pronounced by Isaac on Jacob and Esau. "By thy sword wilt thou live; yet thy brother wilt thou serve. And it will happen, when thou wanderest free, thou wilt break his yoke from thy neck." (Genesis xxvii, 40.) So, to this day, if the nomad Arab enters the cultivated lands he is enslaved by his blood-kin and their different life. To save his soul he must return to his deserts and his wanderings; whatever the life there is it is a free life. That the philosopher had seen and knew. Consider, too, that these men and women with whom he is thus impartially dealing are the founders of his race; the pilgrim fathers and mothers of a people that for him meant everything in the world. Yet his instinct as an artist will not permit him to idealize them; he takes them as the stories give them and simply makes plain of what manner they must have been. It is a family chronicle like the family annals in which Thackeray loved to work from Esmond down and like Thackeray, too, he knew well the persistence to type of the women of a family. It is with such novelists as Thackeray and Galsworthy of the older, direct type that his kinship lies, rather than with the more modern novel of psychological character analysis. Yet he is as subtle in his little touches as Henry James and a great deal clearer. And in it all the marvel is that he was able to produce such living men and women out of the given material of a folk-tale. Does this throw doubt on the historic reality of these people and their lives? Are they only like those vague pre-patriarchal figures—Adam and Eve, Cain and Abel, Noah and his descendants—out of which he drew the foundations of all human life? The very characterization shows that for him there was a difference; that these earlier figures were no such real persons, were, at the best, types. Our "Adam" is not a proper name, but mankind in a single person, and our Eve is the Living One, only personified. But with Abram all that changes. The philosopher knew that Abram was an historic man and he treats him accordingly. Are we, then, only under the spell of his art when we feel that Abram and Sarah and all the rest lived lives, then and there, as true as those of David, Saul, and Jonathan? That is a hard question and is not really of the matter of this book. But if they were not real how explain the people who sprang from them and who felt sure about them? How explain, above all else, the evidently complete faith in them of their rehearser in these pages of Genesis? His own attitude was plainly that of the modern historian who tries to re-create, freely but truly, the figures of his history. And we must explain his faith.

The third element in his great artistic re-creation is the story of Joseph and in it his work culminates. Broadly, it is an adventure story and of the type so well beloved everywhere and at all times, of the young man, thrown upon himself, and finding his fortune in a new environment. But Joseph, while very much of a real person, is more than that; he is the type of the Hebrew race over against the world. The world consists of Hebrews and those who are not Hebrews and this is how the Hebrews face that alien world, make their fortune in it, are a supreme influence upon it and stamp and turn it to their mind. Thus the story tells the triumph of the Hebrew race; Joseph is Prime Minister in Egypt like Disraeli in England. And behind it all is the guiding will of Jehovah; Joseph sums that up to his brethren, "So now it was not you that sent me hither, but God" (xlv, 8). The story presupposes the existence of the Diaspora, the Dispersal of the Jews in foreign lands, but that certainly went far back. The kernel of the story has been sought in an Egyptian folk-tale, which is possible. But the same folk-tale is found everywhere. It is more noteworthy that in this adventure of a young man seeking his fortune in the world there is no real love-interest. This Hebrew was out for himself and his race. But later expanders of the story, which has become famous in Muslim literature, have felt that human need and filled that gap, rather to the upsetting of the meaning of the story. In it the Hebrew race had come to its own and its influence ruled the world. And, so, with it the philosopher-artist could feel that his work was done.

CHAPTER X

OTHER HEBREW STORIES

FROM the great reading of eternal history which gave us Genesis we turn to a unique little effort of Hebrew art which gave us the first true "short story," in the exact sense, which literature knows. It is also, in all probability, the first "dialect story," for in it dialect is used to point the effect. A "short story," in the literary sense, is not simply a story told shortly, but a story which, by its nature, can best be put in short form. Arabic literature is full of them, with all manner of motifs, and some have found a resting-place in the great collection which we know as the *Arabian Nights*. This Hebrew story is our Book of Ruth and in its kind it is unique in the Old Testament. In the King James Version it comes in its strict chronological sequence as history between Judges and Samuel; this is derived from the Greek translation of the Old Testament, through the Latin Vulgate. But the Jewish editors of the Old Testament felt that it was not history in any exact sense and so they put it in the third great division of their Hebrew Scriptures called the Writings, a sufficiently broad term. Even among the Writings, it comes in a further subdivision called the Five Rolls, which are the Song of Songs, Ruth, Lamentations, Ecclesiastes, Esther. These five, it will be seen, are distinctly different from any other books of the Old Testament. They bear a more literary and almost personal stamp and quality than most of the others, and their precise literary quality is different in each. It will be necessary, hereafter, to deal with some others of them and this personal difference will come out more plainly. The Book of Ruth, then, is an historical anecdote developed into a short story. Historically it is dated broadly at the beginning, "in the time when the Judges judged," and at the end it closes with the birth of Obed, the grandfather of David. Historically it also asserts that the great-grandmother of David was a Moabitess, named Ruth. This Ruth is not mentioned elsewhere in the Old Testament, but it is tolerably certain that there was a Moabite strain in David's genealogy. So, for example, David, in his flight from Saul, took his father and mother and gave them into the care of the King of Moab (1 Samuel xxii, 3, 4), his father, Jesse, being a grandson of this Ruth. The nucleus, then, may have been a tradition such as we have several times in the Books of Samuel, but that tradition has been handled very freely and with a loving care and refined art which have made it the unique thing it is. It is written in very pure, simple and careful Hebrew and with picturesque realism of detail. Thus Boaz, the wealthy and elderly farmer of Bethlehem, talks countrified dialect as contrasted with the more literary Hebrew of Ruth. It is almost as though a distinction were intended between these country folks and the young lady from a distance. We are living in that atmosphere of romance which produced "la princesse lointaine" and "das Mädchen aus der Ferne"—the opposite of the realistic attitude of Proverbs to "the stranger woman." And so we can see, with Keats, Ruth standing "among the alien corn." Our own short-story writers at one time made much of such contrasts. The writer, also, is evidently looking back on what for him and his readers was a quite primitive situation. He has to explain the antiquarian law and it is quite possible that he did not understand it or explain it rightly. The usage of drawing off the shoe (iv, 7) persists to this day in outlying Syria, but it is to confirm the giving up the right to marriage with a cousin. ("She was my shoe, and I have drawn her off.") He handles, too, with the greatest delicacy the possibilities that came in the country, during the night after a harvest-home. Our commentators either have not seen this or have wilfully obscured it, but to the folklorist the scene at the threshing-floor of Boaz is quite clear as part of the ancient rites of fertility by which the gods of vegetation were propitiated. And Boaz is shown quietly handling the situation like a gentleman, and not either as an old fool or a village lout. He may be countrified but he has dignity and restraint. This is the real center of the story and to this the care of Naomi for her daughter-in-law and the pretty scenes in the harvest field lead up. Yet throughout it all there are tones of color and beauty. The first chapter, though it begins so far back, strikes the note of family unity and affection, and on the same note the book ends with Ruth's baby laid in the bosom of Naomi. We have here, then, a literary artist using an historical tradition because he saw how he could develop it into the thing of abiding beauty which we now read. And he did his work well, for through it all are scattered phrases which have rooted themselves in the English language as deeply as anything in *Hamlet*. He was therefore an artist in language, but, most curiously and almost uniquely for such a Semitic artist, he studied simplicity and avoided elaborate rhetoric. He knew the tone which was needed for the story he wished to tell. All the above is very plain to the lover of literature who can read those few pages with fresh eyes as though for the first time. And that being so, there is no need to consider whether he had any ulterior object and a position to maintain. Certainly both the legislation of Deuteronomy xxiii, 3, and the ferocious racial exclusiveness of Nehemiah xiii, 23*ff*. must have been entirely repugnant to him. He would also see how impossible such a position was. But he enters into no polemic against it. He lets Ruth of Moab, the great-grandmother of David, testify for him.

For the next type of Hebrew story—that of the religious artist —we have four full examples and these, while all handled with conscious art of one kind or another, are all distinctly didactic with one purpose or another. These are the separate Books of Jonah, Job, and Daniel, with the Story of Balaam as inserted in the Book of Numbers xxii, 2-xxiv-end, and each is based on a popular legend. The Book of Jonah, although not in the least a prophecy, has been put among the twelve Minor Prophets. There, a moral apologue, it stands entirely by itself. Its place is probably due to the fact that Jonah, the son of Amittai, was a recorded, historical, prophet in the days of Amaziah of Judah and Jeroboam of Israel (2 Kings xiv, 25). There is another reference to Jonah which is still more significant for our book. It is in the Book of Tobit in our Apocrypha. There (xiv, 8) Tobit warns his son to flee from Nineveh for he is quite sure that all the things prophesied against Nineveh by Jonah will yet be fulfilled. That means that in the time of the writer of the Book of Tobit—on which see below —there was extant a prophecy by Jonah against Nineveh. In order to throw the time of his own story farther back, the writer of Tobit represents this prophecy as still unfulfilled and Nineveh as still existing. But Nineveh fell 608-607 B.C. and the author of Tobit (chapter xiv) knew of the destruction of Jerusalem (586) and the rebuilding of the Temple (515). He knew, too, the Book of Ahiqar which, as has been shown by those precious papyrus fragments found at Elephantine, existed in Aramaic in Egypt in the fifth century B.C. But he could hardly have known our Book of Jonah. The moral lesson of that book could not have gone over his head and certainly the book cancels out Jonah's prophecy. We are left therefore with these facts: (i) a real prophet Jonah and his prophecy against Nineveh; (ii) the writer of our Book of Jonah speaks of Nineveh as still existing. But it must have gone centuries before; so long, indeed, that it could be restored in order to point a moral. The Nineveh of the Book of Jonah is a city of the imagination. What, then, of our book? It begins with a straight piece of folklore: Jonah's attempted flight by sea to Tarshish; the storm and his being thrown overboard; his being swallowed by a great fish appointed by Jehovah. The story is very vivid, clear, and well told. Then comes Jonah's prayer inside the great fish, a very derivative psalm, dependent on Psalms xviii and xlii, with evident reference to a deliverance from drowning but none at all to his immediate predicament in the belly of the fish. It is, therefore, quite possible that this psalm was by the historical Jonah, son of Amittai, and was inserted here. But why this grotesque episode with the fish which has next to nothing to do with the point of the book except, perhaps, to bring out Jonah's obstinacy? The answer can only be that, in the popular mind, Jonah would not be Jonah without his great fish; they were as identified with one another as St. George with his dragon. That is the unfortunate side of deriving a moral lesson from a folklore tale. As the philosopher of Genesis found, you have to take in more than you want. Then, Jonah, having learned at last that he must do what he is told by Jehovah, starts for Nineveh. He must have been a most astonished prophet at the effect of his preaching—the simplest denunciation of woe to come—on the Ninevites. They repented with all the three marks of repentence, confession, contrition, and determination of amendment. Then Jehovah repented too of His purpose of punishment. But Jonah was sore displeased. He wanted Nineveh to be destroyed and had evidently enjoyed his message of destruction. Now it was all spoiled by the people's repentance, and Jehovah would say nothing to him but, "Are you good and angry?" It must have seemed like derision. That Jehovah had changed His mind was nothing to Jonah, nor to any Hebrew prophet; the theological difficulty involved never troubled the Hebrews. But Jonah had set his heart on the destruction of Nineveh. So he went and sat and waited in the hot sun and the sharp east wind, hoping still for the destruction of Nineveh. He was a pig-headed man. Then there grew up the gourd and there perished the gourd and the sun was hot and the east wind blew and still he hoped and waited, fainting and wishing for death. "And God said unto Jonah, 'Art thou good and angry on account of the gourd?' And he said, 'I *am* good and angry even unto death.' And Jehovah said, 'Thou hadst pity on the gourd on which thou didst not labor nor make it grow, which in a night came and in a night perished. And I, shall I not have pity upon Nineveh, the great city, in which are more than twelve myriad human beings who know not between their right hand and their left, and much cattle?' "

We are not told that Jonah ever saw the point. He is left sitting there and waiting for Jehovah to keep His word and avenge His people on Nineveh, that arch-enemy. Perhaps he is sitting there still beside the mounds and gloating over the accomplished destruction. Of course, Nineveh is a city in a parable and Jonah is a prophet in a parable. But we can imagine both Nahum and Habakkuk behaving much as he did. So the author of the Book of Tobit in his day still poses as waiting for the prophecy of Jonah against Nineveh to be fulfilled. From that we can draw only one conclusion: that he did not know our Book of Jonah with its warning that God was very compassionate towards all His creatures and could change His announced purpose on their repentance. For he, it is plain from his book, was no such hopeless preacher of vengeance as this Jonah. The Book of Jonah, then, is directed against those who clung to Jehovah as a God of vengeance, sure to avenge Israel, and who could not see that He was the God, the maker and father, of all peoples upon earth; that any people, on repentance, could find Him. The bitterness of the feeling against Nineveh may be seen in the Book of Nahum. So we are still left with the question how the Book of Jonah—so strange and different—found its way into the company of the other eleven Minor Prophets. We have no clue as to the origin of the story of the great fish, and

Jonah's association with it in the popular mind. Semitic mythology knows a great sea-serpent, subdued by Jehovah in the old days, and now at His command (Amos ix, 3), but the Hebrew word is different and that serpent does not swallow but bites. It is strange irony that has brought together and preserved this story and Jonah's psalm but blotted his prophecy, which Tobit knew, from the Hebrew record.

In Jonah we have the combination of a folklore story, a psalm, perhaps authentic, and a moral apologue, all welded very skilfully together and connected with a recognized prophet. In the Book of Daniel we have a different combination, not welded together with nearly the same skill and working out to a very dubious conclusion. This book, too, is in no such respectable company in the Hebrew canon. It comes among the Writings, not among the Prophets, and late even there. For it comes after the Five Rolls and is lumped at the very end of the Hebrew Bible with Ezra, Nehemiah, and Chronicles. It is also the only example of a straight Apocalypse to find its way into the Hebrew Canon. Yet Daniel was a great name in Hebrew tradition. He is mentioned in two passages in Ezekiel as an ancient sage, a righteous man and a wise man. In Ezekiel xiv, 14, 20, it is said of the people of the time that they are so wicked that though the three men, Noah, Daniel, and Job were amongst them they could not deliver the land by their righteousness, neither their sons nor their daughters but only themselves. We know from Genesis how Noah was a preacher of righteousness in his evil generation, but could save only himself and his family. Evidently there were similar stories about Daniel and Job, men of old time. It may be that there is an allusion, too, to Abraham's entreaty for Sodom (Genesis xviii, 23*ff*.) in which he gradually beat Jehovah down to ten righteous men, who were not to be found in Sodom. Again, in Ezekiel xxviii, 3, it is said ironically of the Prince of Tyre, "Behold thou art wiser than Daniel; no secret can they hide from thee!" For Ezekiel and his age, then, we may conclude that Daniel was an ancient sage and a righteous man of old time. This Daniel we may call Daniel I, although we know nothing more about him than those allusions tell us. But according to the asserted chronology of our Books of Ezekiel and Daniel, the Daniel carried, as a youth, into exile at Babylon by Nebuchadnezzar in the third year of Jehoiakim, King of Judah, must have been a younger contemporary of Ezekiel. This Daniel, then, we can call Daniel II and with evidently folklore stories about him the first part of our Book of Daniel (chapters i-vi) is occupied. That these stories have an historical basis is quite certain although the exact accuracy of that basis has been called in question. They are all concerned with the wisdom and visions of this Daniel II but we have no means at all of fixing their date. These visions pass over into an Apocalypse (chapters vii-end) and an Apocalypse can always be dated. For there is always a point in it where it passes from narrating events which can be verified in history to foretelling events of which history knows nothing. That point in our Book of Daniel comes at xi, 40, which means that the Apocalypse was written between 167 and 165 B.C. The writer of that date may be called for convenience Daniel III. There are thus in the history of Hebrew literature three Daniels, the ancient sage, the Daniel of folklore stories who was carried off by Nebuchadnezzar, and the writer of the Apocalypse who wrote between 167 and 165 B.C. Of these the last is the only one of definite, historical personality and all that we know of him is his date and that he used as his starting point folklore stories about Daniel II. Was Daniel II a real personality at the court of Nebuchadnezzar and his successors and did tradition give him for his wisdom the name of the ancient sage? Was there a book of stories about Daniel II which Daniel III used? These are questions to which no positive answers can be given, no such answers, at least, as would satisfy an exact historical and philological critic. But the student of creative literature may make guesses and some of these will seem sound to him. He will certainly ask this question. If the book was intended from the first to be an Apocalypse why was so much space given to the early stories about the wisdom of Daniel? The stories, too, of that wisdom in the first six chapters are incomparably superior to any of the stories and pictures in chapters vii to xii. There is Nebuchadnezzar's dream of the great image of different materials—the dream which he could not remember; all its details are vivid and impress the mind. Then the actual image which he set up and the whole tale of the fiery furnace with the three men walking in it, guarded from the flames by one of the Sons of Elohim, a messenger from Jehovah. Then Nebuchadnezzar's dream of the great tree and of how it was cut down, presaging his own madness, the pathos of the story and his recovery. Greatest of all, the scene of Belshazzar's feast and the hand which came forth and wrote upon the wall. And last, the trick played upon Darius and the scene of Daniel in the Den of Lions. All these have passed, by their inherent reality, into universal literature and allusions to them are everywhere. In contrast with this, few but professed students of historical puzzles and theological mysteries can read with patience the chapters that follow with their jumble of beasts and horns, little and great, and Kings of north and south. The writer of all this could never have written the early stories and, so, it seems safe to assume that he used an already existing collection to introduce his Apocalypse. In a sense we may be grateful to him, for without his Apocalypse, probably these earlier stories would have perished.

With the story of Job we have already dealt in considering the use made of it by the poet of the Colloquies. It remains only to underline some hardly answerable questions. Job, like Noah and Daniel, was a figure from the remote past. His characteristic was patient resignation, which was counted to him as righteousness. For Ezekiel he had held fast to his righteousness in an evil generation. It is a characteristic of folk-tale virtues, as it was of virtues in the literature of medieval Europe, that in the most grotesque excesses they are still virtues. Even for the humane Chaucer the patience of the patient Griselda in his *Clarke's Tale* is virtue still. The Renaissance, with the Greek doctrine of the golden mean, changed that for Europe. The poet of the Colloquies saw, too, that the patience of the Job of the folk-tale was driven to the point where it was monstrous and immoral. In the Epistle of James (v, 11) all had "heard of the patience of Job." There is evidence that this was the conception of Job which reached Mohammed and which still persists in Islam, just as it has persisted among us. He resisted the temptation of his Friends just as he had that of his wife and, in consequence, the Friends at the end are rebuked by Jehovah and Job is praised. From this original story, only chapters i and ii and xlii, 7-end, as preserved in our book, survive. Of these fragmentary survivals, xlii, 7-end, was certainly untouched by the poet. Some one tacked it on to make a finish to our book. There, therefore, existed a written prose book about this patient Job, and from it chapters i and ii were taken by the poet. Did he make any changes or did he give them exactly as they stood? If he made no changes, then the writer of the prose book was a great prose artist; the story could not have been better told up to the arrival of the Friends. The whole is perfectly balanced and coordinated and the Hebrew is beautiful. Then came the poet of the Colloquies and used the work of this earlier artist in a way of which he would have heartily disapproved.

The fourth full example of a story constructed by a religious artist on the basis of legend has not reached us as a separate book but is imbedded in the Book of Numbers xxii, 2-xxiv-end. The figure reconstructed before us in it is one of the most enigmatic in the Old Testament. Balaam was a diviner of the old Semitic type, of whom we know several in the stories of the desert before Mohammed. He was not only a diviner who prophesied the future but he uttered blessings and he hurled cursings, and his blessings and cursings were of sure effect. His words like all utterances from the Unseen World fell into a rude form of staccato verse. Those given in his story are the nearest in form and type in the Old Testament to the recorded fragments in Arabic of the similar utterances of the poet-soothsayers of the desert, prophesying, blessing, cursing. It was part of the system of desert warfare for the poet of the tribe on the day of battle to come forth to the front and solemnly call down the curses of the Unseen on the enemy. Such power Balak believed that Balaam had and so he sent for him across the desert from his own country of Pethor beside the Euphrates. But Balaam, in this story, also knew Jehovah, obeyed Him and called Him his God. Jehovah, on His part, comes to him at night, gives him commands and puts words in his mouth. Thus Balaam's figure in this story is a curious blending of a heathen diviner and such a Hebrew seer as Samuel.

Then there is the very picturesque episode with Balaam's Ass who sees the Messenger of Jehovah in the way and whose mouth is at last opened to protest to Balaam. This is evidently part of the legend of Balaam, like the Great Fish in the case of Jonah, and any later teller of his story had to work this in. That, however, was hard to do, for Balaam in this telling of his story is acting in obedience to the direct command of Jehovah and the most that could be done with this incident was to use it to impress upon Balaam that there must be no faltering in his obedience to Jehovah. Balaam is obedient and in his successive attempts to satisfy Balak, turns finally from his automatic methods of divination, encounters Jehovah Himself personally and receives from Him the words he is to say, as might any Hebrew prophet (xxiii, 15, 16; technical expressions belonging to the art of soothsaying are used here). What is the point of it all? It is not simply to tell a story of the old days before Israel had crossed the Jordan. It is to bring home and underline the fact that all soothsayers and all the avenues of contact with the Unseen World are in the direct control of Jehovah. That Jehovah *is* the Unseen World and that there is no means of divination or blessing or cursing except through Him. For this reteller of Balaam's story this position was as absolute as it was for Amos; for him, too, the hand of Jehovah was doing everything, everywhere in the world. But it may be doubted whether Amos would have liked the idea that a seer from outside the people and the land of Israel could be a fully commissioned prophet of his Lord Jehovah. Yet that is part of the teaching. Israel need not think that the will of Jehovah is expressed only through the people of Jehovah. As Jonah had to learn that Jehovah accepts the repentance of any people, so Israel had to learn that Jehovah can speak through the mouth of so-called heathen seers. That their oracles may not be due to evil and lying spirits but may convey the Word of Jehovah Himself.

But all this must have been a very hard saying and that it should have been incorporated in the very Book of the Law is more than strange. It is like the Book of Jonah existing alongside of those of Nahum and Habakkuk in the collection of the Twelve Prophets. For the Old Testament has several other references to Balaam and he was most plainly an inimical and abhorred figure. This separate story sends him back to his own land in peace (xxiv, 25), but in this same Book of Numbers (xxxi, 8) Balaam, along with the Kings of Midian, is slain by Israel with the sword and in verse 16 he is made responsible for the sin of Israel with the women of Midian. In Joshua xiii, 22, this slaying of Balaam is again recorded and he is called contemptuously "the soothsayer," a term (*qosem*) that could never be used of anyone divinely inspired, as in the separate story. Again in Joshua xxiv, 9, 10, Joshua himself gives the kernel of the story as recited by Jehovah: "Then Balak the son of Zippor, King of Moab, arose and fought with Israel and sent and summoned Balaam the son of Beor, to curse you. But I was not willing to listen to Balaam and so he kept blessing you and I delivered you from his hand." Part of the primitive legend of Balaam evidently was a certain supernatural intervention on the part of Jehovah to nullify his curses. Similarly in Deuteronomy xxiii, 4, 5, we have the hiring of Balaam from Mesopotamia to curse Israel and Jehovah's turning of the curse into a blessing. This last is quoted verbatim in Nehemiah xiii, 2. Even in Micah vi, 5, we have a reference to this same intervention of Jehovah. "O my People, remember now how Balak, King of Moab, directed and how Balaam, son of Beor, answered him, from Shittim unto Gilgal, for the sake of the knowing of the loyal doings of Jehovah." There is no mention of these two places in the story but it is evident that there is a reference here to the renewed attempts from one altar and then from another. And even in the New Testament there are three similarly hostile references. In 2 Peter ii, 15, 16: ". . . went astray, having followed the way of Balaam the *son* of Beor, who loved the hire of wrongdoing; but he was rebuked for his own transgression: a dumb ass spake with man's voice and stayed the madness of the prophet." In Jude 11, he is joined with Cain and Korah: "ran riotously in the error of Balaam for hire." And in Revelation ii, 14, there is a reference in detail to the story in Numbers xxxi, 16. These New Testament references, because of their animus against Balaam, are probably due to the scattered references in the Old Testament, and not to the story in Numbers xxii-xxiv, just as the reference in James v, 11, to "the patience of Job" must be to the abidingly patient Job of the original legend and not to that most impatient Job of our Book of Job.

From these references it is possible, in a broad way, to construct the original and hostile legend and to see how the artist of the story has dealt with it in order to bring out his point. But there is evidence in the story itself, not found elsewhere, as to the status of Balaam as a foreteller in the memory of the people of Israel. We have to think of him as such a legendary figure for Israel as was

Thomas the Rhymer, "true Thomas," for Scotland. There are few of the old families of the south and east of Scotland for the destinies of which true Thomas did not leave scraps of prophetic verse. Something of the same kind seems to have held of Balaam in the folklore of Israel, and the writer of the story has gathered up and used the existent scraps of verses as his basis. He must have had some basis for those which bear directly on the situation between Balak and Israel and from xxiv, 14 on, he has preserved a series which have nothing to do with that situation, but are oracles dealing with Edom, Amalek, the Kenites, and even Assyria and Cyprus and the Greek coasts. He throws these into a frank appendix: "And, now, behold, I am going my way unto my people; come, I will admonish thee of that which this people will do to thy people in the latter days." "Thy people," though addressed to Balak of Moab, means, as the following verses show, all those who are not of Israel; it is Israel against the world.

Is it too fanciful, then, to see in all this three separate accounts of this mysterious Balaam and three attitudes towards him? First we may place the folklore memories of him preserved by the populace of Israel. For it he was the great seer and man of magic from the distant East who was drawn into the conflicts between Israel and the peoples of the lands invaded by Israel. In that connection he uttered many prophecies as to the future of Israel, reaching out into distant times. And as the years passed prophecies to meet the new situations would be ascribed to him. There was a strange story told, too, of how the ass on which he rode was instrumental in showing him that there was a divine and overwhelming leading in the advance of Israel. Probably the folklore memory of Israel regarded this figure with awe and without hostility. Had he not prophesied what was true and good? But, secondly, for the religious chroniclers and prophets of Israel he was an irregular and unauthorized intruder from beyond their ring-fence of national and religious feeling. His memory, therefore, had to be blackened and the essential truth of his prophecies minimized. And, thirdly, there was the philosophical and broad-minded literary artist of the separate story who took the popular legend and the prophecies in circulation among the people and reshaped them all for the purpose and in the meaning suggested above. How this apologue of his came to be imbedded in the quite alien context of the Book of Numbers and thus in the Book of the Law itself is only another of the mysteries connected with the building up of our Old Testament out of the fragments of the Hebrew literature.

And that gives the tragedy of Hebrew literature. It is not only in fragments, but it consists greatly of reused and quoted fragments—fragments at second hand. The assured remains of David are only the scraps quoted in the Books of Samuel, unique and enigmatic enough. The equally unique Song of Deborah we have only as used in the Book of Judges. That there was a story about Naamah, the daughter of Lamech, and stories about the three daughters of Job who are named we are left to gather from these mere references to them. Was there a story that began, "And it came to pass in the end of days that Keren-happuch rose up in the midst of her brethren and said . . . "? We are left to conjecture something of the kind. Jonah and his Great Fish cannot but make us wonder how many other such strange tales about prophets there were. These occurrences are all so haphazard and casual. And the sponge seems to have passed over the memory of the Hebrew race very far back, for rabbinic literature has saved practically nothing that can be added to our Old Testament with safety. But there do survive in some additions in the Greek version of the Hebrew Bible, called the Septuagint, bits of folklore story which may easily have existed at one time in Hebrew. One of these is in the Greek additions to the Book of Daniel. It tells how the Prophet Habakkuk was carrying food to some reapers in the field in Palestine, but was seized by an angel and carried with his bowl of food through the air to Babylon to feed Daniel who was in the Den of Lions. But this story found no Hebrew artist to work out its meaning. That was reserved for the poet Longfellow who used it as the *Introitus* to his *Christus: a Mystery*. The next division of the story will bring all this out still more clearly.

It may be called the historical romance in Hebrew and the best example is our Exodus. The contrast in artistic structure between Genesis and Exodus has already been suggested. Apparently the philosopher-artist who made our Genesis what it is had tired of his task when he reached Exodus. Yet there may be traces of his hand even there. In the naïve narrative in chapter iii, verse 14 comes in very curiously and in the still more naïve story of Moses seeing Jehovah in chapter xxxiii, verse 19 looks like a similar expansion and explanation. Chapter iii, 13-15, runs:

See, I am going to the Sons of Israel and I shall say to them, "The God of your fathers hath sent me to you." Then they will say to me, "What is His name?" What shall I say to them? And God said to Moses, "I become what I become." And He said [further], "Thus shalt thou say to the Sons of Israel, '*I become* has sent me to you.'" And God said again to Moses, "Thus shalt thou say to the Sons of Israel, 'Jehovah, the God of your fathers, the God of Abraham, the God of Isaac and the God of Jacob hath sent me to you. This is my name forever and this is my memory to generation of generation.'"

Apparently this means that Moses asks God for His proper name. Every god has a name and to call this god simply the God of their fathers is not enough. In the original form Moses is told that the name is Jehovah and that sufficed. Probably it was pronounced Yahwé. But the philosopher wishes to put a meaning into the name, and a meaning which expresses God's manifesting of himself in constantly changing forms of working and becoming; God "becomes" and shows himself as this and that, in this way and that. So the philosopher plays on the sound of *Yahwé* and turns it into *Ehyé,* meaning "I become" and expands this into "I become what I become," i.e. I show myself under many aspects and you must take me as you find me. Compare Psalm xviii, 25, 26. That he could so play on the sound of the divine name Yahwé suggests that the original meaning, by derivation, had been lost in his time. In chapter xxxiii, verse 19 expresses a similar varied changing and working on the part of Jehovah. Moses has entreated that God would show Himself visibly to him, especially His glory. But this is too crude for the philosopher—and the narrative *is* very naïve—so he inserts: "I will make all my goodness pass before thee, and I will make proclamation using the name of Jehovah before thee, and I will be gracious unto whom I will be gracious and I will show compassion unto whom I shall show compassion." The grammatical form of the clauses here is the same as "I become that which I become." These are particular exemplifications of the things which Jehovah becomes in his manifestation of Himself to men.

Genesis is a great artistic whole; Exodus consists of a chaotic débris of brilliant fragments of historical romances. Egypt for the Hebrews, as for the old Greeks, was the land of marvels. It lay at the end of an easy caravan journey from Palestine, but its people were essentially as queer to the Hebrews as they were to Herodotus. Things went there, and people did them, in a different way. The natural phenomena even were very different. Amos had seen the inundation of the Nile and it was for him a picture of the quivering of the soil in an earthquake (viii, 8). Signs and wonders, then, were fully in place in such a land. And it was with signs and wonders that Jehovah had brought His people up out of Egypt. But the narrative which tells this is jumbled, broken, repeated, to the despair of commentators. Yet there survive brilliant pictures in it: Moses holding out his rod against the sky; a glittering net of hail and lightning flashes. Thus chapter ix, verses 23-24, may be translated:

> And Moses stretched out his rod against the sky, while Jehovah gave thunders and hail; and the fire went its way earthward and Jehovah rained hail upon the land of Egypt. So there came hail with fire in a network in the midst of the hail, very heavy, such as the like had not come in all the land of Egypt since it became a nation.

Such pictures show the work, surviving in scraps, of a conscious, descriptive artist. But the confusion is there, too. What lies behind this confusion? We may conjecture a combination of historical romances such as those in which Arabic abounds and which mean history for the masses of the Arabic-speaking population of the Near East. When the present writer went about in Cairo he was told long tales by his donkey-boy about its medieval buildings; mosques, tombs, palaces. These tales were very puzzling, for the names were historical and also the places; the great events were historical, too, but over everything was the glamour of romance with its stage-setting and lighting. Then the clue was found. The donkey-boy's history was drawn from the historical romances he had heard in the coffee-houses, much as, with us, history often goes back to Shakespeare and Walter Scott. It is hardly necessary, nor would it here be profitable, to give details on these Arabic historical romances. They are very numerous, very long and are constructed on almost no plan except the necessity of going on and on. Many are in print in Arabic, but few have been translated into any European language except one or two, shorter, which had found their way into recensions of the *Arabian Nights* and so have been translated. But when they are truly historical, and do not deal with ancient patriarchs and prophets or with lands of romance beyond the mountains, their characteristic is that they are constructed around more or less historical figures, move in known cities, countries, even buildings, and keep a rough contact with historical events. The present hypothesis is that we must posit such a group of early Hebrew romances as lying behind the stories of the Exodus and the desert wanderings. This would explain the often picturesque phrases and elaborate detail; the very popular heaping up of wonders; the confusions and repetitions. It enables us to retain the broad historical event, guaranteed again and again by the Hebrew tradition; the outstanding historical figures; the essential reality of the spiritual fact. The imagination of the people, working on the known marvels of Egypt, would furnish the wild tangle of the rest. No one who has read far in these Arabic romances can miss the broad resemblance in method if not in events. That the result can often border upon history is true. Sometimes it is not easy in Arabic so to distinguish, and some Arabic romances have deceived European historians.

Our next type of Hebrew story is the fable. A fable, in the technical sense, is a short story in which animals and inanimate things talk and act like human beings and all to point a definite moral or general truth. Our best example is in the *Fables of Aesop* known to us from childhood. Does this type of story exist in the Old Testament? It does, but not as native to the Hebrews. In the extant Hebrew literature there are only two such fables and they are both tree-fables and associated with the Forest of Lebanon. They are part thus of the frequent allusions in Hebrew to that forest and are part also of the still more frequent allusions to trees and plants unknown to the desert. For the singular fact is that in the old Arabic literature—the literature of the desert—the fable in the technical sense did not exist. When an Arab speaker, or writer, of the old days, wished to point a moral and adorn it with a tale he had to use another quite different literary device. He quoted a proverb and then told the story of the origin of that proverb. In consequence there is in Arabic an immense literature of such proverbs and of wise sayings and moralizings, neatly expressed, extending sometimes to short paragraphs. Their substitute, then, for the fable was the anecdote illustrative of these moralizings and much like our after-dinner story. But it was never a fable in the technical sense. It is true that in later Arabic literature the fable appears, but it was always foreign and exotic; the desert did not take to it. It came into that later Arabic literature from two directions; from the Indian birth-stories of the Buddha transmitted through Persia, and from the animal stories of African mythology transmitted through Egypt. These last we all know from Uncle Remus and it is a curious illustration of story-transmission that the Egyptian recension of the *Arabian Nights* has one of the stories told by Uncle Remus to the little boy in Georgia. Out of Africa, it went, in one direction, through Egypt, to the whole Arabic-speaking world and, in another direction, in the hold of a slave-ship, it went across the Atlantic to America. As an Arab tribe, then, we may take it that the Hebrews knew nothing of the fable. It they must have found in Palestine. In consequence, one of the most singular things in the Book of Judges, which has gathered up so much primitive material, is what is called the Fable of Jotham; and it is a true fable in the technical sense. It runs thus in Judges ix, 7-15.

> And they told Jotham. And he went and stood on the summit of Mount Gerizim and lifted up his voice and cried out and said to them, "Hearken unto me, ye owners of Shechem, that God may hearken unto you. There went forth the Trees to anoint over them a King and they said to the Olive, 'Reign thou over us!' And the Olive said to them, 'Shall I give up my oily fruitfulness which gods and men honor in me and go to wave over the Trees?' And the Trees said to the Fig-tree, 'Come thou; reign over us!' And the Fig-tree said to them, 'Shall I give up my sweet good produce and go to wave over the Trees?' And the Trees said to the Vine, 'Come thou; reign over us!' And the Vine said to them, 'Shall I give up my new wine which rejoices gods and men

and go to wave over the Trees?' And the Trees said to the Thorn-bush, 'Come thou; reign over us!' And the Thorn-bush said to the Trees, 'If in sincerity ye are anointing me King over you, then enter and take refuge in my shadow; but if not [if ye are making jest of me] then may a Fire come out of the Thorn-bush and devour the Cedars of Lebanon!'" [May your jest turn to the destruction of all the Trees even the highest!]

It is quite plain that this story is not Jotham's invention but is a well known fable applied by him to the folly of the men of Shechem in making Abimelech King. Further it is of heathen origin; the references to gods and men show that. The only other fable in Hebrew literature is also one that is quoted, but in the shortest possible form, and is also connected with the trees of Lebanon. It is in 2 Kings xiv, 8, 9:

Then sent Amaziah messengers to Jehoash, the son of Jeho-ahaz, the son of Jehu, King of Israel, saying, "Come, let us look one another in the face!" And Jehoash, the King of Israel, sent to Amaziah, the King of Judah, saying, "The Thistle in Leba-non sent to the Cedar in Lebanon, saying, 'Give thy daughter to my son to wife!' And there passed by a wild beast in Lebanon and trod down the Thistle!"

Those are the only two cases in the Old Testament of the true fable. There is much use of imagery drawn from nature and espe-cially from the plant world. There the luxuriant plant life of Pales-tine made its mark on the Hebrews coming in from the desert. And there is often association in those plant-pictures with the Lebanon. For Ezekiel especially the Garden of Eden and the Trees of Jeho-vah were clearly associated with the cedars of Lebanon (xxxi, 3, 9, 16). And he extends this, in chapter xvii, to an almost apoca-lyptic image of the cedars in Lebanon and the great-winged eagle with feathers of many colors there. In Isaiah li, 3, Zion is to be made like Eden and like the Garden of Jehovah; and Israel is often a vine or a vineyard (Isaiah v, xxvii, 2; Psalm lxxx). In these pictures we have personification and exhortation, but never the free speech and action like human beings which is the mark of the fable.

We are driven, therefore, to conjecture in order to explain the phenomenon of the two fables which do occur. They are both tree-fables, connected with the Lebanon, and of heathen origin. Are they a survival from Canaanite literature and are we to posit that there existed among the Hebrews a book of Canaanite origin with some such title as "The Book of the Stories of the Trees of Lebanon"? The evidence suggests something of the kind and this would mean that there was a third primary source for the fable—besides Buddhist India and Africa—in northern Syria. This conjecture may have importance for the still unsolved problem of the origin of the Greek Aesop, the collection which we all know in one form or another. These Greek collections are all late and have, in Greek allusions, Egyptian associations. There is a tree-fable also in the Aramaic papyrus fragments found at Elephantine in Egypt and belonging to the fifth century B.C. Callimachus, an Alexandrian poet (about 310-235 B.C.) tells, as a Lydian story, of a dispute for superiority between the olive and the laurel, much like Jotham's fable. There appears to be no more evidence. But the existence among the Hebrews of tree-fables connected with the Lebanon stands fast and seems to be the solitary survival from the lost Canaanite literature which must have existed. It may be that recent finds in Syria, and finds still to be made, will add to this.

Our next class of stories is of still more markedly foreign origin. It is on the Persian side and consists of a group of four stories, closely linked up together, which have had fates almost the most diverse conceivable. They can also be roughly dated by the fact that fragments of one of them (The Story of Ahiqar) are on the papyrus scraps found at Elephantine and dated in the fifth century B.C. The dating of one gives a rough date of existence for them all. The four stories are: our Book of Esther; our Book of Tobit; the framework story of our *Arabian Nights*; the Story of Ahiqar. The Book of Esther got into the Palestinian Hebrew Canon; it is one of the Five Rolls in our Hebrew Bible. The Book of Tobit got into the Greek Canon, the Canon of Scripture for the Greek-speaking Jews, and hence into the Old Testament Canon of the Christian Church. We all know it, whether fully in that canon, as for the Roman Church, or in what we call the Apocrypha; it is a distinctly more moral tale than that of Esther and better told too. Tobit's Fish and Dog and the Demon Asmodeus are as good as anything in the *Nights*. The framework story of the *Arabian*

Nights we all know also; but its early history is still very obscure. It began apparently as a folklore tale in Farther India, where many forms still survive, worked its way west into Persia where it was transformed into a national Persian legend and associated with early Persian history and there took at least two forms. One turned into a Jewish nationalistic tale in our Book of Esther, and another, later, turned into the Persian original of the framework story of our *Nights*. Another somewhat different form of the original folklore tale is the framework story of another Arabic collection of stories, *The Hundred and One Nights*. The whole *nexus* is a very complicated bit of literary history and hardly belongs to our subject except as showing the non-Hebraic origin of our Book of Esther. The Hebrew of that book is very peculiar and suggests that it has been translated from some non-Semitic language—Persian, it may be. It evidently owes its place in the Hebrew Canon to its ferociously nationalistic character and to its association with the Feast of Purim. The history of the Story of Ahiqar is, if anything, even more curious. It existed, as we have seen, in Egyptian Aramaic in the fifth century B.C. and was read by the Jewish colony at Elephantine. The scraps of papyrus prove that; and it will be remembered that Aramaic was the official language of the western half of the Persian Empire. But Ahiqar was a friend of Tobit (i, 21; xiv, 10) and Tobit refers to his story. Thereafter the Story of Ahiqar went on its way and was translated into many languages of the Near East. Probably it began life in Persian and was translated into Aramaic and so spread. At present it is in popular circulation in Syria in an Arabic form and has even passed into some manuscripts of the *Arabian Nights*. Its persistent vitality and constant popularity are very remarkable for us with our literary point of view. There is very little story in it, and what it has is of treacherous political intrigue. The greater part of the book consists of sententious admonitions, in the style of our Book of Proverbs, addressed by the Sage Ahiqar to his worthless nephew, ending with that nephew's undignified demise. Finally, it may be said that the links of connection between those four great stories and their ultimate Persian origin are quite certain, but to trace them in detail would involve an amount of learned apparatus out of place here. Yet this is the one point where literature current amongst the Hebrews takes us out into the wide field of world literature. The Hebrew Old Testament is here found rubbing shoulders with Farther India, Persia, and the whole Arabic-speaking world.

We can now turn to the question raised at the very beginning of our consideration of the Story, the question as to the existence of true history among the Hebrews. That they were, by nature and by art, a story-telling people is abundantly clear. We have found among them all manner of stories, beginning with the almost untouched folklore tale. They developed the philosophical myth, the true artistic short story, the artistic use of the religious legend in different ways and for different ends and the historical romance. They adopted the fable and turned to their own purposes some very curious Persian stories. Unhappily the oldest layer of all, the most characteristic legends of their earliest days, has come to us only in strange transformations or in the most tattered fragments. A line or two of verse sticking in the national memory may be all that remains of a national crisis. And all those forms of the story have a deceptive air of taking themselves as true narratives of past events. So we have become accustomed to call collections of Hebrew legends, variously worked up by art for its own purposes, the Historical Books of the Old Testament. Even the later Hebrews had a truer feeling when they lumped them all together as Earlier and Later Prophets and as Writings.

We have already seen that the Book of Judges is constructed according to a rough philosophy of history. But a philosophy of history is not history, whatever some even of our modern historians may try to maintain, and the method of the Book of Judges is too suggestive of the still freer and infinitely more philosophical and artistic method of the writer who lies hidden behind our Genesis to be reckoned as historical. Yet we can be thankful to the compiler of Judges that, in spite of his ideas, he saved for us so much excellent old material.

Let us, then, having cleared those matters away, ask ourselves definitely, Did the Hebrews reach true history? That brings us to the further question, What is true history?—a question of no easy answer. We can say very decidedly what history is not. It is not stories about the past. If it were, every people would have reached history and any tribal narration would be an historical treatise. It is not inscriptions; or chronology; or genealogies; or religious prescriptions and rites. All these are the materials of history, what the historian uses in his work; but without his work there would be no history. The oriental peoples were strong in chronology and inscriptions, but until modern scholars used these there was no history of Egypt or Babylonia or Assyria. The Hebrews were weak in chronology and have left us strangely few inscriptions, perhaps by accidental causes, but, like all Arab tribes, they were strong in genealogies and stories of their past. The Greeks had their early epic stories in Homer and Hesiod; they had some genealogies linking them in absurdly few generations up to the gods, as the Egyptians told them; they were weak in chronology and in inscriptions. But they did reach the only true history and Herodotus shows us how it came about. Our word "history" is derived from a Greek verb used by him at the beginning of his *Histories* to describe how he learned by inquiry and investigation as he went about the world. "History," therefore, is by derivation "investigation" and, although our word "story" has been split off from it and used in a very different sense, "history" in the true sense, is still "investigation." It uses as its materials those elements given above and attempts by comparison and examination to reach the facts as to affairs of the past. Without such investigation there can be no history. Did the Hebrews reach this?

It will be observed that this is different from the attempt to impose an idea on the stories of the past and to see that idea there working itself out. That is to construct a philosophy of history before history itself has been reached, and is a fatal handicap on reaching the historical truth. In physical science we have the method of the provisional hypothesis which is often exceedingly useful and not dangerous so long as it can be tested by ascertained physical facts. But this method as applied to history has far greater dangers; it is so easy to pick out the facts which suit your hypothesis and ignore the others. So are built up our modern hypotheses of racial superiorities, and even so, it is too plain, the Hebrews fostered their racial pride.

We have already observed some of the ideas which the Hebrews, writing of their past, made dominant in that past. These ideas had all been working there, in the past, to one degree or another, but schools of Hebrew thought chose them, each its own, as its guide in the labyrinth of the past. One of the most important of these schools of thought was embodied in the prophetic guilds, commonly called the schools of the prophets. Amos has given us very exactly their philosophy of history and their point of view:

> But I destroyed the Amorite before them, whose height was like the height of cedars and he was strong as great trees; and I destroyed his fruit above and his roots below. I made you come up from the land of Egypt and made you go your way in the wilderness for forty years to enter into possession of the land of the Amorite. I set up some of your sons as Prophets and some of your choice young men as Nazirites—Was it not thus, O Sons of Israel?—Is the utterance of Jehovah. And ye gave the Nazirites wine to drink and upon the Prophets ye laid command, "Ye shall not prophesy" (Amos ii, 9-12).

This, for Amos, was the philosophy of the history of Israel in a nutshell. Jehovah had appointed two orders to keep his people in the right way and the people had persistently rejected both. It will be noticed that there is nothing here about the priesthood and the service of the altar. Amos apparently took it for granted as we, a generation or so ago, took for granted going to church; that belonged to ordinary life and living. But the two militant orders were the Prophets and the Nazirites. Contrast this position with that in the so-called historical books of the Hebrews. From 1 Samuel to 2 Kings there is not a single Nazirite mentioned; all the moral guidance and discipline of kings and people is in the hands of the Prophets. The one clear case of a Nazirite in Hebrew history is that of Samson in the Book of Judges, and in the other historical books the exercise of the Nazirite ideal belongs to the tribe of the Rechabites. It is based on obedience to the command of their ancestors and is not an order established by Jehovah. But Amos is perfectly clear on the equality of those two orders and he himself belonged, by direct commission, to that of the Prophets. The conclusion is unescapable that Hebrew history from 1 Samuel to 2 Kings has been written to the greater glory of the prophetic order and with complete suppression of the order of the Nazirites.

In Amos's time, and accepted by him as a normal institution and part of his life, there existed the priesthood and the service of the altar. It was corrupt as priesthoods always tend to become, but Amos accepted it. The contrary view is based on glaring mistranslation of the Hebrew. His case against the altar service was that the people were led to believe that they could propitiate Jehovah by increasing their offerings instead of by bringing to him, with the normal required offerings, pure obedience and true devotion of heart and mind. Later the service of the altar came to be central for the national life and its ideals, and the Hebrews reconstructed the philosophy of their history round the priesthood. This shows itself, of course, most markedly on the return from the exile. The Law became the palladium of Israel and, still later, we find the protective hedge of rabbinic precept constructed even round the Law. So all the history of the Hebrew past had to be remade from this point of view, and it is impossible to say how much the narratives from the past were affected in this reconstruction.

A third idea, and one apparently different from both of the above, was the racialism of the philosopher-artist of Genesis. That has already been developed above and it will be observed how completely it is a philosophy of history—sociological, psychological, nationalistic. It is history only in that modified sense.

Behind all these ideas there lies that fundamental and fixed idea of the Hebrews, the personality of Jehovah. That was no discovery of the prophets or invention of the priests; it lay in the innermost make-up of the Hebrew consciousness; it was taken for granted by them as simply as they took their own personalities. And we, looking now at the Hebrew phenomenon and miracle, can only accept it with the same simplicity.

These dominating ideas are all plain in the Hebrew record. But we have there, too, certain criticisms of these ideas in the Books of Job, of Ecclesiastes, and of Jonah, and in certain scattered fragments. As criticisms of philosophies of history, these will have to be considered as part of the philosophy of the Hebrews. But already it will be evident that the Hebrews never reached that history which is unbiased investigation; that when they wrote of the past with consciousness they were always dominated by some guiding or misleading hypothesis.

CHAPTER XI

THE HEBREWS AND THE WEIRD

INTO the above considerations of poetry and story certain general ideas have kept obtruding themselves and it will be well to deal with them separately and definitely. They are the relation of the Hebrew to the two worlds which he accepted: (i) the world of physical nature before his eyes and (ii) that generally unseen but equally real world of spirits which kept breaking in through the thin shell of custom and affecting his life. The Hebrew was very primitive, but in his relations to both those worlds he was also very modern and of our own near kin. He was both these things because he was a romantic.

The attitude of any people towards an accepted Unseen World can be viewed from several different points. For philosophy it is a part of their metaphysic; for mythology it is a part of their cosmology; for theology it connects with their doctrine of God; and for literature it is their feeling for the Weird. That last feeling is the essential of our present subject, but any investigation of it will of necessity lead us through the realms of philosophy, mythology, and theology. The instinctive shudder that goes with perception of the Weird cannot in the end be explained; it is a primary emotion. It is true that it exists far more strongly—for reasons developed below—in connection with a romantic attitude and civilization, and that it is indeed one of the marks of romanticism. But it is fundamental to all human nature, and so a recent school of theology has even tried to make it the basis for the whole religious attitude. But that is entirely to confuse the imagination of the poet with the perception of the mystic, and to find in Coleridge's *Kubla Khan* and the road to Xanadu the City of Zeus and the way thither. They are akin but not the same. The Hebrews of the Old Testament knew their kinship and were sure that the inspiration of the poet and of the prophet interlocked.

But for us, with our inbred feeling that there is some difference between the world of the Bible and the world of our human life, it will be well to grasp firmly and hold clearly that our present subject is that same human susceptibility to overwhelming emotion in response to a sudden in-breaking from an unknown and unknowable world which we feel, to take some widely differing examples, in the *Wandering Willie's Tale* of Walter Scott, in the first part of the *Inez de las Sierras* of Charles Nodier, and in *Das Majorat* of E. A. Hoffman. In essence, in all of them, there is the immediate confronting of our human minds and bodies by something outside and beyond our world of sense.

Why does this influence affect peculiarly the romantic mind and its environment? There can be little question of the fact. For a classical civilization and attitude clearness and system are essential; and that clearness is not only of this world but of the world also of gods and ghosts. The mapping of the world of the ancient Greek extended beyond the lands of men to the abodes of the gods and of the dead. The mountain of Olympus was real for them if inaccessible; the heaven of their gods was a measurable distance above. When Apollo rained his shafts of death on the Greek army before Troy they were seen falling and "terrible was the clang of his silver bow." When Odysseus went on his long voyage to consult Teiresias in the Land of the Dead, where the poplars grow by the pale of Proserpine, there is no clear break between the world of living men and that of the dead; his black ship was rowed with human arms across human seas until it crossed the River of Ocean and was beached on that shore of the Dead. And there, when he has dug his trench, there is no shudder of the unknown; his sword keeps the feeble ghosts at a distance. Even for Virgil, his pious Aeneas, guided by the golden bough, enters the regions of the dead by a cave in Latium and moves through humdrum shades, a prosaic narrative relieved only by the beauty of the Virgilian phrase. There is no touch of strangeness, of fearful novelty. The system and the scenes that picture it are clear and definite. There are ghost stories in Greek, and even in Latin, but they have no shudders. Almost the only supernatural shudder that the old Greek knew was that of the presence of Pan in the mountain solitudes, which gave us our word "panic."

But when we come later to Lucian and to Apuleius the change has begun. The East with its strange, exotic ideas has broken in upon the West and the old, clearly mapped, classical world is struck into fragments. The system has crumbled; its definiteness is gone; vagueness has arrived and terror with it. Lucian views it all as a materialistic sceptic, but he is evidently living in a world of ghost stories and spirit appearances. Apuleius is half under the spell of the new ideas and, as an artist, knows well the shudders into which they can be worked. So his *Golden Ass* is not only the first Latin book with a feeling for what we now call piety—very, very strange piety and most different from that of the pious Aeneas—but is also the first great collection of folklore stories in which the gods are not gods any longer. To put it in a word, new ideas, like the stone cut out without hands in Nebuchadnezzar's vision, have smitten the fair, clear structure of the classical system and it is fair and clear no more. A romantic world has taken its place, and the gods of Greece and Rome are in exile and are even transformed into the demons and spirits of the wilderness. A barrier has risen between the two worlds. Beyond that barrier is the Unknown but that Unknown sometimes and terribly strikes through and touches our lives. This was already the condition of the classical world when Christianity went out to give it peace. And its peace was that beyond the barrier was the Risen Christ sitting at the right hand of God the Father. So for the early Christians the Unseen was friendly and death had lost its terrors.

Another illustration of this arising of romanticism on the destruction of an ordered, clear, classical scheme, covering both worlds, might be found in the destruction of the Scandinavian mythology under the impact of Christianity. In that mythology all was clear and definite from the mountain of the gods, through middle earth to the very roots of the tree Ygdrasil, and the Norse warrior could fight his way, sword in hand, wherever his courage led him. Then came the change, and all that was left was a débris of mythological fragments settling down into popular superstitions. The gods became devils and Odin rides the night winds and their terrors.

All this is exactly parallel to the situation we find among the Hebrews of the Old Testament as we have it. Once there existed a fixed, Semitic, mythological system. Clear and precise, we know it in the Assyrian-Babylonian literature. It had heaven and hell and middle earth; a mountain of the gods; and an ordered existence for all. It had a mythological scheme of gods and goddesses, demons and devils. The paths that led all through this universe were clear and well trodden. How this was in the desert, among the Arab tribes, we do not know in anything like the same way. There are no records for them and the Arab, also, has never been religious-minded; he always, until Islam became patriotism for him, tended to materialistic doubt. But with the Hebrews came a great and unexplained change. So far as we can see it and put it, the conception of the personality of Jehovah in His uniqueness and reality smote the Semitic mythological system and destroyed it. What was left was the two worlds, the Seen and the Unseen, with a thin shell between them and a jumble of mythological débris which had in itself neither unity nor vitality and was used by the Hebrews only for purposes of poetry and picturesque ornament. They might depict Jehovah as coming in storm from a mountain; the lightnings might be His arrows and the rainbow His bow; they might speak of Him even as possessing a palace; but they were very careful to avoid any conception of a fixed abode for Him which could be called Heaven. Only the implicit absoluteness of His personality keeps the beginning of the One Hundred and Fourth Psalm from being an expression of Wordsworthian pantheism. In spite of these words used so often in our English versions there is neither Heaven nor Hell in the Old Testament. The great Mountain in the North survived but only as a poetical ornament. The Babylonian mythological sea-monster survived but only as a foreign word (Tehom) used for the great abyss of waters under the earth and for the watery chaos in Genesis i, 2. The mythological sea-serpent which rebelled against the gods, but was subdued by them is for Amos (ix, 3) a serpent in the depth of the sea which Jehovah commands. Most suggestive of all is the problem which existed for the Hebrews as to an abode for the dead. They had refused to give Jehovah a special dwelling-place for fear of mythological confusion; therefore they had no Heaven for the blessed dead. But there had come to them out of the Semitic past two broad and entirely different conceptions as to the condition of the dead. One belonged to the desert and may be called the solitary-grave conception. It is that which has survived as orthodox in Islam to this day. According to it when a dead man is buried in his grave it becomes his eternal house and he is there as a whole, not only his body but whatever we may think behind the words "soul," "spirit." His body decays but his identity survives and he knows. There is thus no spiritual world of the dead, but each abides eternally, and as a whole, in his own grave. The other conception connects with the Babylonian Kingdom of the Dead, corresponding, as nearly as could be, to the Greek Hades. There men had only a shadowy existence, lacking in all that belongs to true life and, above everything, removed from God's care and knowledge and the possibility of praising Him. The two conceptions are in origin and in essence entirely separate, but in the Hebrew mind they had become confused together and the terms Sheol, grave, pit, seem to be applied indiscriminately. But, if anything, the solitary-grave conception was the most immediate and real to the Hebrews because of their desert origin, and the conception of an underground Kingdom of the Dead belonged rather to mythology and poetry.

But the crisis came for them when devout souls faced the problem of their personal relation to Jehovah. For long, to all appearances, there was no problem; it was accepted that physical death was the end and no one dreamed of any continuance of any kind. So far as we can judge from David's extant fragments that was his position—exactly the position of the old Arabs before Mohammed. However closely David had been the friend of Jehovah in life, all that ceased with death and apparently there were no regrets. If there had been regrets, the change in Hebrew thinking which came later might have come for him. Very curiously, but again in close accordance with the Arab parallel, the Hebrews never seem to have thought, or guessed, that at death men might be taken over among the miscellaneous inhabitants of the Unseen World. The two kinds of intelligent beings, the Sons of Adam and the Sons of Elohim, were too different for that to be conceivable. So the desert Arabs while they accepted the possibility of sex-intercourse between men and Jinn—like that of the Daughters of Mankind and the Sons of Elohim in Genesis—never dreamt of men turning into Jinn at death. Yet there are at least two exceptional cases in the Old Testament. In Genesis v, 24, "And Enoch walked with God and could not be found [i.e. he vanished], for God took him." Into what existence did the Hebrews think he had thus entered, body and all? The other case is that of Elijah. The story of his passing in 2 Kings ii, should be read as a whole for its wealth of significant detail as to the Hebrew thinking about the prophets and the Unseen World. The culmination is in verse 11, "And it happened while they were going their way, going and talking, that behold a chariot of fire and horses of fire. And there came a division between the two of them and Elijah went up in whirlwind into the sky, in Elisha's sight, while he was crying out, 'My father, my father, the chariot of Israel and his horsemen!' and he saw him not again." We are left with the question as to how the old Hebrews pictured to themselves the future existence of Elijah. Judaism has thought of him as still journeying invisible in the world, endowed with strange powers and doing God's commands; as a spiritual guest for whom a place should always be kept. This may well have been the old Hebrew conception and is, as closely as could be, that of the world of Islam as to a similar immortal, invisible and ever helpful saint, al-Khadir.

These are manifest exceptions; these men had neither died nor were buried, and in their end there is no promise of future continuance, after death, for mankind in general. But it is plain that in the time of Ecclesiastes and even in that of the philosopher who created our Genesis, there had arisen a belief in a future spiritual existence of man which distinguished him from the lower animals. It was based on the "spirit" element in his created nature, but both Ecclesiastes and the philosopher of Genesis rejected the inference (Ecclesiastes iii, 18-22; Genesis iii, 19). Yet the theory existed in their time. Again the poet of Job, reaching out from the situation of his hero and spokesman, has a very strange and wild surmise. Job has reached the point of being well assured that he must die; his physical condition will not permit him to look for any possible recovery. And his view of existence in death is that of the solitary grave. Chapter xiv is deeply significant both for man's condition after death and for the wild hope rising in Job's mind. There is hope for a tree, even if it is cut down, that at the scent of water it may sprout again. Has this any analogy for man after he is laid away in the grave? "His sons may come to honor but he knows it not; they may be brought low but he distinguishes not as to them. Only his flesh, on him, is in pain; and his soul, within him, mourns." So is his condition in the grave; but is it conceivable that some change may come to him, as to the tree? That God may wait until His wrath is past; and may summon him forth from where he lies in darkness? Should He have a desire for the work of His hands and call, how gladly Job would answer. This renewal of life, then, would be a physical resurrection and a living again here on this earth. At the end of chapter xix a precisely similar hope is expressed. Would that, Job cries, his words were written; graven in rock as a perpetual remembrance! "For I know assuredly that my Deliverer [the avenger of blood and redeemer of family estates] lives and hereafter by the dust [of my grave] He will stand erect, and after this, my skin, is destroyed, then from my flesh I will behold God, whom I will behold for myself and mine eyes shall see, and not as any stranger." His own kindred may have cast Job off and none will take the blood-duty of deliverer on him. But in the end God will. He will bring Job up out of his grave and with his human, fleshly eyes Job will behold God and God will be no stranger to him. Nothing comes of this—for no theophany lay in the poet's plan—but it is the high-water mark of Job's re-approach to God.

In Ezekiel xxxvii there is the great vision of the Valley of Dry Bones and the point of it is much the same. The bones are the bones of the whole House of Israel; they are dry and Israel's hope is lost. "Therefore prophesy and say unto them, 'Thus said my Lord Jehovah, "Behold I am opening your graves and I will bring you up from your graves, my People, and I will bring you in unto the soil of Israel. And ye shall assuredly know that I am Jehovah when I open your graves and bring you up from your graves, My People. And I will put My Spirit in you and ye shall live" ' " (verses 12-14).

A very obscure passage in our Book of Isaiah xxvi, 12-19, seems to point to the same hope that the dead and buried may be raised up physically and live again in their own land. This may, of course, be only prophetic imagery for a restoration of the people to their own soil, but the picture shows that the idea of a physical resurrection existed. It developed naturally from the conception of the separate solitary grave as the eternal home of the dead man. It is a straw showing how the winds of hope and yearning were blowing, yet it is equally as far as the picture of the Semitic Hades from being a basis for a doctrine of spiritual immortality. But it did fit thereafter into apocalyptic visions of a new heaven and a new earth.

For any hope of spiritual immortality the Hebrews had to go back to their unique sense of immediate personal intercourse with Jehovah. How David should have missed this is very strange to us. He assuredly knew Jehovah, as we have seen, in the closest intimacy of reciprocal friendship, but the tradition of the desert that death was the end of all intimacies seems to have made even Jehovah a God only of the living and not of the dead. And David's position must have been tenable for very long. In a quite late Psalm, cxlvi, a devout soul teaches it explicitly. For him death ends all, "on that day his thoughts perish," and the psalmist is content with the constant providence of God in this life. But it is only in the Psalms that we meet the note of personal and spiritual exaltation which goes beyond the bar of death. In it there is no reasoning; there is only the deep assurance that the soul that has known God and been known by Him can never be separated from Him, even by death. There *must* be some way in which that communion will remain. Naturally the expressions of this, while assured, are obscure. But let the reader consider Psalm xvi, 7-11; xlix, 14, 15; lxxiii, 23-26, preferably in the Revised Version and remembering always that Sheol in such passages means simply the grave, and not the old Semitic Hades. This note of spiritual aspiration and this assurance of an unending communion with God were the beginning of our doctrine of immortality, spirit with spirit and far removed from the scene of our sorrow. The other conception of a restored physical existence here upon this earth ran its course and passed away in millennial apocalyptic dreams, Jewish and Christian. By this development the classical view of the universe—Heaven, Earth, Hades—of Semitic mythology, the Hebrew romantic conception of our earth and of a vague spirit world beyond, passed away into the presence, everywhere and for all, of a single completely spiritual Being and into His friendship and love for His children of the race of men.

So much it was necessary to say on this one aspect of the relation between the two worlds of the Hebrew. It has led us far away from the Weird—for there can be nothing strange or new or terrible in this abiding communion with God—and it has led us back to the personal Jehovah as Hebrew thinking always did. But Hebrew thinking, when it was not thus brought to the great leap of the mystic, was faced by the fact of its two impinging worlds and by the breaking in upon our commonplace life of portents from the Beyond. The spirit world, because it was so vague, could be very dreadful. And the vagueness was more than uncertainty as to the paths to it and from it. Except as to Jehovah, the spirit world of the Hebrews was severely impersonal. There were in it Elohim and Sons of Elohim, meaning individuals of that class. These are sometimes called "spirits" and sometimes "messengers"—in our versions "angels"—for Jehovah so uses them, but there is never among them an individual who can be called by a personal name. The farthest that identification reaches is the use of a descriptive epithet, "the messenger," "the adversary." This shrinking from personal identification may be illustrated from two curious passages. One of them is in Judges xiii, the account of the promise to Manoah and his wife of the birth of Samson. Manoah (verse 17) says to the Messenger of Jehovah who has brought the message but whom he does not know to be a spirit messenger, "What is thy name? When thy word comes to pass we would honor thee." And the Messenger of Jehovah replies, "Why dost thou ask about my name, seeing it is a mystery?" And the sacrifice which follows is accordingly offered to "Jehovah who works mysteriously." Jehovah not only does wonderful things but He does them through mysterious agencies. The other passage is in the story of the Blessing of Jacob in Genesis xxxii. The member of the Elohim who wrestles there with Jacob is called at first only "a man," meaning "a person," "an individual," but later it appears that he belongs to the spirit world. Jacob (verse 30) asks him, "Tell, pray, thy name," and he replies in exactly the same words as to Manoah, "Why dost thou ask about my name? And he blessed him there." But though his name is here also withheld it is not said that it is a mystery. This attitude, it may perhaps be well to notice, is different from that of Herodotus where he shrinks (ii, 170) from naming Osiris. That shrinking in him was due to a really religious awe and reverence. But the Hebrew attitude was rather akin to that of the Pelasgians of whom Herodotus tells (ii, 52), who spoke of gods but did not give them names. It was still closer akin to that of the old Arabs of the desert. These had their spirit world of the Jinn but the Jinn were a class, not differentiated into personalities. The tribal gods of the desert Arabs, on the other hand, were personal and had local sanctuaries and names. That they had worshipers and were personified seems to have been the great difference between them and the vague mass of the Jinn. The analogy here to the separateness of Jehovah is very close. And Amos, as we have seen, went even further and seems to have left in his spirit world only one Being, Jehovah Himself. The only approach, even, to the beginning of a personality apart from Jehovah in His court is that singular figure, the Satan, the official Adversary, or prosecuting attorney for Jehovah. We have seen him going about his business in the beginning of the Book of Job. He appears again in Zechariah iii, doing his duty against Joshua, the high priest. Opposing him and defending Joshua is a vague Messenger of Jehovah, who is at one time called that and at another called Jehovah Himself; so Jehovah and His Messenger melt into one another. But the Satan because of his office has acquired a certain permanent distinctness. His personality continued hardening until in the New Testament we have Satan repeatedly as a proper name. But that he was an accuser in the presence of God still stood firm. In that singular passage, Revelation xii, 7-12, he is "the Accuser of our brethren . . . who accuseth them before our God day and night"; he is also for the Book of Revelation the Great Dragon of the Prophets (e.g. Ezekiel xxix, 3; Isaiah xxvii, 1) and the Old Serpent of the Genesis story. In our Bible this is the one identification of the Serpent who tempted Eve with the Devil. The overthrower here is the Archangel Michael whose cross is still erected by the Roman Church in its cemeteries as a symbol of his guardianship of the believing dead against Satan; cf. further Jude 9, along with Zechariah iii, 2. But in our Old Testament angels with names do not occur until we reach the apocalyptic part of the Book of Daniel written between 167 and 165 B.C. There we have angels as the guardian spirits of kingdoms and Gabriel (viii, 16; ix, 21) and Michael (x, 13, 21; xii, 1) contending in behalf of Israel. But all that is utterly un-Hebraic; the only approach to it is in the four chariots of Zechariah's vision (vi) which are "the four spirits of the heavens going forth from

THE HEBREWS AND THE WEIRD

standing by the Lord of the earth." There is grandeur in the picture of the control thus exercised by Jehovah in all the earth; but, still, these have no names. The complicated angelology and demonology of later Judaism was not developed from the spirit world of the Hebrews but imposed upon it. We return, then, to some illustrations of its vague terror.

One of these we have already seen in the story of how the Witch of Endor evoked the ghost of Samuel (1 Samuel xxviii). As a straight ghost story it could hardly be better told, and Charles Lamb has left on record the effect which it produced on his childish mind. It is reduced to the utmost simplicity and in that is its strength. "And the woman said unto Saul, 'Elohim did I see coming up from the earth.'" She means that through the beaten clay floor of her house something ascended from the spirit world. "And he said to her, 'What is his form?' and she said, 'An old man is coming up and he is covered over with a mantle.'" That was enough for Saul; he recognized the familiar figure of the aged Samuel with his mantle drawn over his head. For us, in trying to reach the Hebrew feeling for the Weird, the significant thing here is that the world of spirits is in immediate contact with our world of sense. There is no journey between; space does not exist; spirit and its world are as close to us as our own bodies. The only touch left of physical relation is that the ghost comes up; but folklore ghosts always do. "Why has thou brought me up," says Samuel, "disquieting me?"—literally, "making me quiver." But the story is evidently cut to the bone. With the appearance of Samuel, something told the woman that it was Saul himself who had come to seek her aid. Like a modern "medium" she was prepared to summon any spirit from the vasty deep, but like a modern "medium," too, she gained knowledge with their coming. Yet it is possible that something has dropped out at that point just as it is probable that Samuel's message has been expanded. He is too loquacious for a true ghost.

Another spirit appearance is described by Eliphaz to Job (iv, 12*ff.*). It is led up to, very skilfully and delicately, with nuances of Hebrew expression which are hard to render:

> But unto me a word was given stolen-wise, and my ear took a murmur from it, as thoughts come from visions of the night when

deep sleep falls on men. Fear befell me and quivering and all my bones it made to fear. Then a spirit before my face was passing, while the hair of my body began to stir. It was standing still but I could not distinguish its appearance; a form was over against my eyes; a quiet sound I was hearing: "Can a man be more just than God or even a strong man more pure than his maker? Lo, he puts no trust in his servants and to his messengers he ascribes folly. How much less the dwellers in houses of clay whose foundation is in the dust; crushed more quickly than a moth, from morning to evening they are being cut off, and none regards; for ever they perish."

This is an entirely different kind of spirit from that which came to Saul. Eliphaz suggests that he, like a prophet, has had his revelation and describes how it came and the effect upon himself of this touch of contact with the spirit world. But he does not venture to say, "Thus said Jehovah"; an unnamed spirit from the world of spirits speaks. That is where the terror of the Weird comes in. When Jehovah speaks to His prophet there may be fear in His presence, but not this quiver which makes the hair bristle and rise.

Still another such nameless manifestation is in the sacrifice which sealed Jehovah's covenant with Abram (Genesis xv). Apparently in a conventional sacrifice the parties to the covenant passed between the severed pieces of the sacrifice as a sign of confirmation. In this case the parties to the covenant are Jehovah and Abram and the confirmation must be in darkness that Jehovah's manifestation may be seen. Abram has divided the animals of the sacrifice and laid them, each part over against the other. Then he waited, waked and watched. "And the birds of prey came down upon the carcasses, but Abram drove them away. And it happened when the sun was about to set that a deep sleep had fallen upon Abram, and lo, a horror, a great darkness, was falling upon him. . . . And it happened when the sun had set that thick darkness came on and lo, a smoking furnace and a fiery torch which passed between the pieces." Thus the covenant was ratified by this manifestation of Jehovah in fire and smoke to Abram. The story has probably suffered some interpolation of pious phrases, but a unique element has survived in it from its folklore origin. In the Old Testament there are several manifestations of Jehovah by fire: at Elijah's sacrifice on Carmel and otherwise in Elijah's life; at Solomon's dedication of the Temple as told by the chronicler (2 Chronicles vii, 1); the fiery column of the nights in the desert; many times in thunder and lightning. But in this, as with Eliphaz, the nerve of the supernatural is touched; the horror of human flesh in contact with the Unseen is shown; and a great darkness falls on Abram that is not due to any setting of the sun. So, some Hebrew thought, must be the unseen background and reality in any such covenantal sacrifice. In singular contrast with this quiver before the Unseen is the calm detail of even so strange a story as that of Manoah's sacrifice in Judges xiii. Manoah feared, but it was only death that he feared.

The picture of Apollo raining from a clear sky his arrows of death on the Trojan camp has been cited above as an example of the immediacy and clarity with which the supernatural entered life for the Greeks. With it may be contrasted in the Old Testament, 2 Kings xix, 3-5, what was a precisely similar situation, pestilence falling on the camp of a besieging army. But the Hebrew puts it differently. First there is Isaiah's prophecy of deliverance; then: "And it came in that night that the Messenger of Jehovah went forth and smote in the camp of Assyria one hundred and eighty and five thousand, and when men rose early in the morning, behold they were all dead corpses." For the Hebrew it was a blow out of darkness, in darkness, sudden and unexplained; the Unseen World had reached out and smitten our world of sense. But the Greek must have his picture and see the shafts fall and Apollo dealing them and hear the clang of his bow; his world of gods was clearly joined with the world of men.

But the best example of all is in the great story in Daniel v of Belshazzar's feast and of the doom pronounced on him. The whole story should be read for the consummate art with which it is told from the beginning, "Belshazzar the King made a great feast" to the inevitable end, "In that night was Belshazzar the King of the Chaldeans slain." Was there ever in history a Chaldean King Belshazzar? There are grave doubts. But there are no doubts that his story belongs to great literature and in it he lives and will live for ever, even as his Queen prayed for him. Why has the story so tremendous an effect? In part it is the art with which it is developed, but, above all, it is the mystery and terror of the handwriting on the wall. "In the same hour came forth fingers of a man's hand, and they were writing, over against the candlestick, upon the plaster of the wall of the King's palace; but the King was seeing only the part of the hand that was writing . . . and the God in whose hand thy breath is and whose are all thy ways hast thou not glorified. Then from before Him was sent the part of the hand, and this writing was written." It was the fingers only that came, but the writing remained—and remains. There is no other writing on any wall that has had such effect as this. And its working is that the sudden immediate contact with the Unseen suggests such vast, untold and untellable possibilities. Gazing with Belshazzar at that wall we are also standing "silent upon a peak" as Cortes in Keats's great sonnet, with all the ocean of the Unseen before us. It is the silent form that teases us out of thought; it is the unheard melody that is sweetest of all. And the untold mysteries of the Unseen brought thus in momentary dignity before us have more effect upon us than the plastic beauty of detail in the Greek world. For us, as romantics, a touch on that nerve is all we need.

CHAPTER XII

THE HEBREWS AND NATURE

THE Hebrew attitude to the world of nature—that world before their physical eyes—was like their attitude to the world of spirits in that their philosophy, theology, cosmography, mingled almost inextricably with their esthetic perception, appreciation and reaction. The fundamental ideas which made up the background of their minds were always present, as help or hindrance, when they looked out on the manifold, multitudinous world spread out before them. And those fundamental ideas were sure to culminate, sooner or later, in the overwhelming personality of Jehovah.

That personality meets us at once when we use the word "nature" in relation to the Hebrews. We have personified Nature and have moved from the *rerum natura* of Lucretius to the *natura benigna* and *natura maligna* of our modern poets. For us, it is now quite simple to look out over natural scenes and think of a personality behind them, a personality that lurks in the life of the joyous earth or in the death of icy peaks and stormy winds. We hardly remember that behind our thinking there lies a long development from some one divinity in a polytheistic system who personified this ever renewing life—the "life-giving earth" of the Greeks, the *alma Venus* of the Romans, "Mother Earth" of the Teutonic peoples. But such a beginning to a development was impossible for the Hebrews who had definitely cut themselves off from the conception of different divinities with different attributes and associations. For them, Jehovah filled the whole background of life in all its phases. We have already seen that the philosopher of Genesis had reached the conception of an order of nature which could be trusted and which was as certain as the return of day and night. But that order was imposed upon the earth by the will of Jehovah and assured by His sanction. It is true that there survive in the Hebrew Bible two or three isolated expressions which seem to point to an earlier personification of an energy in natural things. But these are so purely verbal that they have vanished under the stress of transformation into English. In Amos iv, 7, "and the piece whereupon it rained not withered" is literally "whereupon she rained not." It seems certain that these, like some of our own phrases about weather, are mere verbal survivals and meant nothing to the Hebrews who used them. It may be taken, then, as certain that personified Nature for the Hebrew did not exist. This saved him the trouble of much modern speculation as to the reality of this Nature, by which we are esthetically affected. Can we through the esthetic effects upon us of Nature reach knowledge of the reality of Nature, or do we only excite certain neural effects in ourselves which do not correspond to any external reality? Is there any truth in that which has been called the Pathetic Fallacy, that Nature is affected by our sorrow and responds in comfort to us? Is there any real anodyne administered by Nature or do we ourselves quiet ourselves and lift ourselves out of ourselves by the mere sight of Nature's beautiful but remorseless and unchanging course? The Hebrew would have been much amused and somewhat irritated. "It is Jehovah; He comes as He comes and He does as He does!"

That assuredly being so, what of man in this complex of the world and Jehovah? We have already seen that the Hebrews had at least two opinions as to man's place in the world. One of these— that the world was created as the habitat for man—was worked out in detail by the philosopher of Genesis. For him man was the measure of all things and all things led up to man. But this is essentially a philosophical reflection and could only have arisen as the result of long and conscious thought. The attitude of the masses of the Hebrews, hardly a conscious one, was probably quite different. For them there was the world and Jehovah behind it and they probably stopped at that. Even philosophers sometimes have difficulty in realizing that they themselves are part of the picture at which they are looking and which they are trying to analyze and understand. And it was not only the unthinking masses who were content to look at the world as simply God's creation, created by Him for His own pleasure and in which man was only a part, if sometimes an obtrusive and self-assertive part. Both poets and philosophers loved to think of the world as God's vast toy, spread out before Him and in which He, like a child, took His delight.

That is made very plain in Psalm civ. Psalm ciii gives the relation of God and man and has strange echoes in it of the Genesis story; the Psalmist devoutly loves and trusts and adds human pathos to the physical tragedy of man's life. In his love and trust he is different from the severe self-repression of the philosopher of Genesis, content to register the evident facts. And he is still more different from Ecclesiastes who has neither love nor trust, and accepts only because he must. To Psalm ciii, Psalm civ was evidently added in order to give the relation of God to the whole world and to leave out entirely the troublesome problem of the life and destiny of conscious, self-responsible man. It is a view of creation the opposite of that in Genesis.

Bless Thou, O all my Being, Jehovah! Jehovah, my God, Thou art very great; with glory and majesty Thou art clothed. Covering Himself with light as with a garment; stretching out the sky like a curtain. He that lays in the waters the beams of His roof-chambers; He that setteth the clouds as His chariot; He that goes His way on the wings of the wind; making His messengers of winds, His ministers of the fire of a flamer. He set the earth on its foundations; it cannot be moved for ever and ever. The Abyss like a garment Thou didst spread upon it; over the mountains the waters were standing. From Thy rebuke they were fleeing; from the sound of Thy thunder they were quivering away—while the mountains were rising, the valleys sinking—unto the place which Thou didst set for them. A bound Thou didst place; they cannot pass beyond; they cannot return to cover the earth.

He that sendeth forth water-springs in the valleys; between the mountains they go their way; they give drink to all the wild things of the field; the wild asses quench their thirst. The trees of Jehovah are satisfied; the cedars of Lebanon which He planted; where the birds make their nests; for the stork the fir trees are her house. On them the birds of the sky dwell; from amongst the foliage they sing.

Watering the mountains from His roof-chambers; from the fruit of Thy work the earth is satisfied. Causing green grass to sprout for beasts and herbage for the service of man; to bring out food from the earth. Wine which rejoices the heart of man;

to make his face shine from oil; and bread which props the heart of man.

The high mountains are for the wild goats; the craggy peaks are a refuge for the wild rock-badgers.

He made the moon for appointed times; the sun knows well his place of setting. Shouldest Thou put darkness, then night comes; in it all the wild things of the thicket swarm; the young lions are roaring for their prey and to seek their food from God. The sun scatters its rays; they are gathered together; and unto their abiding places they go and couch; while man goes out to his doing and to his labor until evening.

How many are Thy works, Jehovah! All of them with wisdom Thou hast wrought; the earth is full of Thy making. There is the sea, great and wide; there are the swarming things without number; living things, little with great. There the ships go their way; yonder Leviathan whom Thou didst form to sport with him. All of them hope unto Thee, to give them their food in its time. Thou givest to them; they gather it; Thou openest Thy hand; they are sated with good. Thou hidest Thy face; they are troubled; Thou gatherest in their spirit; they expire; and unto their dust they return. Thou sendest forth Thy spirit; they are formed; and Thou renewest the face of the soil.

The glory of Jehovah be forever; Jehovah rejoices in His works. He that looks at the earth and it trembles; touches the mountains and they smoke. I will sing to Jehovah while I live; I will make music to my God while I yet am. Sweet in Him is my meditation; I will rejoice in Jehovah. Bless Thou, O all my Being, Jehovah.

It will be noticed how small a part in this picture is played by man. He is intentionally minimized; and the strange reference to the ships seems to be meant to parallel and surpass them with Leviathan. But if man is only a small part of it all he yet is needed, in the person of the psalmist, to praise Jehovah and rejoice in Him. Man is nature's priest and voices the response that the dumb creation cannot render. Jehovah is glad in all the multitudinous hosts of the earth, and man is glad in Jehovah. The "spirit" in the living creation is their vital principle; it is sent out by Jehovah and again gathered in by Him. For Jehovah Leviathan is a peculiar plaything; that great creature exists only for God Himself. But with all His creatures Jehovah is in close relationship; they are immediately dependent on Him for food and for breath. He is even pictured as a child looking out over the earth as a great toy before Him and touching it here and there. This is to make vivid His joy in it all. The wealth of loving detail in the natural descriptions and the exactitude of the words used also stand out. There is in them, too, that greater wonder of creative imagination which carries us beyond the words into vistas of memories and of pictures. With the picture of the river among the hills we are carried on to "Yarrow, a river bare that glides the dark hills under." But it will be noticed that the Hebrew picture has neither "bare" nor "dark." Hebrew has no real adjectives and does very well without them. It has only nouns which are like epithets, names, that is, which carry descriptives in them. With these it makes its pictures—concrete, direct.

For the poet, then, Jehovah was a person looking at the earth before Him. But He was also very strangely a part of the structure of the earth, and that not simply by His sympathy with it and liking for it. In the early verses certain aspects of the universe are made a veil for Jehovah. The light that fills all the interspace of earth and heaven is a garment which covers Him who is Light of Light; through the clouds, the winds, the heavenly fires, He works His works and goes His way. If He were similarly behind and in the hills and rivers we would have the pantheism of Wordsworth. But that has not yet fully come.

In Job xxxviii-xli we read the answer of an unknown poet to the poet of the Colloquies. The poet of the Colloquies, speaking through the mouth of Job, had taken it for granted that man was the head and end of creation; that the world existed for him and that all things should work together for his good; also that righteousness and justice should be the outcome of all things in the world. That, if there was unmerited suffering in the world, the maker and ruler of the world was responsible and to blame. But if man were simply an insignificant part of the world, and if the world did not exist for man but solely for the pleasure of God, then the ground would be greatly cut from under Job's feet. To bring that view of the world home is the object of the poet who wrote the speeches of the Lord to Job. He is not greatly concerned with Job's accusations of moral slackness against the Ruler of the World. He would have been quite prepared to accept the alternative in Plato's *Euthyphro* that a thing is right because Zeus does it. And he was the unconscious ancestor of that school of Muslim theology which explicitly held that abstract right and wrong depended on the will of Allah. But the question simply did not exist for him any more than it does for so many mystics. His point was that Job thought a great deal too much about himself; that he and all mankind were a quite insignificant part of the great world and that God had a perfect right to do with him what He pleased. So an elaborate picture of that great world is painted and held up to Job. How small must Job feel himself as he looks at it; how incapable of taking a part in directing it and in reforming its abuses! But our present subject is not the calm impudence, or at least, moral blindness of this—which suggests most to us Boss Tweed's "What are you going to do about it?"—our subject is the picture of nature and of the interest, liking and care of God for all the natural world, animate and inanimate. And from that picture man is carefully excluded. It ranges from the morning stars of creation, singing together, to the rain falling in the wild places where no man is and causing the green grass to sprout and spring, but not for man. Then there are the pictures of all the creatures of God which live their lives by themselves out in the wilds: the lions, the wild goats, the hinds, the wild ass; the wild ox, the ostrich, the hawk, and the eagle. It is unnecessary to retranslate all this; it is admirably done, with some few inevitable blunders in the natural history in the King James Version. Further, the little vignettes of pictures—and the delight of this artist in them—can be paralleled again and again in the poems of the old poets of the desert. These poets, like the Hebrew poets, were, in this, modern and romantic. For the classical poets animals were either for use or for toys. But there was one thing that these old Arab poets did not have and that was the Lord Himself. They described what they saw and did it very beautifully; but there was nothing behind their pictures except the external mountains and the desert wilderness. For the Hebrew, these pictures were always combined with God or with man. Over them brooded the seeing eye and the perpetual care of God, or through them the yearnings of man looked up to God. In the one case man might be completely excluded or regarded as an intrusive and hostile figure; in the other case there were present the three abiding elements which made up existence for the Hebrew—God, man, and the world.

It will be observed that the references to man in these speeches of the Lord are always as to a discordant and disturbing element in life. Let man keep his hand off his fellow-creatures or it will be the worse for him; even the horse can rise against his rider. This, of course, is partly a speaking to his brief by the poet and is directed against Job and his poet. But it voices a deeper and more universal feeling; that man *has* disturbed the peace of Nature and is outlawed by Nature. That Nature can do very well without man and would like to be let alone. In this respect these speeches are entirely different in spirit from the One Hundred and Fourth Psalm and man here is not in the slightest Nature's priest. Rather, we are at the beginning—if it is the beginning—of that glorifying of the physical operations of Nature and of the non-human animal life of the world which culminated in the savage satire of Swift's Gulliver among the Houyhnhnms. For our modern poets it is purely physical and nakedly natural, but for the Hebrew it had of necessity to be under the eye and fostered by the care of Jehovah. This, on its different sides, is one of the most singular aspects of the relation of the Hebrew to Nature. Nor is it isolated here. It will be remembered how the philosopher of Genesis elaborately includes all living things in the covenant which seals the order of nature. And how Jehovah in the Book of Jonah concludes His rebuke of Jonah with, "and also much cattle." And how repeatedly in Joel (i, 18, 20; ii, 22) the beasts of the field groan and suffer with man; cry out to Jehovah with man; and are of good courage because the pastures of the wilderness spring again. There is a similar feeling for wild life in Ecclesiastes ix, 12, where man, knowing not when his fate will fall upon him, is compared to "fish taken in an evil net" and to "birds caught in a snare." It is true that there is not separation in those passages between man and the beasts of the field, but the beasts are full copartners with man in the life and perils of the world. They may be the toys of God, but they are never, for the Hebrew, the toys of man. The Old Testament does not know anything like the cats of the Greek anthology or the sparrow of Lesbia.

Again, some, at least, of the Hebrews came to have yet another way of looking at this threefold combination of God, man, and nature, a way of looking in which God was lifted so high above everything else that He was pictured as solitary on a single peak looking out on a plain of lowness and prostration. The Jehovah who delights in the beauty of the earth with all its differences of life is gone, and a Jehovah has appeared whose sole characteristics are separateness and loftiness. This, to all appearance, was one of the effects on Hebrew imaginative thinking which were wrought by the Exile with its contact with elaborate worship of divine images in lofty buildings. Amos had not been disturbed by the Calves which represented Jehovah at Bethel; they were of no importance to him. But the Hebrews in the Exile, face to face everywhere with worship of multitudinous images which did not represent Jehovah, seem to have been stung to a kind of madness on the whole question of idols and became the iconoclasts, which we so commonly think them. The change, too, from the hills and valleys of Palestine to the Mesopotamian plain had its effect on their minds. So Ezekiel in the midst of that plain, was haunted by the thought of the mountains of Israel (vi; xxxiv, 13, 14; xxxvi, 1*ff.*). In that *omnium gatherum* of prophetic fragments which we know as the Book of Isaiah there are several expressions of the iconoclastic fury. But one passage combines it most curiously with the feeling for the plain and for the solitary figure confronting and dominating it. It is a fragment in Isaiah ii, 10-22, and comes immediately after a context, real or accidental, describing a land filled with idols and men prostrating themselves to them. There are some imperfect refrains in it which suggest that it is part of a longer poem.

> Enter thou into the rock and hide thyself in the dust from before the fear of Jehovah and from His glorious loftiness. The high eyes of man are low, and bowed down is that exaltation of men, and Jehovah alone shall be lifted up in that day. For Jehovah of Hosts has a day against everything lofty and high and against everything lifted up; and it shall be low. And against all the lofty and uplifted cedars of Lebanon; and against all the oaks of

Bashan; and against all the lofty mountains and against all the uplifted hills; and against every high tower; and against every guarded wall; and against all the ships of Tarshish; and against all pleasant sights. And the height of Man shall be bowed down, and low shall be the exaltation of men, and Jehovah alone shall be lifted up in that day. And the idols shall utterly pass away and men shall enter into the caves of the rocks and into the hollows of the dust from before the fear of Jehovah and from His glorious loftiness, when He arises to confront the earth. In that day shall man cast away to the moles and bats his silver idols and his golden idols, which he made to bow himself down thereto, to go into the holes of the rocks and the cracks of the crags from before the fear of Jehovah and from His glorious loftiness, when He arises to confront the earth. Cease ye from man in whose nostrils is wind. At how little is such as he to be reckoned?

In this fragment the resources of the language are strained to produce synonyms enough to express loftiness and lowness. For the whole point is that Jehovah, "high and lifted up" in the phrase of the Isaiah of Jerusalem (vi, 1), confronts the whole earth, spread before Him in uniform lowness. This is far on the way to the absolute separateness of the Muslim Allah and even to that awful scene in Muslim eschatology where Allah, on the Day of Resurrection, high and lifted up on his throne, confronts the throngs of those arisen from their graves, standing, standing, standing on a vast plain before him. Hence the scene is called *al-Mawqif,* "The Standing." This is an absolutely different conception of the relation of God and his world from that of the philosopher of Genesis, or that of the poet of the One Hundred and Fourth Psalm, or that of the poet of the speeches of the Lord in Job. This is the work of a half-mad theologian, driven by the dominance of a single idea to the picturing of a half-mad deity.

Let us look at this again from another point of view; not of God over against nature, but of man looking at nature. When we look at a landscape spread before us we do so, probably, in one or other of two ways. We think of it in connection with human life and interests, as a setting for man. Because of this many of us feel that a picture should contain something linking it with our own life, if it is only a trodden path on a hillside or a bit of wreckage on a storm-beaten shore. But for others, Nature—and here we begin to personify—is a mighty mystery and exists for her own sake. She may be beneficent to man, a fostering mother; or she may be malignant, a brooding fate; or she may be indifferent alike to our joy and tears; but she is apart and no one has lifted her veil. There is much of this feeling of the impenetrability of Nature to man in those speeches of the Lord in Job. Whatever we may think of their moral attitude they are the work of a very great poet and thinker and they have many sides. But when the Hebrew looked at nature, however keenly he might see it and however closely the beauty might come home to him, his mind always passed beyond, for whatever he saw spoke to him of Jehovah. Everything belonged to Jehovah; almost was Jehovah. David—if it is David—in the roar of the waters of the wild north country, longing for the peaceful streams and pastures of the south, cries out, "Deep is calling unto deep in the sound of thy cataracts; all thy breakers and rollers have passed over me!" (Psalm xlii, 7) and these very resounding waters, "blowing their trumpets from the steep," are Jehovah's. He is looking at these waters; their roar is in his ears; their spray is drenching him. But his emotion carries him beyond to Jehovah whose they are, and in the subjectivity of his imagination he transforms them. It is his emotion which he sings to us—his emotion and all it carries and means—and the scene before him is only incidental imagery. And so too always. When the Psalmist (cxxi, 1) lifts up his eyes to the hills, perhaps the long, straight range of the mountains of Moab which walls that eastern sky, he goes beyond them to the help which their stubborn, abiding strength images and which comes from Jehovah. For the old Arab poet, "still against time abide Tiyar and Yaramram [mountains of the desert] and the stars marching on all night in procession," but they brought to him only the feeling of the abiding, unchanging world and of the fleeting life of man. To the Psalmist the mountains meant Jehovah and his assured help. And the Psalmist never stopped to analyze what this assurance meant. He was no theorist and to him such terms as pantheism and immanence would have meant nothing. He was on the way to the Wordsworthian pantheism, if he had not reached it; but Jehovah was also a person whom he knew and trusted. The world was very nearly the Face of God to him, but many centuries were to pass before Mohammed, whose Allah was as much a person as Jehovah, could say, "Wherever ye turn there is the Face of Allah." We would say that Nature was instinct with divinity; which is only another phrase.

Again, in all Old Testament descriptions of nature it should be noticed how simple is the diction. As was said above, Hebrew has no adjectives in our sense; it has only nouns which involve descriptive ideas. We say "wise," "good"; Hebrew can only say "a wise man," "a good man" or "thing." In consequence all description is direct and concrete. The sea is the sea; and that is all. There are several words for different kinds of clouds, dust clouds, rain clouds, morning clouds, but each word involves "cloud." This makes any translation which tries to give all that is in the Hebrew, difficult and elaborate, and so the translation may contrast unhappily with the simplicity of the Hebrew. Free recasting is often necessary and in the King James Version has sometimes a singular felicity. But with that simplicity there is often combined a curious subtlety of allusion. A touch of description may make us see pictures, as so often in Virgil, "all the charm of all the Muses often flowering in a lonely word." And, above all, there is nowhere description for its own sake. All description comes in of necessity, woven, as it were, in spots of color into the fabric of emotion or thought. This economy in description is like that of the artists of the classical world and is not at all modern. The elaborate natural descriptions of some of our modern novelists, pages long and apparently written, as one of them indeed has confessed, for their own sake and not even as a necessary background to the story, would have been impossible for the Hebrew. The nearest we have are the descriptions in Job, and they, too, are meant as an argument. They may be elaborate pictures, but they are pictures with a purpose.

There is yet another significant phase of the Hebrew mind face to face with nature. However long he may have been settled in Palestine as a tiller of the soil, he never acquired the eyes of the peasant who sees only the things about his feet and in a narrow range round him. He retained the far-reaching eyes of his Bedawi ancestors, fixed on the horizon, looking to distant things. His position on the ridge of the Judean uplands, facing the desert, the sea, the height of Carmel and the peak of Hermon, the lofty plain of Bashan and the mountain range of Moab, must undoubtedly have helped him to see far. But he had the inherited eyes to use that position. Amos, coming from his sheep and sycamore-fig trees, could still stand up and look round the horizon at all the encircling peoples, pointing to each, and denouncing each. In this he is in singular contrast to Robert Burns, otherwise very close to him, called from the plough and given a message in song. Burns passed his life on the uplands of Ayrshire which look across the sea to the peaks of Arran against the western sky. One of the great views in Scotland is sunset over those peaks, and Burns must have seen it most of the days of his life. But he did not see it; he never lifted up his eyes to those hills and that sky. There is no single allusion to that view in all his poems. His eyes were the eyes of a peasant fixed on the glebe at his feet and the farthest he could see was along a moorland road. This contrast carries far; for the Hebrew mind, like the Hebrew eyes, looked to distant things and to a heavenly horizon.

CHAPTER XIII

THE PHILOSOPHY OF THE HEBREWS

WE COME now to a more systematic consideration of the philosophy of the Hebrews. Such a study is made difficult by the prevailing prejudice that the Hebrews had no philosophy—that the Hebrew mind was essentially unphilosophical—and the whole subject is further obscured by a myth which has been built up that, instead of philosophy, the Hebrews had something called Wisdom which is expressed in a part of their literature commonly called the Wisdom Literature.

How baseless is the prejudice as to the essentially unphilosophical nature of the Hebrew mind has been shown again and again above. The artist who reconstructed for us our Book of Genesis and made it what we have was one of the great philosophers of the world. He looked at the fundamental institutes of human life, tried to see them as they exactly were and then explained them in their bearing on the conduct of life. The relation of man to the world, of man to the lower animals, of man to woman, of man to the scheme of nature, of man to the apparatus of life and living, and the whole deep, pathetic mystery of the continuity of the human race and its existence of necessary toil, from the dust and to the dust—"from the great deep to the great deep he goes"—all that he had faced objectively with clear vision. He had faced, too, with the keenest psychological insight the characteristics of his own race as they showed themselves in Abraham and the succeeding generations. He saw, too, his race as it faced the world and its manifest destiny in the world and all the philosophy of human history which was therein involved. And we have seen, too, how when he turned in Exodus to illumine the conception of the nature of Jehovah Himself he knew, as well as any Greek, the difference between a philosophy of abstract "being" and a philosophy of concrete, living, developing "becoming"—that things are in a perpetual flux and that Jehovah Himself is in that flux. We have seen how the whole temper of the Hebrew mind in its attitude to the world was Platonic and not Aristotelian, an essentially philosophical distinction. We have seen, too, in the homely philosophy of the Wise Woman of Tekoah the fundamental Hebrew mind facing and stating the pathos of the short human existence in the hand of Jehovah—"we are as water spilt on the ground, and, yet, doth God devise means." We have seen in the Book of Jonah and in the Story of Balaam the results of straight thinking about a situation and a universalizing of it, until it becomes a rule for life and a clue through the mysteries of existence. All that is true philosophy and Plato would have known these Hebrews as his spiritual kin.

Yet in all these passages there never occurs that mysterious word, Wisdom; these thinkers were philosophers and never knew it. For what is philosophy in its ultimate analysis? Is it not thinking, as clearly and rationally as we can, about all the sides of life as we know it; about ourselves and this world in which we find ourselves, our relation to it, our knowledge of it, along with our own whence and whither? Is it not, in a word, the application of our reason to life? There will come from this rational investigation certain results, schemes of existence, mental and physical, systems of psychology and ethics and ultimate being and becoming. These will lead to further questionings and even ultimate uncertainties. But it will all be under the rule of the power of the mind which we call Reason; that will be the permanent and characteristic element. There will also be positions which will be accepted as certain and axiomatic, to prove which no attempt will be made, for they are the bases of all things. Every philosophy has such a system of accepted bases; even a system of scepticism knows that it is sceptical.

For the Hebrew there were three such accepted bases: God, in the personality of Jehovah; man, the thinking percipient; and the world, the physical universe which surrounds and conditions man. In a sense the Hebrew could have no metaphysic for he was absolutely certain that behind this physical universe in which man exists was an ultimate personality, Jehovah, the maker and ruler of the universe, and that beyond Jehovah there was nothing. But on another side the Hebrew could have a metaphysic. Jehovah was his metaphysic and his metaphysical problems dealt with the nature of

Jehovah. The absolute certainty about Him was that He was a person, with all the marks of personality; He was no impersonal force or fate, although in His actions and their motives He might often be inscrutable. But was He, in character, good, bad or indifferent to both? And was His reason and thinking like the reason and thinking of man or something entirely different? These were possible and ultimate questions, and Hebrew philosophy had to thresh them out. Second, as for man, Jehovah was his maker and to a great extent controlled him through His rule of the world; the life and thinking of man were mysteriously connected with the life and thinking of Jehovah. But the Hebrew was also absolutely certain that man, mentally and morally, was free. He could choose for himself and his choice could anger and irritate Jehovah. It was true that he was very largely controlled by his physical environment; on that side he was part of the material universe and controlled as such by Jehovah. But, on another hand, no Hebrew sceptic ever doubted that he possessed the power to choose for himself between two alternatives; that he had what we call roughly free will. As to that, no Hebrew was a fatalist or even determinist. And, further, all Hebrew thinkers accepted that man had a clean-cut conception of the two ideas, right and wrong, good and bad, and knew that this thing, or action, was the one, and that that thing, or action, was the other. All Hebrew sceptics even were sure that these categories corresponded to an ultimate reality, but, most paradoxically, some of them doubted the existence of these categories in Jehovah, maker of all and ruler of all as He was. This logical contradiction was a most curious and interesting blind spot in Hebrew thinking. There will be more upon it hereafter. Third, the physical universe is an abiding, objective, reality. The generations of men come and go, but it stands fast, so long as the sun and moon endure means forever. It may be in the toil of perpetual change; the seasons, the winds, the waters, all in their ceaseless tasks; but it itself abides. It is real and concrete and no phantasmagoria of thought, divine or human. We are told that it was shaped and made by Jehovah in words that imply a material something out of which it was made. Only exceptionally, are words used that imply a fresh bringing into existence, as of light in the First Creation Story. And only exceptionally, in the language of ecstatic devotion, are words used which imply any unreality in the physical world as over against the absolute reality of the personality of Jehovah. The conception developed into dogma by the Muslim theologians, and even found in the Koran, that God is the only absolute reality and that the physical world, His creation, beside Him is unreal, may be present in germ in some utterances of the Old Testament but was not part of the Hebrew philosophical thinking. These three things, then, all Hebrew thinkers accepted as self-evident and as needing neither proof nor even statement.

As has been said above, the consideration of Hebrew philosophy has been greatly obscured by the creation of a myth that instead of philosophy the Hebrews had something called Wisdom which was of a more theological and religious character than any human philosophy worked out by applying reason to life. The English word wisdom occurs very many times in our translations of certain books of the Old Testament—Proverbs, Ecclesiastes, Job—and a certain number of times elsewhere. Words from the same Hebrew root—wise men, wise man or woman—in multifarious applications also occur. But behind all these there lies one Hebrew root, and behind wisdom there is always one Hebrew word, *hochmá*. This word the Hebrews used to indicate two ideas which for us are very different. It was their word for reason, that power in man by which he thinks things out—"reasons them out," we say. This is a part of man's nature as a created being and has nothing in it theological or religious. It may be, of course, applied to theology or religion. Theology, in fact, is largely reasoned out religion. But the other thing for which this word *hochmá* was used is exactly what we call wisdom, the ripened fruit of experience and reason. It is more than knowledge and different from reason; "knowledge comes but wisdom lingers" and even rationality is often very far from wise. Let the English reader read in Proverbs or Ecclesiastes or Job and pause at every occurrence of the word "wisdom." Let him experiment putting "reason" in its place—or some cognate word, "rational," "rationality," to suit the construction and he will see how often the meaning flashes out in new reality. Often, too, he will find that he has to retain the word wisdom: that it is that curious combination of ripened experience and conscious thinking which is meant. The two meanings of the word *hochmá* will thus become assured to him.

But what lies beyond the Hebrew word itself? It is plain from usages of the same root in Arabic that the idea behind it is that of something which controls, directs, rules, guides. That is, the Hebrew primarily thought of reason on that practical, governing side. So we have it applied to arts and crafts—the skilled mind and the trained hand. Ezekiel (xxvii, 8, 9) uses it of the pilots and shipbuilders of Tyre and (xxviii, 3, 4) of the business men of Tyre. Jeremiah (x, 9) uses it of goldsmiths and their work. It is used of technically trained and skilled women in Exodus xxxv, 25, and of women who are trained lamenters in Jeremiah ix, 16. What exactly was the art or skill or training of the "wise women" in attendance on the Mother of Sisera in the Song of Deborah (Judges v, 29) is obscure. They may have been the ladies in control of her household or they may have been magically skilled as the magicians at the Egyptian court (Genesis xli, 8; Exodus vii, 11) where the word is the same, only masculine. The precise meaning, also, in the case of "the wise woman" of Tekoah (2 Samuel xiv, 1-5, 14) and of her of Abel (2 Samuel xx, 16 *ff.*) is obscure. A Hebrew village evidently could contain a woman who, for some endowment, had attained a local reputation which led to her advice being sought and taken. She may have been a woman of strong mind and dominating personality—such the East has always known—or she may have possessed some occult powers such as to gain her the respect rather than the fear or dislike of her fellow villagers. These local wise women were evidently quite different from such illicit practitioners as the Witch of Endor. In all such cases, however, some form or other of this Hebrew word was used.

It will be noticed that women had their full share in it and that it could be used in very practical ways. The art of life, in the widest sense, was the material in which it worked and its workmen and workwomen had to be skilled in all that belongs to life. But this need not tie down the user of this reason to simply material things. All material things, all art, all skill of hand, heart and mind, led for the Hebrew back to Jehovah and to the question, What part had *He* in it?

As far as regards the practical art of living and of making a success of life the answer was simple enough. Almost all our Book of Proverbs is occupied in answering this question and in a way, on its premises, most simple and logical. That book is a compilation into which everything seems to have been thrown that the editors could find bearing on that point of success in life. It is a late compilation, for the arrangement of the separate elements which make it up is somewhat different in the Greek translation from that in the Hebrew; when the Greek translation was made the compilation had not yet a fixed order. It consists partly of paragraphs of exhortation, written in rather ornate and artistic prose (chapters i-ix). The writer—or writers—was half an artist who enjoyed using words and half a moralist with a distinct didactic purpose. Arabic literature has many little books of exactly the same kind and combination of objects and interests. Partly, it consists of collections of proverbs, some of which may be real popular proverbs, but many are evidently of artificial origin. Arabic literature, again, has parallels to both of these kinds. Chapters xxx and xxxi are of a more miscellaneous character. The first few verses of xxx are evidently sceptical; we shall return to them. The rest of the chapter shows often a bitter and sardonic humor different from the general tone of the book. But the purpose otherwise of the book is unmistakable and could almost be thrown into the form of a syllogism. Jehovah is good; Jehovah is in complete control of the world; therefore if you are good you will be successful in life. That is the background and the burden of the exhortations throughout. The point is repeated so skilfully, so frequently, with such complete assurance, that the general impression of certainty is tremendous. There is no shadow of doubt in the minds of the different authors—admittedly there were many—as to the moral goodness of Jehovah and as to the completeness of His control of the world. This must have represented the philosophical position of a great body of the Hebrew people. It is philosophical because it is reasoned throughout and driven home by argument, almost, one might say, by dialectic. And it furnishes a philosophical basis for life which is not in the least to be despised. Once grant its premises and it can amply take care of itself. And that basis for life touches the widest extremes. In one extreme it is almost repulsive, because it is so much a doctrine of worldly success; goodness is to be pursued because it leads to success. It does not say only, "Be good and you will be happy," but "Be good and you will be successful." It goes farther than "Honesty is the best policy," because it draws into worldly prosperity ideal goodness itself. That is the one extreme. The other in its development and application lies at the root of our Christian creed.

Throughout the whole book the conception of reason—wisdom in our version—is ever brooding in the background. It is to the reason of man that the appeal is made and from time to time it is Reason that makes the appeal. Reason addresses men individually as "My Son" or collectively as "My Sons." And thus enters the higher, the more ideal extreme of the teaching of the book. This means at the least that the whole material world is instinct with reason; that the world is rational and that man by the use of his reason can put himself in harmony with nature and thus, at one with the whole structure of things, live happily and securely. But the conception goes much further than this, which might be a merely rhetorical personifying of the reason that is in all things speaking to man. Behind the world is Jehovah, its maker and ruler, therefore the Reason which speaks to man in Jehovah's creation must have some relation to Jehovah and to His conceptions—His thoughts.

Can man think the thoughts of God? Is human reason of the same kind as the divine reason or has God kept the ultimate, ideal reason for Himself and given to man only some practical guide sufficient for his daily life? Is philosophy really possible or must man content himself with the fear of Jehovah and turning from evil? On this the Hebrews were of a divided mind. The most complete denial to man of any power to reach absolute reason is in a little poem which stands as the twenty-eighth chapter of Job, but which has no relation at all to the argument of the Book of Job. Its subject is, Can man reach reason? There is an elaborate description of all the hidden treasures which man can find in the earth and draw forth from it with a refrain, "But Reason, whence is it found?" Finally there comes a summing up of the whole situation and of the relation between God, Reason, and Man.

But Reason, whence does it enter and where is the place of Understanding [power of distinguishing]? It is covered from the eyes of all living and from the birds of the sky it is hidden. Only Destruction and Death say, "With our ears have we heard something of it." It is God who has distinguished its way and He knows its place. For He looks to the ends of the earth; under all the Sky He sees, to give to the Wind a weight and the Waters He adjusts with a measure. When He made for the Rain a limit and a way for the Thunderbolt, then He saw it and reckoned it; He established it and also searched it out. But He said to mankind, "Lo, the Fear of Jehovah is Reason and turning from evil is Understanding."

This little poem shows the philosophical thinking of the Hebrews struggling towards a synthesis of their old reference of everything to the will of Jehovah and the questioning which their own meditation upon themselves had raised. They were acute psychologists with an especially ethical interest, if they were not thoroughgoing metaphysicians. But their self-analysis had led them to the fact that they had in them a power, reason, which was a power of distinguishing. The philosopher of Genesis had called it "knowing good and evil." Was this reason absolute? Was it the supreme guide in life and could they apply it to everything, including Jehovah Himself? What was its relation to that fear of Jehovah which their fathers had accepted as the supreme guide? They knew very well what the searching and acquiring powers of man were; physically there was no limit to them. Could man search and acquire *beyond* the physical world? But beyond the physical world there was only Jehovah. Whence, then, was this reason and distinguishing ability of which they were conscious? And so, with that strange personifying power of the Hebrew imagination, which never reached true drama, for that is action, they conceived Reason as one of the entities in the universe and worked out a relation between it and Jehovah and themselves. It is a strange relation because it implies that Reason is something outside of Jehovah. He found it in the universe when He was setting all things in order and giving each its place, measure and weight. So He did with it; He counted it over, established its nature and investigated it thoroughly. Hence Jehovah knows all about Reason—this absolute, metaphysical entity, before all worlds—and He has kept it for Himself. Man must be content to draw his guidance from the old doctrine of the fear of Jehovah and from a conscious turning from evil. Is this irony or true pious submission? The Hebrews, like all Semites, were very capable of both.

But, irony or not, it raises the inevitable question of the relation of the fear of Jehovah to reason as rival guides in life. In how many ways is that phrase "the fear of Jehovah" used and how many emotions did it represent and excite? It plainly goes back to the very roots of the relation between Israel and Jehovah. It is Jehovah revealing himself in the Mount and putting His fear on all the people. The prophets have no part in the picture; this is Israel face to face with its God. There is no intermediary; no need of a "Thus said Jehovah"; the facts of life are plain and the commands of Jehovah are known. Each man knows all this of himself and must work it out for himself in the guidance of his own soul and what powers of reason he has. For the philosophy of the Hebrews was psychological, individual, personal. Even at its most sceptical it was that curious mixture of crass common sense and devout intuition which we know best in Quakerism. We shall see immediately, even in our hard-headed Book of Proverbs, how that relation of the soul of man to the reason of God was working itself out.

But, to return, how did that soul of man react to the fear of Jehovah? We have seen already the severe self-repression of the philosopher of Genesis towards a God who could not be called attractive but who must be accepted as He is and who can fairly be trusted. We shall see in Ecclesiastes an explicit acceptance because there is nothing else that man can do; but in his case there is neither love nor trust. But contrast Psalm i and Psalm ciii as to their devotional attitudes; they mark absolute extremes of possibility. Psalm i is exactly in the tone of those hortatory little paragraphs which open the Book of Proverbs. The author must have regarded himself as a devout person; he certainly feared Jehovah and delighted in His Law. But his whole attitude is so logical as to be businesslike. Be good and you will prosper; be wicked and you will be destroyed; the Lord will see to both. The pathos of human life which even Genesis recognizes has never reached him.

Life for him is one thing or the other—open or shut. But Psalm ciii is full of the physical tragedy of man's life. Its author knew well the inevitable tears of human things. The blessing in it, too, is for those that fear Jehovah, but how different is the fear! And how often the mercy and pity of Jehovah is felt and told! From generation unto generation He remembers for good, He forgives and helps. If man's days are as grass that the wind passes over and it is gone and gone forever, yet the Lord with His love abides and it will be well with the generations as they follow, each the other. The whole relation of God and man is sublimated through affection, devotion, and trust.

And through it all the well worn phrase, "the fear of Jehovah" is on its trial. The One Hundred and Third Psalm is a valiant and quite successful effort to relate that fear to the kindness and love of Jehovah. What, then, of its relation to the ultimate test of this reason which, in one way or another, is in both God and man? That was the problem which the Hebrew philosopher, when he was devout, had to face. These two things were his guides in life; Godly fear and reason both existed for him; they had both to be accepted and must be brought together. In consequence there arose a supposedly healing and uniting phrase which was ambiguous in more ways than one. In Psalm cxi, 10, stands, "The beginning of Reason is the fear of Jehovah." But "beginning" here may mean also "principal part." The fear of Jehovah is either the starting point or the sum and substance of reason. If reason cuts itself loose from that fear it has neither basis nor reality. This allows reason an existence but subordinates it to the fear of Jehovah. In Proverbs ix, 10, this is put without ambiguity. "The beginning [another word with no double meaning] of reason is the fear of Jehovah and knowledge of the Holy One is understanding." This is absolute. All reason and all understanding—that is, power of distinguishing and realizing—are in the fear of Jehovah and in knowledge about Him or derived from Him. It is almost a way of saying, If you do not fear Jehovah and do not know Him and His teaching you are not a rational being. And many Hebrews evidently liked this way of putting it for in Proverbs i, 7, we read, "The fear of Jehovah is the beginning [or, sum] of knowledge; reason and discipline only fools [the word means exactly pig-headed, self-conceited fools] despise." But others felt that this was much too absolute and that reason existed for itself. This is the point of Proverbs iv, 1-9, with its emphasis upon, Get reason, be rational and understand (verse 5). And it culminates in a direct challenge of contrast in verse 7, "The beginning [or, the sum] of reason is 'Get reason'; and in all thy getting get understanding." Evidently for the Hebrews the point was a burning one and even the devout could look at the matter in two ways. While as for the undevout, and not all Hebrews were devout, it gave occasion for a frankly agnostic attitude as to our knowledge of Jehovah. There was no doubt as to the existence of Jehovah; the evidently created world was a proof of that. But what could we know about Him? He was outside of reason and inaccessible in His heavens. This is expressed ironically in Proverbs xxx, 1-4, a fragment worded as a parody of a prophetic oracle of the oldest type, as those of Balaam:

I have wearied myself, O God, I have wearied myself, O God, and can no more. For I am too brutish to be a man and the understanding of human kind is not mine. I have not learned reason and the knowledge of the Holy One how can I know? Who was it went up to the heavens and came down? Who gathered the wind in His two hands? Who tied up the waters in a mantle? Who established all the ends of the earth? What is His name and what is His son's name—so that thou [anyone] shouldest know it?

This ironical fragment quotes and ridicules the commonplaces of devout faith. The description of God's working is exactly like those with which Job's friends sought to crush him and may be a literal quotation. What of it, this sceptic asks, and how do you know all that? That there is a person behind the world we may accept, but what more do you know about Him? And as for the reason which must begin in His fear and as to "the knowledge of the Holy One"—a literal quotation—this sceptic can make nothing of it. Evidently he, the sceptic, must be a mere brute beast! Such echoes and answers this famous phrase had found.

But there was yet another way of bringing together Jehovah and reason and one which had nothing essentially to do with the fear of Jehovah. Hebrew rhetoric loved to personify and its personification could easily be theologically hypostatized into actual and separate personalities. We have seen in Job xxviii how the Lord "found" Reason in the universe, examined it thoroughly and kept it for Himself. In English we have to say "it" but the Hebrew word is feminine and so for the Hebrews Reason was "she." This merely grammatical detail that Hebrew has no neuter undoubtedly helped the Hebrews in their personifications. In consequence we find again and again in the Book of Proverbs Reason speaking like a kind of Minerva or Athene, a goddess of wisdom. As such she addresses men as "My Son" or "My Sons." There are passages where it is hard to say whether it is some mere human teacher or this ideal Reason who speaks. But there can be no doubt as to Proverbs i, 20 *ff*. and viii and ix; in these the ascription is precise. And in all these what may be called the *mise en scène* is the same. Reason appears speaking and addressing whoever will listen to her. Wherever men congregate or pass on their way she is there, whether in the field or the town, trying to attract their attention. The universality of her presence and her eager desire to instruct are the characteristic marks of this representation of personified Reason. She addresses men as her sons; all her being goes out to the human race, to seek it, to capture its attention, to teach it and guide it in the right way. Her attitude is full of yearning, full of love and desire towards those wandering children of hers. Yet indifference and rejection may provoke her to scornful laughter to the hiding of her face even when, in repentance, they seek her again (i, 24-28). In another representation (chapter viii) Reason is less easily provoked; she rejoices in the habitable earth and has delight in the sons of humankind. And in yet another (chapter ix) this Reason offers education and training in her house which she has built for herself with its seven pillars—an allusion apparently to some sevenfold scheme of schooling, a trivium and quadrivium combined. As to that we know nothing. There had even grown up a contrasting picture of a personified Folly, trying similarly to attract men (ix, 13 *ff*.).

From all this it is plain how the picture of Reason, speaking to men in and through the world, had attracted Hebrew thinkers and became for them an expression of a rational and practical creed. Again, here, there is no allusion to possible guidance and instruction through prophetic ecstasies; that is ignored. The revelation in the Mount is minimized; all that is left of it is the assurance of the reality of Jehovah behind everything. These philosophers were convinced theists, but they were developing their theism in the light of the revelation which the world itself brought. This was an analogy of religion which they were trying to work out. And the teachings of nature were voiced by that same Reason who had been with Jehovah in the beginning and with whose aid He had framed the universe. That Reason was now in the universe and was always speaking through the universe; in the world of men by the hedgerows and in the country paths, in the city streets and squares and gateways. On the one hand this Reason belongs to Jehovah; on the other it is in the world beside each one of us. The world is instinct and clamant with the divine spirit of Reason. And men can hear, understand, and accept the guidance of this Reason. This Reason is intelligible to men because men are her children and product. The Reason by whom God made the world is the Reason in whose light men walk in the world. So these thinkers bridged the gulf between the absolute Reason of God and the conditioned Reason of man. And so, too, they swept away all difficulty as to the relation between the fear of Jehovah with its demand of unconditional obedience and man's intellectual faculties and their claims upon him.

In all this there is another illustration of the fragmentary nature of Hebrew literature. In that literature we have no systematic treatise on Hebrew philosophy. In the Book of Ecclesiastes there is the nearest approach to a systematic statement, but it is still more a contribution to the literature of self-revelation. In Job we have a jumble of attempts at the solution of a single problem, that of unmerited suffering. And here, in this Book of Proverbs we have all kinds of fragments, thrown together with little attempt at arrangement, surviving fragments from the intellectual life of the Hebrews pursued through many generations. With patience and some imaginative reconstruction—following the analogies of developments of thought elsewhere—we can see certain dominant ideas which rose amongst them and how these must have been related to one another. But we must beware of trying, out of such remains, to construct a definite and dated history of Hebrew philosophy. Some Hebrews at some time or other thought such and such things and lived therein their intellectual life. Thus this idea of the divine Reason speaking to men in the very structure of the world came to some of them and was worked out by them in these three surviving pictures (Proverbs i, 20 ff., viii, and ix). Probably to it all there was a much vaster background of thought which we have lost, but these at least have been saved for us.

Because of its future importance and influence on the theological thought of the world it will be well to give a translation in full of the longest of these, in chapter viii. It is the key to the Fourth Gospel and the key, too, on another side, to a dominant conception in the theology of Islam. It links up with Butler's *Analogy*, with Wordsworthian pantheism and with the inner light of the mystics of all lands and ages, the divine Spirit that lighteth every man.

> Doth not Reason cry out and Understanding utter her voice? At the head of the heights, beside the road, between the paths, she has taken her stand. At the side of the gates, at the issue of the city, at the entry of the gateways she crieth out shrilly. "Unto you, O Men, do I cry out and my voice is directed to the sons of human kind. Understand ye, O simple ones, shrewdness and, O stupid ones, mind!
>
> "Hear ye, for splendid things do I speak and the very opening of my lips is sincere. For trustworthiness doth my mouth murmur and the abomination of my lips is wickedness. In loyalty are all the words of my mouth; in them there is nothing tortuous or crooked. They are all straightforward to him that understandeth and straight up and down to the finders of knowledge.
>
> "Take ye, then, my discipline rather than silver and knowledge rather than refined gold. For better is Reason than strings of jewels and there are no desirable things equal to it. For I, Reason, dwell with Shrewdness and knowing schemes do I find out. The fear of Jehovah is hating evil; so, too, do I hate pride and haughtiness with evil conduct and blatant perversities.
>
> "Mine is counsel with effectiveness; I am understanding; mine is strength. It is by me that kings execute their office and worthy judges render true decisions. By me princes do their part and nobles—all the judges of the earth.
>
> "I love them that love me and those who seek me diligently shall surely find me. Wealth and honor are with me—possessions abiding and true. Better is my fruit than gold—fine gold; and my increase than refined silver. In a loyal way I go on steadily through

just paths, to put those that love me in possession of substance; and their treasure-houses do I fill.

"It was Jehovah Himself who got me as a possession at the beginning of His course, before His works of old. From eternity was I enthroned—from the beginning—from the antecedents of the earth. When there were no abysses was I begotten, when there were no fountains, heavy with water. When the mountains had not yet been moulded with a stamp; before the hills was I begotten. When He had not yet made the earth and the spaces beyond and the sum of the particles of the inhabited world. When He established the sky, there was I; when He inscribed its circuit on the surface of the abyss; when He made firm the vault above, in hardening the water-springs of the abyss; when He set for the sea its mark and the waters shall not pass over its edge; when He thus enscribed the foundations of the earth. Then was I beside Him as a skilled workman and I was in delight, day by day, laughing before Him for every occasion, laughing for His inhabited world and my delight was in the sons of human kind.

"So, now, Sons, listen to me, and oh, the happiness of those, who keep my ways! Listen to discipline; be wise and reject it not. Oh, the happiness of the man who watches at my doors, day by day, while he listens to me; who guards, as it were, the posts of my doorways. For he who finds me finds Life and receives good favor from Jehovah. But he who misses me does violence to his own self; all those that hate me love Death."

In so far as Reason here is described as a separate possession of Jehovah we seem to have the same situation as at the end of Job xxviii. But really the situation is very different, for this Reason is a separate personality from Jehovah, was with Him in all his acts of creation, rejoicing in them all and especially in the achievement of the inhabited world, in the creation of man. Because of her part in it all, these sons of humankind are her sons and she rejoices over them and yearns towards them, seeking to draw them to herself. With her, listening to her, they will find happiness and life, but whoever of them for any cause fails to come to her does violence to his own self and goes to death. This is no Reason that Jehovah has kept to Himself, but an eternal being that was with Him before the world was and who now through the very structure of the world seeks to reach men, to teach them and give them the true, abiding life.

As we read those verses do there not rise before us others in the New Testament, in the Prologue to the Fourth Gospel? Read "Reason" there instead of "Word" and the first fourteen verses of that Prologue are in substance verses 22-36 of this chapter in Proverbs. It is unnecessary to reiterate that the Greek word Logos is as much Reason as Word; our English word "logic" is evidence for that. Nor need we try to unite the two meanings by calling, with Coleridge, the Logos "the communicative reason." Simply read that Prologue, putting "Reason" for "Word" and see how it looks! "In the beginning was Reason and Reason was with God and Reason was God. The same was in the beginning with God. All things were made by Him and without Him was not anything made that hath been made. In Him was life and the life was the light of men." Then there come verses on John, the Witness, and on the relation of this light to men. "There was the true light, that lighteth every man, coming into the world. He was in the world, and the world was made by Him and the world knew Him not. He came unto His own. . . . And Reason became flesh and dwelt among us and we beheld His glory . . . the only begotten of the Father."

What is there here that is not in Proverbs? Four things especially: "In the beginning" carries us to the first verse of the Book of Genesis and "the light of men" carries us to that first divine act in Genesis, the creation of light, the absolute entity light, not the light produced by any luminary of sun or moon or stars. And, third, this Reason is masculine, as is the word "logos," and is the only begotten son of the Father. Yet of that conception "begetting" we have a trace in verse 24 of Proverbs, "when there were no abysses was I begotten." And, fourth, and this is the great historical movement forward of the Gospel revelation, "And Reason became flesh and dwelt among us and we beheld. . . ." This Reason, who through all the ages since the Creation had spoken to all men through that Creation, was now incarnate and visible in the human form of Jesus of Nazareth, and the words that He speaks are the words of that divine Reason so now incarnate.

Between chapter viii of the Book of Proverbs and the Fourth Gospel there lie centuries of philosophical development. We know nothing as to the process of that development, but we can see in

Proverbs, combined with the first verses of Genesis, the germinal ideas from which that Gospel and especially its Prologue sprang. The old explanation that the Christian Logos had connection with the Logos of Philo is now generally abandoned; they are essentially different in nature. Any connection of the Christian Logos with the later Jewish Memrá is equally impossible and for the same reason. The Memrá was the authoritative utterance of Jehovah, as in the recurring phrase, "Thus said Jehovah," and not the divine Reason, planning the world and then speaking through the world in rational appeal to men. The conception of a special sonship of this divine Reason must have developed in the gropings of those unknown centuries of thinking. Is it possible that in the words of the sceptic (Proverbs xxx, 4) "What is his name and what is his son's name?" there has survived an allusion to one of those early guesses?

The Fourth Gospel itself lies outside the scope of this book but the philosophy of the Hebrews in its whole range lies within that scope and the culmination of one phase of that philosophy lies in the Fourth Gospel. Apply, then, this key to the problem of the difference between that Gospel and the other three. Read the words of Christ in it as the utterances in space and time and through lips of flesh of that hypostatized divine Reason, who from all time has spoken to men through and in the structure of the created world—the Reason who had wrought creatively therein. The strangest and most difficult of these words of Christ assume meaning and reality at once. "No one cometh unto the Father but by Me" (xiv, 6) is true of the inner light of the mystic and of that inner light only. "Other sheep I have which are not of this fold" (x, 16); only the light that lighteth every man has those uncovenanted folds scattered among the peoples and through the ages. "In My Father's house are many mansions" (xiv, 2); are these many mansions for the different "folds"? "The glory which I had with Thee before the world was" (xvii, 5); "For Thou lovest Me before the foundation of the world" (xvii, 24). And reiterated throughout the whole book there is the sending of Jesus from the Father with the gift of eternal life which is the knowledge of God and of Him whom He did send, and of the return of Jesus to the Father with His commission accomplished. It is only necessary to read through the Gospel and, page by page, its words fall into place. For the author and for his community—whoever these were —the Prologue expressed clearly the fundamental conception of the Christ which was later to be developed in the book. For this is not simply a life of Jesus but a constructive theory of the meaning of His life. Is it, then, a philosophical theory imposed arbitrarily on the life and figure of Jesus and are His utterances most skilfully and artistically forged to uphold that theory? Or is it the work of a follower who understood more fully those true utterances of his Master, who realized the meaning in them and from them built up his picture? For Luke and Matthew also have utterances which are exactly in the tone of those supposed to be peculiar to the Fourth Gospel. Compare Luke xi, 49 and its parallel in Matthew xxiii, 34-36; Luke x, 21, 22 and the parallel in Matthew xi, 25, 27. These are in what is supposed to be the unassailable kernel of the Gospel tradition. Consider, also, the cases we possess of different biographies of the one man. How different these are simply because the biographers and their governing ideas were different. Yet they are each pictures of the same historical figure. It is possible, therefore, to hold that the writer of the Fourth Gospel was the last for us in the line of development of that phase of Hebrew philosophical thought which we have found in Proverbs and Genesis; that he worked out his life of Christ in full honesty of intention; and that we may take it as one of the possible interpretations of that life by a man who had himself known the Master. For, however late may have been the reducing of the whole to its present form, the book in its great design and in the minuteness of its details, the immediately seen and heard, has all the marks of a contemporary record.

But there were other Hebrew thinkers who applied other tests to the theory of the world and of living in it which is upheld throughout the Book of Proverbs. In that theory the world, as in the first chapter of Genesis, is "very good." It is a perfect structure according to the will and wisdom of God and has received His approval. Viewed philosophically the world is rational; it has Reason behind it and in it; and that Reason is the divine Reason. It is, therefore, because of the current view of the character of Jehovah, a benevolent Reason. It purposes the happiness and prosperity of man. All this, as we have seen, is *a priori* reasoning from the accepted nature of Jehovah. And it leads up to a natural theology, independent of any authoritative revelation through prophets. The eternal divine Reason speaks through the structure of the world and speaks, also, as an inner light in the soul of man as part of the world.

But the whole foundation of this scheme can be assailed by a different interpretation of the facts of life. Is the world, when we look at it carefully, "very good" and is it of a nature to foster virtue and goodness? Is the world rational? Does it hang together, intelligibly, in a scheme understandable by man's reason, which, on this same hypothesis, is man's ultimate test? For this hypothesis is really akin to one form at least of our modern humanism, "the intention of men to concern themselves with the discovery of a good life on this planet by the aid of human faculties" (Walter Lippmann quoted in *Isis*, xvi, 2, p. 452). This hypothesis is akin to humanism, as so defined, but differs from it in that the Hebrew humanists were perfectly certain that behind the whole scheme was a personality, that of Jehovah.

Criticism, then, of the scheme goes back through examination of the facts of life to criticism of Jehovah. In the Old Testament we find such criticisms in various stages and forms. There was a primitive scepticism on the part of those who did not put their trust in Him, because they believed that some other god was stronger and more reliable. Secondly, there were men of insolent profanity like Lamech. Their god was the sword in their hand and they were not really sceptics but simply godless; yet they would have admitted that some divine being existed. In Islam, their attitude is called "feeling secure from Allah" and is reckoned as "unbelief." The correlative, "despairing of Allah," is also reckoned as "unbelief." Again in our version of Psalm xiv, 1, and liii, 1, we read, "The fool hath said in his heart, There is no God," but that is an error of translation. What the fool really said was, "God is not present"; He is not beside me, taking account of what I am doing. So, here too, the fool admits the existence of God but thinks that he can escape His notice.

Reasoned scepticism is another matter and amongst the Hebrews it took the form of two questions, "Is God good?" and "Can we really know Him?" Both of these began by looking at the plain facts of life in the world. The scheme of the Book of Proverbs asserted confidently that because God was good and wise and completely controlled the world, the good man must prosper and the evil man must fail in life. The sceptical philosopher began at the other end with life and was quite sure that in point of fact the good man did not always prosper and that the wicked man often did prosper. Then the whole moral character of Jehovah came into question or, alternatively, the possibility of man's really knowing Jehovah. The combination of a natural theology and an inner light in man was thus assailed.

The scheme in Proverbs was further complicated by its combination of evil and folly. Reason, speaking in the world, is a moral guide; Folly, similarly speaking, is a guide to evil. This, of course, is very modern with us, but it was also deeply rooted in the ancient Hebrew mind and not a product of philosophical thought or observation. It tended, further, to produce a hopeless attitude towards evil. If a wicked man is so because he is a fool what can you do about it? A fool is a fool and it is folly to waste effort upon him. In Proverbs xxvi, 4, 5, we are given two contradictory rules on answering a fool which evidently mean, "Don't answer him at all." In ix, 7-9, there is specific warning not to waste effort on a fool, but rather to teach the already wise. This emphasis on foolishness as the essential evil in the world led to a linguistic development of various words for "fool." The fool bulked so largely in the Hebrew mind that he was distinguished and classified with some care. Thus there is a word for the simpleton—the least hopeless kind. There is a word for the pig-headed, self-conceited fool and another for the big, stupid, useless fool who tends to be impudent and defiant. Another is for the fool who is by nature a blunderer and cannot help putting his foot in it. This word means literally "one who misses the mark." It, with other words from the same root and with the same essential idea of blundering, occurs very often in the Old Testament and is most frequently translated in our version "sinner." This has come about because the Old Testament writers use it in two entirely different ways. This is not like the two meanings of the word *hochmá*, reason and wisdom, because the two different ways go back to two different attitudes towards evil and the users knew that. The first meaning is undoubtedly "blunderer"; it is used with that meaning in the ritual law and in the early stories of the Books of Samuel. And to this original meaning the Hebrew philosophical writers always held. Ecclesiastes, for example, uses it as the opposite of the word for "wise," "rational." But when the Prophets developed the idea of the moral holiness of Jehovah— i.e. His ethical separateness—they took over this word as meaning one who persistently violates that moral separateness. The development for the Prophets seems to have been from one who makes a mistake as to the ritual law to one who wilfully sets himself against the moral law. The certain point is that the word is used differently by philosophical and by prophetic writers and that this difference is obscured by our version which translates generally "sinner."

This combination of wrongdoing and folly, which might be called a hard-headed, rationalistic attitude towards evil, ignored its deeper, spiritual and emotional sources. It was much like some of our more optimistic systems of penology which think that the evil of the world may be done away by a comparatively simple change of habit or law or training. Such systems are brought up short, from time to time, by unexpected revelations of an abyss of wickedness in the human heart. The general thinking in the Book of Proverbs is similarly superficial, but it is not optimistic. The Hebrews, that is, felt very sure that man, left to himself, would grow steadily worse. His very created nature—from the unclean earth— led him constantly astray. Yet there was also working on man and in man a certain divine influence which sought to guide and to hold him. As to the nature of this divine influence and its success in dealing with man the Hebrews were plainly of many minds. That man, mysteriously but assuredly, was free and could set himself against the will of God they seem never to have doubted. That was one of the axioms of life which needed no proof. For some Hebrews that divine influence was exercised authoritatively, once for all through the Law or continuously through a succession of prophets. These all, in one way or another, brought the specific commands of Jehovah and were the mouthpieces of His Word to men and the interpreters of His actions. The Law was absolute, once for all delivered, but the prophets were more flexible in their adjustments to the varying times. All spoke with authority. But on the other hand, for many Hebrews the divine influence spoke from within through a mysterious spirit implanted by God in the created nature of man, or through a divine influence in the voice of nature itself. As both the external world and man were the direct creation of God some movements of divinity must have passed into both. That man was in the image and likeness of God lay behind this as a fertile and provocative thought.

So there was man in the midst, a self-determining being exposed to all these influences and having to find his way as best he could. When the Law ceased to hold and the prophets fell into disrepute with thinking men, what was there left? The Book of Proverbs, with one voice but in many different keys and modes, tells us to rely on the witness of life itself and on the divine Reason which speaks through the facts of life.

So we come back to the interpretations of the facts of life and the criticisms which thence arose of the basal position in the Book of Proverbs. The Hebrews who looked straight at the facts of life without any preconceived scheme of God's working through them saw very plainly that there was much unmerited suffering in them. How, on the pious hypothesis of God's working in the world, could this be? We do not know at all how the consideration of this problem came to center round the legendary figure of Job. All we know is that in our Book of Job there is gathered up a number of considerations of the problem from different points of view. The Job of legend, of course, was a conspicuous example of such unmerited suffering. Apparently the poet of the Colloquies seized the opportunity to make him the mouthpiece of the existence of the problem. Then others took up the challenge and the fight was on. As to when, where, and in what environment all this took place, we have no clue. The protagonists of the conflict are as anonymous as the folklore author of the legend. On all this it is unnecessary to go into further details. The book has been treated at length in Chapter III under Poetry (pp. 20-32 above); also in Chapter X under Story (pp. 128-9); at several points in Chapter XI on the Weird; in Chapter XII on Nature (pp. 163-5). But in putting the book here in a general consideration of philosophical thinking among the Hebrews one point asserts itself. How far does the book take us in the history of Hebrew thinking, if it be allowable to use the word "history" when we have such broken remains? Does it leave us in a blind alley or on a summit with a prospect before us? Elihu, from this viewpoint, may be disregarded and the speeches of the Lord also with Job's overwhelmed repentance. The question is as to the outcome of the Colloquies culminating in Job's long, final apologia. The poet, in so many words, posits this as Job's or his own challenge to Jehovah. Could Jehovah on a basis of fact and reason have found any answer? There are two possibilities here. The poet knew the Prologue; Job did not. For the poet, taking the Prologue as heavenly fact, Jehovah had no possible defense. Jehovah could only have said, "I used you as a pawn in a bet which I made with the Adversary. I had to give him complete control over you, short of your life, and it led to all your misery of body and mind and to the destruction of your children. I am very sorry. Can you forgive me? Is it possible that we can start again on the old footing?" But such a statement is unthinkable, easy and humane as the Jehovah of the Hebrews was. It might have crossed the somewhat cynical brain of Ecclesiastes, although his Jehovah was far from being so good-natured. And Ecclesiastes would have been very careful not to put it in words. For the Hebrew mind a confession on the part of Jehovah that He had made a mistake was perfectly possible. But even for the Hebrew mind, Jehovah could not confess that He had done wrong, especially such callous, merciless wrong as this. For it gave away the whole position as to the causes of unmerited suffering in the world. According to this it was simply due, always and everywhere, to the amoral caprice of Jehovah. For the poet of the Colloquies, with his sharpened moral sense—and it is of him we must think at this point—such a world under the control of such an absolute rule was ethically impossible. That might be the world of fact—it is plain that he suspected as much—then, so much the worse for the ruler and for the human beings whom he controlled. The poet, thus, was very near the position in which we shall find Ecclesiastes; the difference is that the poet was still in protesting revolt but Ecclesiastes had reached philosophic conformity. Ecclesiastes was so sure of the facts of the situation that he had adjusted himself, his theology and his philosophy to them and had worked out a possible plan of life under them.

So much for the poet. But Job himself, this dramatized figure, through whom the poet has been speaking, knew nothing of the Prologue and of the action in the Court of Heaven. He knew only that up to a certain point Jehovah had been his friend and that then, suddenly, a series of shattering blows had wrecked the lives of himself and of all his household. He had gradually steadied himself under these shocks, but they had opened his eyes to the fact that such inexplicable and unmerited sufferings did often happen in the world. Yet he had held to the memory of the friendly and trustworthy Jehovah of the past and was still open to an explanation of it all from Jehovah. But in that explanation they must meet as equals; "as a prince I would draw near to Him." We have seen how in Psalm xviii David bears himself to Jehovah as one gentleman to another. So evidently Job felt to Jehovah; he would be no crushed worm in even that Presence.

Such being Job's knowledge and standpoint had Jehovah any possible answer, valid for him? Job had come through self-torturing meditations to the point where he would meet Jehovah halfway; the old memories were strong and had reasserted themselves. A very little would reawaken the old tenderness and trust, if Jehovah would only show Himself tender and trustworthy. But one thing was certain, that Jehovah's answer must give some clue and assurance as to the clamant misery of the world which Job now saw so clearly and felt so deeply. The answer must be both rational and moral and not either violent or sentimental. Job was in contact with facts and the answer must meet these facts.

Let us suppose, then, that Jehovah had appeared to Job in a quiet and friendly manner and said: "What you have said of yourself and of me is true, and what your friends have said is not true. For all this has not come upon you because of sin on your part. Be assured of that. But you have gone on to speak of me as though I were devoid of moral sense; that is the real point of your accusation against me. You have done so because you have applied a certain quality of moral sense existing in you to events in the world and you consider that these events are revolting to your moral sense. But consider: Where did you get that moral sense? You know that I made you; that everything in you proceeded from me. Did not, then, that moral sense of yours proceed from me and must it not be present in me? If you are moral I cannot be amoral. If I, then, have a moral sense like yours, I must be governing the world by and with it, just as you would do. Can you trust me, your friend of the old days, that such is the case? This means that you don't know everything and you will easily, I think, admit that."

Such an answer would probably have met Job's personal need. But it was not made. It might have satisfied Job, although it was in so glaring contradiction with the Prologue. Yet, very curiously, this solution or, at least, postponement of the problem of unmerited suffering never seems to have occurred to any of the Hebrew questioners and thinkers. They all accepted in the most absolute fashion that they were the creation of Jehovah and then, in argument about the nature of Jehovah, they left out their own most essential characteristics. But there is this to be said for them that the same holds of the great majority of philosophizers about the universe. They apparently think that they can look at the universe from the outside and do not realize that they and their principles and philosophies and questionings and answers are part of the universe and must be taken in and explained with the universe. But these explanations and solutions never rose for the Hebrew mind. The poet began with the patient Job of the legend and with the scenes in the Court of Heaven which that legend quite naïvely gave and so fatally tied his own hands.

Further, the philosophical problem is complicated with an esthetic one. The poet was a poet as well as an ethical philosopher. He was creating what in his conception such a man as Job in his position would have been and done and said. He was pouring himself into Job and speaking through Job under the modifications of Job's situation. We have, therefore, the poet's position, but the poet's position as expressed through Job. It is exceedingly difficult to separate between these two: what the poet felt Job must have been and what the poet himself certainly was. If the poet had been less of a dramatic artist the problem would have been easier. But the pathetically individual figure of Job with his household and his great possessions—his sons and daughters, his lands and cattle —obscured for his poet the simple, clean-cut issue of Jehovah's government of the world. Still more was that issue obscured by the psychological problem of Job's personal relationship to Jehovah. The issue of Jehovah's friendship complicated that of Jehovah's justice.

And there enters also in the poet another obscuring element. As has already been said he had the defects of his qualities as a Hebrew artist in words. He did not know when to stop and had no conception of the eloquence of silence. It is true that Job had to be given time to steady his aching heart and mind and that we, reading his words, must be led to see through what deep waters his emotional life has been passing. But undoubtedly in the structure of the Colloquies there is repetition that is due to the poet's desire to make beautiful pictures in beautiful words. To paint such pictures for the sake of the pictures has always been the weakness of the Semitic artist, even of the truest and highest. With the Semitic artisan in words it has become an obsession.

Because, then, of all these limitations and characteristics it is not easy to separate out and exhibit in a cold philosophical light the position reached and held by the poet and the other contributors to our Book of Job. The same holds, but in a less degree, of the Book of Ecclesiastes. But it deserves a chapter to itself.

CHAPTER XIV

ECCLESIASTES

THE Book of Ecclesiastes is easily the greatest surviving product of Hebrew philosophic thought. Its philosophical line of connection and development is with the utilitarianism of the Book of Proverbs, which it pursues to a bitter and ironic end. But the book itself, like all Hebrew literature, is a free personal creation, including several literary elements quite disjoint from philosophic systems.

I. As it begins, it is an attempt to evoke Solomon from his tomb and make him tell what had been the experience and the outcome of his intellectual, practical and emotional life. But this occupies scarcely two chapters and is then dropped. The strain of the re-creation of an historical personality was too much for the author who was really and primarily interested in himself. He had evidently taken Solomon as a starting point because of his reputation for wisdom and knowledge, and especially because of his dream and the story of his choice of wisdom rather than wealth (1 Kings iii, 5-15; 2 Chronicles i, 7-13). For the author wished, as one at least of his objects, to try out in his book the practical question of the usefulness of wisdom for life in the world. Solomon had the reputation of having possessed it in the highest form. What did he think of it in the end? From this use of Solomon as a point of departure comes the first verse of the book: "The words of Qohéleth, son of David, King in Jerusalem"; and, also, its Hebrew title, Qohéleth. This word, which means literally gatherer, collector, is used as a name for Solomon and was probably sufficiently familiar for the first readers of the book, although to us it is otherwise unknown. It must have sounded apt enough as a description of a man who was a collector of everything collectible, from facts of knowledge to the women of his harem.

II. But the author very quickly drops Solomon and speaks as himself, for himself and of himself. We do not know in the least who he was. As to his name especially we can form no guess, but it will be convenient to call him Ecclesiastes, the name by which in English his book has so long been known. Ecclesiastes was the Greek word used by the Greek translator of his book to render the Hebrew Qohéleth. But it was a very bad guess, as Ecclesiastes means in Greek a member of an *ecclesia*, an assembly of any kind at all. Similarly our alternative title in English, "the Preacher," is another bad guess, this time as to the meaning of the Greek word Ecclesiastes. It supposes that a member of an *ecclesia* must necessarily be one who addresses an *ecclesia* and, therefore, a preacher. It would have raised in Ecclesiastes an ironic smile to have this conversation with himself, and confession of himself, turned into a sermon.

So much should be said to clear away confusion; hereafter Ecclesiastes is used for convenience to mean the author. What do we know of him and his circumstances from his book, our only source of information as to him? It is plain that he came of an old and noble family; that he was a gentleman farmer of large estates and devoted to the cultivation of them; that he knew, also, the chances and perils of business life and that there was a large export business in his time in which he was interested. He was an old man with old memories to inform and strengthen him; an aristocrat in every fiber and also a true gentleman. As the best type of aristocrat he knew well the sorrows and toils and oppressions of the world; he felt his kinship with all classes and their need not only for a vindicator and defender but for a comforter and consoler (iv, 1). The world for him stood in grievous need of comforting and found little or none. It was a time—and here the aristocrat of old family comes out—of new men, slaves risen to high position in the State and at the ear of the King (x, 5-7). The King of the time was an absolute ruler surrounded by his own favorites (viii, 2-9). So Ecclesiastes had had wide experience of all classes of society and all kinds of life and living and had come to some very definite conclusions as to the art of living. These conclusions will come hereafter by themselves, but at this point in forming some picture of the man himself it is well to notice that his rules for life are always carefully balanced. There is this thing to be said of a quality or for a course of action and there is that to be said against the same. Consider the other side, he always urges; there is something to be said for almost everything, except, of course, folly and blundering—and yet the blunderer does enjoy himself in his own way. Finally there is one point on which he has no doubt and twice at least he brings it out clearly. It is the part of a wife in the daily joy and living of her husband. That belongs to youth and the time of full strength; looking back as an old man he has no second thoughts of that.

And so in his age he came to write his book. It falls in the great and ever appealing literature of self-revelation and puts him beside Marcus Aurelius, Sir Thomas Browne, Pascal, and many others their like. We can see him in it clarifying himself to himself, enjoying the luxury of confession, of talking, if indirectly, about himself and enjoying, too, the creative impulse we all know about ourselves. This self-confession had occurred, again and again, in the Psalms, in a devout form addressed to Jehovah. It belongs, as we have seen, to the very kernel of the subjective Hebrew soul. But here, having no such God of comfort as would respond to confession, Ecclesiastes makes it to himself like Marcus Aurelius in his "conversations with himself." And he enjoyed making it for his own private exercise and satisfaction like Sir Thomas Browne in his *Religio Medici*, and like Sir Thomas Browne, too, Ecclesiastes had a keen enjoyment of skill in phrasing and happy expression in creative words. And of necessity he was forced to a philosophy of life and of what lies behind life, even as Pascal in his *Pensées*. All this, because it was the rendering, full and complete, of a great personality, made his a great book, a friendly, a lovable book—the only lovable book, said Renan, ever written by a Jew—which has caught and held the most varied minds, from St. Paul to Thackeray and Edgar Allan Poe, whether they fully understood it or not. For it is of the quality of great literature to have a myriad meanings for its myriad readers. No one can exactly tell what and all Shakespeare meant; and we have to be content that what each of us finds that he implicitly meant. So with Ecclesiastes; every age has found itself in his book and yet there is no end. It is safe to say, that of the Hebrew literature that has reached us, this book is the fullest and most perfect flowering of the essential Hebrew genius in its strength and in its weakness. Its irregularities of form, even, are significant. It opens with an elaborate and carefully phrased introduction in beautifully clear Hebrew, if evidently of the Silver Age. Then it passes to a chaotic mass of reflections, discharged as though from note-books, to close with an elaborate and pathetic picture of the human body as the House of Life and of the end of all things with the passing of that life. This is the normal sequence in a Hebrew book of care, irregularity, and final care. No attempt can be made to exhaust its contents here; for that there is nothing but reading and rereading of the whole, loaded as it is with meaning. But there is one aspect, personal to its author, that stands clearly out from beginning to end. And that is the calm and steadfast courage with which he faces and directs life in a world, that for him with his theological and philosophical position, must have been a kind of diabolic nightmare. And he does not blink its nightmarish uncertainties. Throughout, his admonition is constant to go on doing your part by life, with open eyes and a clear mind, with courage but without hope—save for the fleeting moment; that is the part to be played by a thinking man. A wise man has eyes in his head, but a fool walks in darkness. It is true that they go to the same end but it is for us to go thither wittingly. Certain consequences are inevitable and unforeseeable; meet them in courage. The penalties for life that must be paid, pay them. Life for Ecclesiastes was an amazing thing, a thing by itself and a thing which made all the difference in the world. He seems, again and again, to hover on the edge of the discovery of that mysterious quality in life which makes us go on; which swings us in an *élan vital* and draws us always to look forward to something beyond, even if foolishly (ix, 4). This feeling was personal to him, part of his psychological endowment, and it is plain that he never worked out its implications and so made it part of his scheme of the universe. It was simply there; he knew it and followed its gleam. But it seems, as an unshakable inner experience, to have given him the courage with which he went on into ever new things.

III. But what was his consciously thought out scheme of the universe? It was a compound of what he had learned from certain passages in his Scriptures—we can hardly call them his Holy Scriptures—and certain observations and philosophical constructions from life. It is evident that he had read and pondered deeply the early chapters of Genesis with their philosophy of life. He can hardly have taken these statements as revealed truth from God, but he does regard them as essential fact. He makes a development from one of them, turning the curse of perpetual and abiding physical toil into a toil in the mind which man cannot escape. And he then shows how it can be transformed. Was there a school of philosophers to which both the editor of Genesis and Ecclesiastes himself belonged? That is a pure hypothesis but the facts, such as they are, point in that direction. Such an hypothesis, too, inevitably demands dates and to date the literature of the Old Testament is a task that the present book consistently declines to attempt. It is characteristic for the situation that the apocalyptic close of the Book of Daniel is the only element that can be fixed within a year or two. But that Ecclesiastes is very late can be taken as certain. The original Hebrew of Ecclesiasticus was written about 190-180 B.C. and Ecclesiastes was earlier; for Ecclesiasticus echoes him but in a different spirit. We know no more. The attempts to find and identify historical references in his book have failed. Still less can we tell when the philosopher-artist who made our Book of Genesis what it is did his work.

But for such a hypothetical school there is no further evidence than in the Books of Genesis and Ecclesiastes. None of the contributors to our Book of Job show any trace of its influence. Nor do we find any other trace of any influence at all from those chapters of Genesis until we reach Paul and he, as we have seen, belonged to yet another school of interpretation. Ecclesiastes, on his part, knew very well what the philosopher of Genesis had meant, although he could not follow him in his devout attitude to his revengeful and self-protecting deity. But the world of the philosopher of Genesis was his world, although the religious reactions of the two seem to have been different. In both is evident a clear insight into the fundamental institutes of life; life for both was a fundamental fact which must go on; for both, God and man are frankly opposed. Both know the toiling, unresting universe and both recognize that there is an order in that universe—what we would call the order of nature—and both recognize too that God has confirmed that order with an oath binding on Himself. To this order it is for man to adjust himself, willingly or unwillingly. Like

Margaret Fuller, in the well known story, both "accepted the universe" and, to vary Thomas Carlyle's words about Margaret Fuller's utterance, Ecclesiastes recognized, "Gad, he'd better!" To Ecclesiastes this toiling, unresting universe suggested an infinite weariness in perpetual transition and recurrence. Man, too, was caught in this weariness and not simply the sun and the winds and the seasons. The senses of man had to keep on working and the mind of man was under the curse of toil more even than his body. That is where Ecclesiastes develops the Genesis idea on the basis of his own experience. In Genesis the curse of toil is on man's body to supply his belly-need; for Ecclesiastes it is also in man's mind, his restless, unceasing, craving mind. For Ecclesiastes, God put "toil" in man's mind in order that man might not be able to understand God's working as a whole (iii, 11). In another passage it is phrased, to make ultimate reality unattainable for man (vii, 24). But both Genesis and Ecclesiastes agree that all this is to put the fear of God into man. Here we come back to "the fear of God," that much used phrase with its many meanings and applications. In one way or another it recurs, again and again, in the Book of Ecclesiastes. In consequence some have sought refuge from the real difficulties of the book in calling it the Song of the Fear of God. In a sense it is that, but what is fear in this book and what is Ecclesiastes' God? For the philosopher of Genesis the fear seems still to be a devout, accepting, godly fear and the God is the Jehovah of the Hebrews. Ecclesiastes has gone far beyond that. This fear for him is prudent caution towards a jealous and easily irritated Being under whose eye he is condemned to live, and this Being whom he calls God is entirely amoral. Yet he must get along with this Being; that is what life and living involve.

But in the stories retold in Genesis there are certain obscure references as to man's created constitution. He was made by God out of dust; that is his fundamental nature; came from dust and he returns to dust (Genesis iii, 19; Ecclesiastes iii, 20). Ecclesiastes seems to have no allusion to the statement in the first chapter of Genesis that man is in the image of God and according to His likeness. But Ecclesiastes does refer to a "spirit" existing in man which bears some relation to God (iii, 21, 22; vi, 10; xii, 7). The common word for "spirit" in Hebrew is ambiguous, for it is, also, as we have already seen, an ordinary word for "wind." Between these two meanings it seems to have been used in Genesis and by Ecclesiastes for a vitalizing wind, a principle of life. In Genesis ii, 7, it is said of man, not of the other animals, that God "blew into his nostrils a breeze of life." The word "breeze" here is another word for "wind," not used of our "spirit." But in the story of the Flood (vii, 32) it is said that there died "all"—beasts and men—"in whose nostrils was breeze of spirit [or "wind"] of life." Here the two words for "wind" are combined. Again, in Genesis vi, 3, Jehovah says, "My spirit will not contend in man for ever, because he is also flesh." Mankind, here, consists of "flesh" and a certain divine spirit, and these two are in conflict in man; but man's life shall be shortened that the conflict may not go on forever.

Let us turn now to the passages in Ecclesiastes. Some development had evidently taken place between Genesis and Ecclesiastes, for an argument had grown up in support of man's immortality based on his possessing the divine spirit. But in Genesis vii, 32, the word "spirit" is used of all living creatures. So a distinction had to be made: the "spirit" in man was of a kind that went up, upwards, and that in beasts was of a kind that went down, downwards to the earth. To this Ecclesiastes simply asks: "Who knows that this is so?" (iii, 21, 22). And he reiterates that everything comes from one place; everything came into being from the dust and everything returns to the dust (iii, 20). This is exactly what is said of man in Genesis iii, 19. So, too, Ecclesiastes says, in the closing scene of all (xii, 7), "And the dust returns to the earth as it was and the spirit returns to God who gave it." The life-principle, blown into man, returns to God and all is over. So there can be fittingly added verse 8, which closes the book: "Oh, how transitory! saith this Gatherer [here the author himself, not Solomon]; all is transitory!" There remains Ecclesiastes vi, 10, which may be translated: "That which is, long ago its name was given to it and it is known that it is Man and he cannot contend with Him who is stronger than he." This is an allusion, through the word "contend," to Genesis vi, 3, and voices Ecclesiastes' constant position that it is hopeless for man, being man, to set himself in any way against God. Man must formally submit, conform, and make the best of it. Job, it will be remembered, held his head high as a prince and came into the presence of God as an equal. But Ecclesiastes, by accepting and conforming, out of the very facts of life devises a way of evading God's curse. His attitude is very close to that of the clever man in our own medieval stories who is under bond to the Devil, but by his wits succeeds in overreaching that enemy.

So much, at least, Ecclesiastes had got from the stories retold in the beginning of Genesis and so far he had expanded them. But he had also looked at the world and its facts and from these he had worked out a definite philosophical scheme of his own. In that scheme the only really traditional element is his unshaken acceptance as self-evident and needing no proof that behind the world there is a personality, whom he calls "God," who made the world and now absolutely controls it. This personality for him is unaffected by moral considerations; the facts of life show him that and he tests these facts of life by a norm of absolute right and wrong which he takes for granted as in his own possession. He gives us no sign as to how he comes to possess and trust this norm; he simply uses it. And in his use of it he finds that "God" does not pay any attention to it. The norm to which God does pay attention divides the people, and things, who please Him from the people, and things, who irritate Him. The first class Ecclesiastes calls "good before God"—a very qualified goodness—and the second class are the blunderers who put their foot in it with God (ii, 26). Here, and throughout his book, Ecclesiastes makes use of that ambiguous word used by the prophets in the sense of "sinner" and by the philosophical writers in its root meaning "blunderer." Ecclesiastes makes great play with it in the latter sense and for him it is the opposite of "wise," "rational" (e.g. ix, 18). For Ecclesiastes, then, there are two norms as to conduct: an absolute moral norm which he himself has and applies, and a very relative norm as to what pleases or displeases God. It will be seen, therefore, that Ecclesiastes' conception of this personality whom he calls "God" is that of an absolute ruler, such as the East has always known, on whose caprice depends not only the happiness and success of those in contact with him but the very laws of right and wrong (v, 1-6; viii, 2-5; x, 4-7). His "God" is, therefore, very close to the Allah of the Muslim schoolmen. Finally, to conform to the caprice of this Being is the first rule for success in life, and the second rule is to be always on the alert and quick to change when that caprice changes. Never commit yourself too far; don't be self-righteous or play the philosopher obtrusively; don't be over-wicked and, above all, don't be a fool (vii, 15-17). And so the pious utilitarianism of the Book of Proverbs works itself out.

But Ecclesiastes had observed much more in the world than this. If this destructive conclusion had been his whole philosophy, he would have had no place among constructive thinkers and would have been fairly open to the charge of cynicism. Chapter iii in the divisions of our text of his book opens with a sentence unique in Hebrew literature and which makes a statement that cuts to the kernel of all philosophical thinking. "The universe possesses time and there is a fit occasion for everything under the sky." In making this statement he is struggling with the Hebrew vocabulary, and laboring to break it in to new usages. "The universe" is literally "the all"; that outside of which there is nothing. "Time" is the abstract conception; not a particular time but Time itself. It was only late in their development that the Hebrews acquired a word with this meaning. They had been content to speak of "time" in terms of "days" and "years." "In the days of . . ." meant "at the time of" and "after many days" meant "after a long time." But eventually they acquired—we do not know when—a word to express the abstract idea and Ecclesiastes uses it here. The form of his sentence is perfectly simple; in the same idiom he could have said, "I possess a book." But the idea is not simple at all. It means that he has observed the existence of the category Time as part of the universe. We have no evidence that any Hebrew ever said anything like that before. Further, he has observed that all events in this world of ours, "under the sky," fall each in their exact occasions. The word "thing" or "event" is a somewhat abstract one, having behind it a flavor of "desire," but "event" will fairly translate it. And these events all fall in situations in which they are in place; that is their fit occasion. God has made everything "beautiful" in its occasion (iii, 11) and so when an event comes it looks exactly suited to its environment. All that is because the universe possesses the category Time. "Occasions" are grains in that extended entity, Time.

But Ecclesiastes, looking at the changing world, has made another observation which is more like a bad dream of Hegel than anything else. All Hebrews were familiar with the conception of the world and things, as being in perpetual change. The world for them was "becoming" and not "being," and this affected Jehovah Himself. But Ecclesiastes observed that these changes could be brought under the classification of a thing and its opposite—A and not-A. Here we have the germ of Plato's doctrine of "the other." And he saw that if A came, then, at some time or other not-A was bound to come. And here we have the doctrine that there cannot be good without evil; a system so good that there is no evil in it, is unthinkable. But Ecclesiastes says only that it does not exist. Each would come, too, in such a way as to fit in exactly to its environment when it came. God had seen to that. Ecclesiastes puts that in his concrete way by giving a table of illustrative opposites: there is an occasion when being born occurs and an occasion when dying occurs, and all the rest. This in Ecclesiastes is pure observation and registers facts in life. But he joins it to one of the fundamental ideas of the school of Genesis that God is bent upon keeping man in his place. To do that, God has put into man's mind the instinct to toil; that is how we must read and render the word which our versions, text and margin, have rendered "the world" and "eternity" (iii, 11). The textual change in the Hebrew is almost nothing and the passage at once has meaning which neither "the world" nor "eternity" can give. Man, therefore, cannot help himself but must keep on working, at one thing or another, and so God has secured that He Himself and His doings as a whole and the ultimate reality behind the appearances of the world should remain a mystery to man. Things, then, being so, what should man do? Get the best out of life he can; adjust himself to the changing events of the world, each by each, A and not-A, B and not-B, and enjoy it all. Because of this drive to work intended by God as a curse, man will find that he can enjoy work; that it is in fact the only real enjoyment in life. Thus the curse is evaded and man can secure a transient happiness. The happiness is not in the results of work—the fruits derived from work—but in the work itself. Whenever man stops and looks at what he has produced and seeks to enjoy it, it turns to dust and ashes—mere transitoriness and chasing of wind. That, in Ecclesiastes' parable, had been Solomon's experience (ii, 11) and it is plain that Ecclesiastes had observed the same thing in himself and universally. For it is a universal experience that the joy is in the doing of the work and not in the product of the work after it is done. So, most ingeniously, Ecclesiastes reached a doctrine of salvation from the divine curse and his gospel was the gospel of work. That it was strictly an evasion of the divine purpose gave him probably a secret joy. But he saw also another relief for the situation of man. These events, the thing and its opposite, came regardless of justice and righteousness. But they were sure to come and in the change was the relief for man from an otherwise intolerable condition. Nothing persisted; everything was transient; and its opposite would come. If there was wickedness now regnant in the place where righteousness should be, by this very law of opposites righteousness would come and in its turn would go. This is what Ecclesiastes calls "judgment"—the change from A to not-A and back again. Otherwise life would be impossible (iii, 17; viii, 6, and often). So he can call the change from youth to age "judgment." The context shows that there is no moral condemnation. When you are young, use youth and its strength, but be quite sure that God will bring upon you the opposite of youth, old age. Meet each and use each; they cancel each other out (xi, 9).

We can now see the meaning of the words with which Ecclesiastes begins his book and ends it, and which recur throughout it. The translation of them in our version is most unhappy. The basal word is the same as Abel's name and means "a breath of wind." But the idea in it for Ecclesiastes, just as in Abel's name, was certainly not "vainness" or "emptiness" but "transitoriness." The world was very far from being "vain" or "empty" to Ecclesiastes; it was very full of the most worthwhile things in the doing of which was joy. But they did not abide; they were in perpetual flux; and man had to toil after them. In that toiling there was joy, but he had to keep it up; the accomplished work was always escaping him. So he could say, "Oh, how transitory; all things are transitory!" and go on to describe the groaning, travailing universe in its perpetual circlings. There was no progress in it and man was carried with it, round and round. But man by giving himself to it; by laboring at each thing as it came could snatch a joy.

But we must never forget that this round of events was not the ultimate. Behind it was God, and it was only a kind of screen that God had erected between man and Himself that He Himself, behind it, might remain inscrutable. So man by foolish blundering can easily irritate God and God in His anger may destroy what a man is trying to do (v, 5), or may destroy a man himself even though his appointed occasion of death has not come (vii, 16, 17). God is not constrained even by this system of opposed events. Here the philosophy and theology of Ecclesiastes meet most curiously. This screen, or wheel on which events go round and round, appearing each in its fit occasion and cancelling each other out, is a product of Ecclesiastes' observation and reflection, but his God is still the capricious, irritable, and absolute Semitic deity. Even the doctrine that a man has two possible terminations to his life, one absolute and the other conditioned by accident, appears in Muslim theology. In certain ways Ecclesiastes was a throw-back to a quite primitive Semitic attitude towards God—any God—and that attitude again reappears in certain phases of the thinking of Mohammed and in certain developments of later Islam. This forces us back to the unescapable fact that there was a certain primitive tradition of thinking and acting which ran through the whole history of the Hebrew race and which kept on—and keeps on—reasserting itself at, it may be, long intervals. In modern Jewish thinking there are sometimes strange reappearances from a supposed dead and gone world. For another and very different phase of this tradition, the continuity of the organizations of the Hebrew prophets through and into the organizations of the darwishes of Islam cannot be doubted by any one who looks at the fundamental and governing motives and ideas in both cases. How the tradition was handed on is another matter.

To return to Ecclesiastes, another point at which he singularly combined, or contrasted, his personal experiences and the teachings of the school of Genesis was in his attitude towards women. The philosopher of Genesis is scrupulously objective and careful in his treatment of Eve, as he is, indeed, of all the women in the book. He handles his feminine characters with sympathy and veracity. But those Jewish writers who, later, refer to the Garden Story and to Eve's part in it show no such restraint and care. For them it was all Eve's fault; they did not think of her as "life" and the mother of all living, but as the immediate cause of death in the world. And in this attitude Ecclesiastes in one passage (vii, 26-28) joins. It is the most outspoken piece of railing in his book; but though it sounds like a personal experience it is simply an echo of an inherited school prejudice. He has been speaking of his endeavor to seek out a rational reckoning, or balance sheet, of life and to see how wickedness is the same as folly and foolishness as insanity. Then comes the singular outburst:

> And I find that bitterer than death is the woman [or, generically, woman] whose mind is like hunting and fishing nets, whose hands are like fetters; he who is good in God's sight [i.e. who is favored by God] will escape from her, but a blunderer will be taken by her. See, this have I found, sayeth this gatherer of one thing with another to find a reckoning—a thing which my desire still seeks but I have not found—one man from a thousand have I found, but a woman in all these have I not found.

It is undoubtedly a singular passage and some have sought to find in it a bit of the *vie intime* of Ecclesiastes, such a glimpse that some of our western poets from time to time give us. Was Ecclesiastes of these? Did he "unlock his heart with a sonnet key"? Is his book of self-communion and revelation like Rousseau's *Confessions*? To think so is utterly to mistake the temper of all oriental literature. It may be healthy or unhealthy in tone, but into that form of morbidity it never enters. The oriental gentleman does not use his own womankind as literary material. What we have here is a literary convention—an unhappy convention—which dictates that references to woman in professed literature should be cynical. This convention is very deeply rooted and produced Job's wife, the *adjutrix diaboli*. But the popular story-teller knew nothing of it and to him we owe the pictures of those magnificent women scattered through the Old Testament. And even here, Ecclesiastes has doubts and in the next verse he writes down his own condemnation. "Only see this which I *have* found, that God made man simple [straightforward], but they have sought out many reckonings." Evidently his judgment above only half pleases him.

But there are two passages bearing upon women in his book which are quite clear and are not based on any literary or philosophical convention but spring from his own experience. In chapter ix he is dealing with the great fact of life, and that life is to be used fully while it lasts. In verse 4 he has noted that unique quality of "trust" or "confidence" which carries us on. It is the only occurrence of the word in Ecclesiastes and is his most distinct allusion to the mystery lying behind life. So he continues: "On every occasion let thy garments be white and oil on thy head, let it not lack." Be always as going to a feast—the feast of life. "See life with a wife whom thou lovest all the days of thy transitory life which He [God] has given to thee under the sun, all thy transitory days, for it is thy portion in life and in thy toil in which thou toilest under the sun." The crown, then, of life is to enjoy life with a beloved wife.

The other passage has been very badly translated in our versions, but the rabbinic expositors knew quite well what it meant although they wrapped their exposition in ambiguity. Chapters xi and xii connect closely and the end of chapter xi is an exhortation to the young man to be glad in his youth and to use his youth and strength while he has them. They, too, are transitory and old age and weakness will assuredly come; God has arranged for that as their opposite. "And remember thy well of water in the days of thy strong youth, so long as the days of evil come not nor the years draw nigh in which thou wilt say, 'There is nothing for me in them' " (xii, 1). Or the last words might be rendered, "I have no desire in them." The "well of water" here means his wife. This metaphorical usage is made quite clear in Proverbs v, 15-18, and Song of Songs iv, 12, 15. In Proverbs: "Drink water from thy cistern and running streams from the midst of thy well [exactly the word in Ecclesiastes]. Shall thy water-springs be spread abroad and be runlets of water in the streets? Let them be for thyself alone and not for strangers with thee. Let thy fountain be blessed and rejoice thou in thy youthful wife." And in the Song of Songs: "A well shut up, a fountain sealed . . . a garden fountain, a well of living waters and running streams from Lebanon." That "creator" in this context has no special meaning is equally clear. Ecclesiastes never uses the word of God, and the attitude which he prescribes towards

God is one of cautious fear all through life. Finally, to this comradeship of a man and his wife it is possible that there is discreet allusion also in the passage on the advantage of comradeship in general (iv, 9-12).

IV. It has already been said that Ecclesiastes largely constructed his book as a guide to life. So his experiences had been and so the conclusions which he had drawn from them; let others profit by them. It has been shown, too, how cautious he was in his practical conclusions and how he liked to express them by putting two flatly opposed results side by side. For him they were both true: under certain circumstances this; under others, that. Truth is manifold and relative, and so, Be careful! To that he returns again and again. "Consider!"; that is, consider how God has constructed the world and arranged its events. Because of this attitude of his, face to face with this astonishing world, many abusive names have been applied to him. But any careful reader will see that his character was too many-sided to be brought under an epigram. He knew himself as himself and cared nothing for literal consistency. So he has been called a fatalist, but that certainly he was not. Man, by exercise of his free will, can act for himself and bring down upon himself the wrath of God. There is no fatalism there. But there is much irony in Ecclesiastes' position as a consistent conformist. When, out of the fear of God, you conform to the situation into which God has brought you, *pecca fortiter*; you may be immoral but conform and be safe (vii, 16, 17; ix, 10). Thus it is only the fear of God that can lead Ecclesiastes to immoral action. Of course, you *can* set yourself against the will of God and be as moral as you please; but that is to play the blundering fool.

Was he, then, a pessimist and does he teach pessimism? Again we must distinguish. The scheme of life, as he saw it, would justify the blackest pessimism. But it was a scheme of *life*, if only in the fleeting days of this world, lived under the sun, and it is plain on every page that he faced life with gallant courage; he tells us, too, to do the same. This attitude may be called illogical, but it is tremendous and it is very real. Ecclesiastes was sure that man could not reach the absolute reality which God has kept to Himself, but he possessed—and knew it—three absolutely final and real things, his moral sense, his freedom of choice, and his sense of life as good and sweet (xi, 7, 8). There were things enough in life to make him a pessimist but he was no pessimist. Nor does he teach it. He tells us to live full, joyous lives in spite of everything and he shows us how we can so guide our lives as to do so. It will require care and much circumspection to keep on the right side of God; it will require, too, that we shall not be awkward and untimely moralists or do our own philosophizing out of season; but it can be done. St. Paul was greatly affected by this book and found in it some strange things which would have astonished its author. And he has transformed the illogical, yet most real, rejoicing of Ecclesiastes into the equally real but fully intelligible rejoicing in the Lord of his Epistle to the Philippians. All the difference lies in the kind of God posited as behind the scheme of life.

Was Ecclesiastes, then, a hedonist, teaching a life of unthinking pleasure? That least of all. He undoubtedly came eating and drinking, but he came, too, with a gospel that the only salvation from the terror of the world was in the joy of doing work. And he came, too, with open eyes and heart for the tears of the oppressed who had no comforter (iv, 1). The terror of the world was far more real for him than the terror of death. And the terror of the world can be met and overcome by his gospel of salvation by work, while whatever terror death might have, he overcame by looking at it steadily. The disabilities which old age brought were far more grievous to him than the oblivion in the gulf of death. The end, there, was complete and man had escaped from his transitory life and all it had brought. He who had lived such a life as Ecclesiastes describes could feel that he had done his part by and in the mystery of life—whatever God might have done. And to do one's part by life meant to make the best of life, to get out of it all that was in it, both for oneself and for others. Let life go on and the joy of living on all its sides. It is true that it is transitory and has to be lived, moment by moment, as each comes and goes. It is true that you can never sit back, fold your hands and enjoy; never say with Faust, "Oh, still delay, thou art so fair." God did not make life in that way. But take it as He made it and it is still worth living. This open-eyed acceptance of the facts of life and of the sureness of its end is not the attitude of the hedonist. He shuts his eyes, folds his hands and consumes his own flesh; and he, for Ecclesiastes, was one of the kinds of fool (iv, 5). The rational man thinks consciously, goes forward wittingly and though he inevitably ends in the same oblivion of death, he has done his part by life and truly enjoyed life.

What of the final accusation against Ecclesiastes that he was a cynic? This comes shrewdly near to him, even though it be modified into calling him a gentle cynic. He was an explicit conformist and had no use at all for the non-conformist conscience, running out into its lunatic fringe of kickers, reformers, and uplifters. He had a conscience, but it was a well trained conscience; he knew the unescapable rules of life and that it is absurd for man to "batter the wheels of heaven, if they roll not rightly by." But he did not tell lies to his conscience; he kept it and its verdicts clear and sound although he recognized that its positions were too often impracticable. That was part of the fundamental insanity of the scheme of life; but life, at any cost, must be lived. Life was one of his realities. This is always the reverse side of the conformist creed. Almost all of us are conformists to one degree or another and the conformist must conform. Ecclesiastes saw himself, like a fish or bird, caught in the evil net of an unchangeable, inexorable world (ix, 12) which is ruled by the terror of a capricious deity of no moral sense, and he had to make the best of it. So he had to be a conformist in the highest degree. In a deeper and fuller application than Carlyle meant, "Gad, he'd better!" Otherwise life could not be lived and it was laid upon him—how, why, whence he knew not—to live life. And inevitably, in proportion as we are conformists, cynicism does enter. The best we can, things being as they are, takes the place of the absolute best. We say it with a shrug, and saying it we face the paradox of life. "Whatever you are, don't be impossible" applies not in politics only and the Duke of Wellington's great dictum, "The King's government must be carried on," was for Ecclesiastes, life must be lived. But the pathos for Ecclesiastes was that for him there was no King to be reverenced and obeyed: there was only this strange impersonal mystery of imperative life. For this cause and to this extent Ecclesiastes was a cynic; a bitter cynic as to God all the time; a cynic, perforce, as to many of the details of life. With life he did the best he could; with God he had as little to do as he could. So he went down to death unafraid, unashamed, and so he left to others his pattern of a livable life.

V. What is his place in the history of philosophy? The following points seem to be clear: (i) He worked out the Hebrew conception that all things are in a process of becoming to a possibly implicated end that all things are passing and vanishing; that nothing is permanent and abiding. But his becoming was not the becoming of an ever forward process; it was the becoming of a weary reiteration. The sweeps of its circlings come back again and again and there is no new thing under the sun (i, 9). Thus he negates all hope of fundamental change; so God has fixed it all that man might fear before Him. Yet his God, too, is under change, the change of caprice. But (ii) he added to this his doctrine that all events in the world are a thing and its opposite and that if the one comes, the other, the opposite, is sure to come. Each comes in a setting into which it fits and so the whole, although thus contradictory, is bound together. To have observed and constructed this scheme is his philosophical achievement. (iii) Psychologically his achievement is to have observed and used the universal fact that everyone has joy in doing something. This, too, he worked into his scheme. (iv) Against the anarchism of his theology he set up as a positive and abiding fact the mystery of life and he posits its basis in the inexplicable "trust" which he had observed as a universal psychological fact (ix, 4). This separating out of life as one of the realities is his own and it culminates in his great picture of the body as the House of Life (xii, 3, 4). This, as a fundamental conception and picture, has made a deep mark on subsequent literature as have also isolated phrases in this same chapter. The culminating pathos of the picture of the end of life, an end that is a final and triumphant escape from the breakdown of the means of real living and from the nightmare of the system of the world, an escape, too, from the fear and will of God Himself, has touched the human mind, consciously and unconsciously, understandingly and misunderstandingly, in all ages. It is the Hebrew expression of the Virgilian tears of things; humanity face to face with the stark realities. This may not belong to the philosophy of the schools, but it is part of the deepest insight into human life and there is no answer to it save the triumphant answer of our Lord, the Christ. The reality and depth of its question poets have mostly understood and theologians seldom. In it another thread of the Hebrew thinking stretched to its end.

After all this, it is hardly necessary to say that verses 9-14 of chapter xii are a quite evident appendix in praise of the book and in deprecation of any further similar attempts. The "one Shepherd" is Jehovah Himself and all the words of the wise are traced back as given by Him. This appendix may belong to the time of the incorporation of the book as part of the latest Canon of Scripture. As to how that came about we have no clue. Ecclesiastes plainly wrote for his own pleasure. Then his book would come into circulation among his friends and, later and guardedly, among a wider public. That, at least, has been the normal way in which such spiritual autobiographies have reached the world. How it came to be canonized is another and much more difficult problem. It begins as the professed words of Solomon and that name, while retaining some rags of sacred authority, would cover much strange doctrine. It is full of the fear of God, a phrase which could be taken with consecrated meaning. It is full, too, of echoes—quotations and applications—of old moralizing and pious proverbs. That these were often travestied would even appeal to the sardonic Hebrew sense of humor. And the evident intimate pathos of it all would appeal, too, even when the implications were not well understood. However all that may have been, in the earliest rabbinic references to the book it is already in the canon. The question at issue was whether it should remain in; some critics evidently had begun to see more clearly its real meaning. That, of course, must always have been plain to the inner circle of Ecclesiastes and his friends. Now the meaning had to be debated in the open, and the book's reiteration of the fear of God carried for it the day. Since then it has been Scripture for both Synagogue and Church—an end which would have infinitely tickled Ecclesiastes himself.

EPILOGUE

AND so, these things assuredly being thus, we are left with the question, What about the Old Testament?

One of the strangest paradoxes of the situation in which the religious public finds itself at present is the indifference which that public has developed towards the Old Testament. The Old Testament simply does not interest it and it has in consequence even reached a point of ignorance where it doubts—or is quite certain—that the Old Testament has neither meaning nor value for modern life. This is largely, or entirely, the fault of the professed Old Testament scholars and students. They have worn out the patience of the mass of readers with their mechanical analyses and verbal details—the sawdust of criticism; they have hunted "documents" until the word has become a joke. They have also, in an attempt at moral popularization, so overemphasized certain sides of the thinking and literature of the Hebrews, such as the prophets, that they have created the idea that there is nothing else worth while in the Old Testament than those prophets, and people have become frankly bored with their monotony. They have also, in an attempt to be truly scientific and evolutionary, degraded the general picture of the God of the Hebrews into a grotesque parody, and the sublimity of Sinai and its thunders into a raree-show worked by priests. That the intellectual and religious phenomenon of the Hebrew race was as great a miracle in the history of the world as that Greek miracle of which we hear so much has been obscured to the point of vanishing.

And the paradox in all this is that while with the religious world the Old Testament has steadily slipped into the background, in the world, on the other hand, of scholars, who are interested in the history of the whole human race, it has equally steadily been coming back to its own. There was a time, the time of our grandparents, when the Old Testament meant the whole ancient world of the East. Then there came a time, the time of the return, into the knowledge of scholars, of India, Egypt, and Babylonia-Assyria, when the Hebrews came to be considered as an insignificant people to be safely disregarded. They were viewed, that is, as Egypt and Assyria used to view them. But now the balance of true proportion has righted itself. The contributions of the Hebrews to the records of history are no longer regarded with primary suspicion. With the passing of bibliolatry, the distinction between traditionalists and critics has also passed, and it has become plain that, through the racial tenacity of the Hebrews, there has been preserved for us in the Old Testament a unique and trustworthy key to the history of the Near East. It is now possible to read together Herodotus, Jeremiah, and Ezekiel and to profit by the comparison of these first-hand records. How exactly true this is any one may verify by turning to the volumes of the *Cambridge Ancient History* which touch even remotely upon the Hebrews. There it will be found that the old "critical" suspicious attitude towards the historical tradition of the Hebrews has vanished and that these records are given equal credence with those—often much scantier—of the other peoples. It is true that this is part of a general reversal of historical attitude from extreme scepticism to a recognition of a basal truth in national tradition. Homer has come back and with him the tale of Troy divine. We need not, then, be surprised that Sinai and Jerusalem have also come back, and that Moses is on his way back.

Why have they so come back? In part it is undoubtedly due to this reversal of a critical attitude towards all tradition. But there is more. Sheer literary reality has made itself felt. Learning for long was too blind, in Andrew Lang's eloquent words, to see the crown on Homer's head of indivisible supremacy. But learning now has learned better and all the East has always known that the book is the life, whatever the book may be. So may the Old Testament, too, come fully back!

The Hebrew records having then won their right to respectful treatment on the part of students of history, what of the Hebrews themselves? Are they an interesting people, a human people; are they in the language of today "folks"? If we can once rid ourselves of the idea that they were perpetually uttering prophecies or singing psalms or smiting Agag before the Lord, and take them as they have written themselves down in their own literature, we will find how many sides of common humanity they show and how fully and artistically they show those sides. We hear much nowadays about Egyptian literature and Babylonian literature. Can anyone who reads those scanty, broken fragments, which are called "literature" because they are undoubtedly in writing, ever dream of putting them beside the contribution of the Hebrew race to real literature? Why the Hebrews reached this preeminence no one can possibly tell; it is part of the mystery of race and national endowment. But when all is said and the dust of learned controversy has cleared away there survive for us only two real literatures in the ancient Mediterranean world, those in Hebrew and in Greek. There may have been others; we know nothing of them; and the surviving records do not suggest that they need be considered. There is even an element of pathos in watching Assyriologists and Egyptologists gathering up the scraps of literature left by those most unliterary peoples and trying to make it rival the literature of the Hebrews. In a single one of the stories about David as told by these there is more of genuine literature than in all the Egyptian and Assyrian annals. The business papers of a trading firm are not literature; law codes may be venerable but that does not make them literature; arid records of campaigns and victories are not literature; school-books, lexicons, and word-lists are not literature. To call those records literature is to debase that word to cover anything in writing. Much of sociological interest may be deduced from these things to show the civilization which produced them; they can do no more and mean no more. But across the minds of the Hebrews there came the mystery of creative genius in words, and the things which they so created were of the kind that refuses to die. Songs of the emotion of a moment they may have been, but they still live in the fellowship of Homer and Pindar. Deborah and Barak sang of some obscure little victory in the plain of Esdraelon, but they did it in words that ring still in our ears and with pictures that are part of the literary inheritance of the human race. The Mother of Sisera still looks from her lattice and still asks her ladies her fatal question. She is as abiding as any tragic figure of Euripides or Aeschylus. Of which of the odes of victory of Egypt or

EPILOGUE 219

Assyria can this be said? And when David laments for Jonathan, "O mountains in Gilboa!" we are carried down many centuries to Byron's heart-cry, "Hills of Annesley!"

Is it possible even now to rescue our Book of Genesis from the archeologists and claim it as the work of a great artist and philosopher? Cannot we read it with his eyes and mind who tried to make it an expression of what for him were the fundamental institutes of human life, of what were the psychological characteristics of the family which began his race and of how that race stood over against the non-Hebrew world? Can we trace out, following him, the varying philosophies of the Hebrew thinkers who were face to face with exactly the same problems as we ourselves, and not recognize in them the breathings and leadings of the one Spirit? We can see how different were their schemes of life and how varying were their methods of meeting life. But life was in every word that they wrote and their life was ours. The rough utilitarian philosophy of the Book of Proverbs is exactly reproduced in the crass moralizing and practical wisdom of Dorothy Dix, and its sententious sayings are not far removed from the wise-cracks of our own homely moralists. And if Proverbs seems often to ignore the real facts of life, the Book of Job abundantly treats, from many viewpoints, the problem of unmerited suffering, and the Book of Ecclesiastes faces with a triumphant *élan vital* a horribly pessimistic faith. We know that Job as the mouthpiece of humanity, is on a higher level and nearer to us than Prometheus on his crag, and that Ecclesiastes preached a practical philosophy richer and nobler than that of any Stoic.

We are often told of the ferocious nationalism of the Hebrews and of the savagery of their Jehovah. Do the people who say such things ever read the Book of Ruth or of Jonah and realize that these same Hebrews not only produced those books but accepted them as part of their Sacred Scripture? That Ezra's denunciation of foreign marriage could not annul the fact of David's Moabite ancestress, and that Habakkuk and Nahum had to see in the sacred circle of the Twelve the apologue of Jonah which reduced to nothing, and less than nothing, their rhetoric of denunciation against Nineveh? Too many of the writers on the Old Testament seem to have eyes to see only one weak and passing side of its multifarious contents.

But results of neglect of the Old Testament do not stop at the Old Testament itself. A considerable part of the New Testament also becomes unintelligible. It is an old truth that there is no absolute beginning in history although there are many beginnings, and you cannot cut away the past of the Hebrew race and expect to understand the phenomenon of our Lord Himself and still less the hypotheses of His followers about Him. The nerve-threads of all that world of the first Christian generation run back into the Old Testament. In older days among ourselves students were students of the whole Bible and were expected to know their Hebrew as well as their Greek. In the specialization of our day it is a rare theologian who can pass from the New Testament to the Old and use both at first-hand. And it is almost humorous how, in consequence, outlying small fry of Essenes and Mandaeans are dragged in to explain phenomena in the New Testament, the source of which is plain in the Old. This will right itself in time, but the laughing Reason of the eighth chapter of Proverbs must be sore put to it to keep up her good humor with men when they persistently ignore her as the Logos of John's Gospel and find that Logos in the entirely different Memrá of Philo. Even Tertullian knew that John's Logos was as much Reason, Strength, and Spirit as Word.

What are we going to do about all this? For one thing let us recognize the facts and try to look at the Old Testament in a broader and saner way. Archeology and criticism, documents and analyses, will certainly be with us to the end and they have their own place and value. But let us give the Old Testament a chance to prove that there is truth in the old belief in the witness of Scripture to itself. Let us hear its witness, a manifold, multitudinous, multifarious witness to the unique endowment, experience and thinking of the Hebrew mind and spirit. And let us do that, recognizing that in the Old Testament as a whole we have the surviving mass of the literature of the Hebrew race and that it is as truly a mass of artistic creation in words as that of the Greeks. What this means for the importance of a constant, living knowledge of Hebrew in the Christian Church I need hardly labor to bring out. It seems self-evident.

A NOTE ON THE OLD TESTAMENT AS THE HEBREWS THEMSELVES CONSTRUCTED IT

OUR English Old Testament, with its Apocrypha which are an essential part of it, was a reconstruction, under the pressure of Reformation controversies, of the Latin Vulgate. It, in its turn, had been a reconstruction from the Septuagint, the Greek translation of the Hebrew Old Testament, which originally was the Bible of all Greek-speaking Jews. When it was adopted as Sacred Scripture by the Christian Church the Jews abandoned it and returned to the original Hebrew.

If we are, then, to consider the Old Testament as containing the surviving literature of the Hebrews we must look at it as the Hebrews themselves put it together and not in any later non-Hebrew forms, however interesting these may be in their witness to theological changes. The Old Testament in its Hebrew form remains today in Jewish usage practically as it was gradually put together. Originally it goes back, as has been brought out above, to an enormous number of fragments, long and short. Some of these were unified books, great and little; others were pure collections of fragments, united only by a broad common subject, but otherwise thrown together; such are Proverbs, Isaiah, Job. The resultant books in their arrangement show how the Hebrews themselves regarded them and are witnesses also to the gradual growth for the later Hebrews of what must be called a Canon of Sacred Scripture. How the earlier Hebrews regarded these, in their earlier, fragmentary and not yet sacred form, we can only guess.

The Hebrew Bible, then, consists of three parts: the Law, the Prophets, the Writings. The Law consists of the five books as we know them, but these are called simply the Five Fifths of the Law. The books have individual names, but these are hardly significant as they consist only of initial or early words. The Law is to be regarded as a unity. Of course we know that it is highly compound.

The Prophets divide into the Earlier Prophets and the Later Prophets. The former are our Books of Joshua, Judges, 1 and 2

Samuel, 1 and 2 Kings. There is no explanation why these are called Prophets. The Later Prophets are Prophets as we understand the term: Isaiah, Jeremiah, Ezekiel, and the Twelve: Hosea, Joel, Amos, Obadiah, Jonah, Micah, Nahum, Habakkuk, Zephaniah, Haggai, Zechariah, Malachi. It will be noticed that Daniel is not among them and that Jonah is reckoned as one of the Twelve.

The Writings are the most miscellaneous. They are Psalms, Proverbs, Job; then the Five Rolls, Song of Songs, Ruth, Lamentations, Ecclesiastes, Esther; then Daniel, Ezra, Nehemiah, Chronicles.

This is the arrangement in printed Hebrew Bibles and also the arrangement, with some slight varyings towards the end, in manuscripts and canonical lists. There has been reference above to some of the differences in order from our English Bibles. The Five Rolls, for example, are grouped together and Daniel is separated from the Prophets and only precedes Ezra at the end. In all this, literary considerations have weighed heavily and also the order in which canonicity seems to have been reached. But the history of the origin of the Hebrew Canon is involved in controversy and is not in point here.

INDEX OF SCRIPTURE REFERENCES

GENESIS   3, 58, 93 ff., 141, 144, 167, 201 ff.
i   28
i-xi   98
i, 1-ii, 4a   99, 109
i, 2   148
ii, 4   103
ii, 4b, 6b   99
ii, 7   203
iii, 14   106
iii, 16   106, 111
iii, 19   113, 150, 202 f.
iii, 22   99
iv, 7   106
iv, 23, 24   37
v, 24   149
vi, 1 ff.   112
vi, 3   203
vii, 32   203
viii, 21, 22   114
ix, 12 ff.   114
x, 5, 20, 31   115
xii-xxxvi   98
xv   156
xviii, 23 ff.   126
xxvii, 40   118
xxxi, 27   36
xxxii, 30   153
xxxvii-end   98
xli, 8   175
xlv, 8   119

EXODUS   59, 96, 133 ff.
iii, 13-15   133 f.
iv, 10-16   72
v, 1   35
vii, 1, 2   72
vii, 11   175
ix, 23, 24   135
xv, 20, 21   35
xxiii, 14   35
xxxii, 5, 6, 9   35
xxxiii, 19   134
xxxv, 25   175

NUMBERS
xi   77
xii   72
xii, 3   73
xiii, 33   113
xxi, 14   59
xxi, 17   38
xxi, 27-30   59
xxii-xxiv   68
xxii, 2-xxiv-end   123, 129 f.
xxiii-xxv   59
xxiii, 15, 16   130
xxiv, 14 ff.   132
xxiv, 25   130
xxxi, 8, 16   130 f.

DEUTERONOMY
xiii, 1-5   71
xviii, 15-22   71
xxiii, 3   123
xxiii, 4, 5   131

JOSHUA
x, 12, 13   58
xiii, 22   130
xxiv, 9, 10   131

JUDGES   41, 95, 141, 143
v   5, 16, 22
v, 29   175
ix, 7-15   137
xi, 34   36
xiii   157
xiii, 17   153

RUTH   121
iv, 7   122

BOOKS OF SAMUEL   3, 41, 45, 51, 66, 70, 83, 95, 143, 191

I SAMUEL
ix, 6 ff.   69
x, 5-12   80
x, 6, 10   77

INDEX OF SCRIPTURE REFERENCES

1 SAMUEL (*Continued*)
xvi, 14-end	76
xviii, 5-xix, 20	76
xviii, 7	37
xix, 18-24	80
xxi, 11	37
xxi, 13-15	79
xxii, 3, 4	122
xxviii	70, 155
xxviii, 10	77
xxix, 5	37

2 SAMUEL
i, 17-27	53 f.
iii, 33, 34	54
iv, 1	79
vi, 14, 16, 20	36, 81
vii	42
vii, 9	42
xiv, 1-5, 14	175
xiv, 14	42
xvi, 5 ff.	42
xx, 16 ff.	175
xxiii, 1-7	52

BOOKS OF KINGS
3, 41, 51, 66, 71, 83, 89, 95 f., 143

1 KINGS
iii, 5-15	197
xviii	82
xviii, 21, 26	35
xviii, 29, 46	82
xx, 31-37	76
xxii, 5-xxviii	74
xxii, 17	87
xxii, 19-23	75

2 KINGS
ii, 11	150
ix	79
x, 15	110
xiv, 8, 9	138
xiv, 25	123
xix, 3-5	157

1 CHRONICLES
xvi	43
xxi, 1	78 f.
xxv, 1, 2, 3	82
xxix, 29	70

2 CHRONICLES
i, 7-13	197
vii, 1	157

NEHEMIAH
xiii, 2	131
xiii, 23 ff.	123

ESTHER
139 ff.

JOB
14, 15, 23, 58, 89, 96, 98, 100, 102, 123, 128, 144, 154, 167, 183, 192 ff.
i, ii	24, 75, 78, 128
ii, 3	24
iii-xxxi	24
iv, 12 ff.	155
ix, 16, 17	29, 31
xii, 6	38
xiv	150
xix	151
xxv	27
xxvii, 13-end	27
xxviii	5, 27, 177 f., 181 f., 185
xxix-xxxi	27
xxxi, 35, 36	25
xxxi, 40	27
xxxii-xxxvii	28
xxxii, 19	71
xxxvi, 27	104
xxxviii-xxxix	5, 11
xxxviii-xli	28, 163
xl, 3-5	31
xl, 7 ff.	29
xlii, 1-6	31
xlii, 7-end	24, 26, 31, 128

PSALMS
18, 44, 55 f., 102
i	179
ix, 2	103
xiv, 1	189
xvi, 7-11	152
xviii	5, 14, 25, 26, 45, 50, 56, 134, 194
xviii, 14	115
xxiii	51
xxiv	36
xlii	56
xlii, 4	36
xlii, 7	168
xlix, 14, 15	152

INDEX OF SCRIPTURE REFERENCES

PSALMS (*Continued*)
liii, 1	189
lxviii, 25	36
lxxiii, 23-26	152
lxxx	138
xc	5
xcvi	43
ciii	161 f., 179 f.
civ	5, 11, 28, 30, 100, 148, 161, 167
cv	43
cxi, 10	180
cxxi, 1	168
cxlvi	152

PROVERBS
	11, 23 f., 176 ff., 197
i-ix	176
i, 7	180
i, 20 ff.	182 ff.
i, 24-28	182
iv, 1-9	181
v, 7	181
v, 15-18	210
viii	34, 36, 100, 182 ff.
viii, 24, 25	103, 186
viii, 30, 31	34
ix	182 ff.
ix, 7-9	190
ix, 10	180
ix, 13	182
xxvi, 4, 5	190
xxx	176
xxx, 1-4	181
xxx, 4	187
xxx, 19	106
xxxi	176

ECCLESIASTES
	23, 58, 97 ff., 102, 109, 111 f., 144, 183, 191, 193, 197 ff.
i, 9	214
ii, 9	43
ii, 11	207
ii, 26	204
iii, 1 ff.	205
iii, 11	202, 205 f.
iii, 17	207
iii, 18-22	150
iii, 19-21	113
iii, 20-22	202 f.
iv, 1	198, 212
iv, 5	213
iv, 9-12	211
v, 5, 6	208
vi, 10	113, 202 f.
vii, 15-17	208
vii, 16, 17	205, 211
vii, 24	202
vii, 26-28	209
vii, 29	209
viii, 2-5	204
viii, 2-9	198
viii, 6	207
ix, 4 ff.	200, 210, 214
ix, 7-9	210
ix, 10	211
ix, 12	165, 213
ix, 18	204
x, 4-7	198, 204
xi, 7, 8	212
xi, 9	207
xii, 1	210
xii, 3, 4	214
xii, 7	113, 202 f.
xii, 9-14	215

SONG OF SONGS
	45
iv, 12, 15	210
vi, 13 ff.	36
vii, 10	106

ISAIAH
	26, 72, 90 f.
ii, 2-4	90
ii, 10-22	166
v	138
vi	75
vi, 1	167
xxvi, 12-19	151
xxvii, 1	154
xxvii, 2	138
xxix, 4	71
li, 3	138

JEREMIAH
ix, 16	175
x, 9	175
xxix, 26	79
xxxi, 4	36
xxxv	110
xxxvi	91

INDEX OF SCRIPTURE REFERENCES

EZEKIEL
vi 166
xiv, 14-20 23, 126
xvii 138
xxvii-xxviii 5, 11
xxvii, 8, 9 175
xxviii, 3 126
xxviii, 3, 4 175
xxix, 3 154
xxxi, 3, 9, 16 138
xxxiv, 13, 14 166
xxxiv, 23, 24 41 f.
xxxvi, 1 ff. 166
xxxvii, 1-14 5
xxxvii, 12-14 151
xxxvii, 24, 25 41 f.

DANIEL
 92, 123, 126 ff.
i-vi 127
v 157 f.
vii-end 127
viii, 16 154
ix, 21 154
x, 13, 21 154
xi, 40 127
xii, 1 154

HOSEA
 2, 72
ix, 7 74, 79

JOEL
 91 f.
i, 18, 20 165
ii, 22 165

AMOS
 3, 8, 52, 67, 72 f., 88 ff.,
 143, 154, 166, 170
i, 2-ii, 13 89
ii, 9-12 143
ii, 11, 12 72
ii, 14-16 89
iii, 2 84
iii, 7 72
iv, 7 160
vi, 5 40
viii, 8 135
ix, 3 126, 148
ix, 11 40

JONAH
iv, 11 123 ff., 144
 165

MICAH
 90
iv, 1-3 90
vi, 1, 2 54
vi, 5 131

ZECHARIAH
iii, 1 78
iii, 2 154
vi 154

MATTHEW
 188
xi, 25, 27 188
xxiii, 34-36 188

LUKE
 7, 188
x, 21, 22 188
xi, 49 188

JOHN
 7, 100, 184 ff.
i, 4, 5 100
i, 1-14 100, 186 f.
x, 16 187
xiv, 2, 6 187
xvii, 5, 24 187

I CORINTHIANS
xii, 3 71

PHILIPPIANS
 212
ii, 6, 7 48

JAMES
v, 11 128, 131

2 PETER
ii, 15, 16 131
iii, 16 109

I JOHN
iv, 2, 3 71

JUDE
9 154
11 131

REVELATION
 7
ii, 14 131
xii, 7-12 154

TOBIT		APOCALYPSE OF EZRA	92
	123, 139 f.	iii, 7, 21	108
i, 21	140	vii, 11, 15, 116-118	108
xiv, 8	123	BOOK OF ENOCH	
xiv, 10	140	vii	112

Now (*October 1933*) in Preparation

THE HEBREW PHILOSOPHICAL GENIUS

A Vindication

Being a companion volume to *The Hebrew Literary Genius*

By DUNCAN BLACK MACDONALD

Recently Issued

THE MACDONALD PRESENTATION VOLUME

$6.00

This is a volume published as a tribute to Professor Duncan Black Macdonald and presented to him on the occasion of his seventieth birthday, April 9, 1933. The representative studies and essays by his former students, which make up the book, deal largely with Biblical subjects and the literature and history of Islam, and are of permanent value.